Finland

modern architectures in history

This international series examines the forms and consequences of modern architecture. Modernist visions and revisions are explored in their national context against a backdrop of aesthetic currents, economic developments, political trends and social movements. Written by experts in the architectures of the respective countries, the series provides a fresh, critical reassessment of Modernism's positive and negative effects, as well as the place of architectural design in twentieth-century history and culture.

Series editor: Vivian Constantinopoulos

Forthcoming:

Britain
Alan Powers

France
Jean-Louis Cohen

Germany
Iain Boyd Whyte

Greece
Alexander Tzonis and Alkistis Rodi

Italy
Diane Ghirardo

Japan
Botond Bognar

Spain
David Cohn

Turkey
Sibel Bozdogan

USA
Gwendolyn Wright

Finland

modern architectures in history

Roger Connah

REAKTION BOOKS

For Nadezna Alice, may this help her trace
  the more than small 'hope' in her name
In the land of her forefathers, The Land that is Not

Published by Reaktion Books Ltd
33 Great Sutton Street
London EC1V 0DX, UK

www.reaktionbooks.co.uk

First published 2005
Copyright © Roger Connah 2005

The publishers gratefully acknowledge support for the publication of the book
by the following:
   Graham Foundation for Advanced Studies in the Fine Arts
   The Finnish Institute in London
   Embassy of Finland

Printed and bound in Great Britain by Cromwell Press Ltd, Trowbridge, Wiltshire

British Library Cataloguing in Publication Data
Connah, Roger
   Finland. – (Modern architectures in history)
   1. Architecture – Finland – 20th century
   I. Title
   720.9'1897'0904

ISBN 1 86189 250 0

Contents

Modern Architecture and the Shape of History

How do I know what sleep is?
  and where the shoulder ends and the breast begins?
Make this poem into an inexpensive winter home for me,
  with lots of cupboards,
and furnish me a room for the soul,
  and I'll live in this line a long time,
in verses that don't flake,
  a liveable voice, a house.
  Paavo Haavikko, *The Winter Palace*[1]

In terms of land area Finland is a mid-sized European state with nearly one quarter of its territory north of the Arctic Circle. With more than 80,000 islands and 188,000 lakes, the country lies on the edge of the Eurasian boreal coniferous zone, with 70 per cent of land area as productive forests of pine, spruce and birch. Finland's climate is extreme, though milder than expected for its northern location. The seasons are radical and different. Light varies in subtler ways, often unrecognizable to those from harsher, lighter cultures. The polar night or *kaamos* lasts 52 days in northernmost Lapland, and in the south the lack of daylight can produce serious trauma, which reaches deep within the cultural, environmental and architectural psyche. The population reached 3 million in 1914 and 4 million in 1950. Then the birth rate sagged as the shift from a rural to urban society produced an emigration to Sweden in search of jobs. Gradually, by 1991 the population had reached 5 million, and by spring 2000 the official census put the population at 5,171,302. More than two-thirds of Finns are of working age (15–64) and over 51 per cent of the population are women.[2]

Architecture has in many ways not only helped to modernize Finland but has proved more than useful in a country adept at making its own from a tradition not its own. Modernism and modern architecture became both myth and reality, both tradition and innovation. To many outside Finland, Finnish architecture and its associated 'Finnishness' represent – albeit loosely – something pure, honest, direct and environmentally successful. The leading critic of the Modern Movement, Siegfried Giedion, was one of

Raili and Reima Pietilä,
Official Residence
of the President of
Finland, Mäntyniemi,
Helsinki, 1984–93.

Helsinki cityscape with J. S. Sirén's Finnish Parliament (*centre*) and the Kiasma Museum of Contemporary Art (*right*).

the first outside the country in the 1930s and '40s to begin to celebrate, through the work of Alvar Aalto, an architecture that was natural, regional, civilized, humane and Finnish. In the 1950s, the banquet years, Finland was the place to be, and Finnish architecture began to celebrate this 'reading' as more people – internationally – took notice of it. Eventually Finnishness would stand in – metonymically – for notions about the whole culture: pure, honest, direct. At the end of the twentieth century, encouraged and realigned by Postmodernism and the rise in the media role within architecture, the Finnish culture had learnt to judge itself by how well it performed to these notions of Finnishness. This not only brought more deserved attention to the small country, it produced a careful solidarity within the architectural profession. Today an architecture encouraged by material polish, tectonic finesse and careful articulation has currently become international again and strangely spectacular. As poetic and professionally seductive as this architecture is, the question has to be posed: is it as natural and humane as in the banquet years of the 1950s?

How, then, are we to approach the history of Modernism and modern architecture in a single country? The critical unity of any era, let alone a century, is, of course, usually an illusion. But if the *modern* agenda implied within modern architecture became an applied art and offered tectonic accomplishment, then surely subsequent psychological and cultural complexities would inevitably invite a self-criticism. This self-criticism has not emerged. Instead, those who know Finland well speak often of the natural silence within what is called the 'Finnish atmosphere'.

For some countries the Modern Movement was more than a shock to the system. It was, often ambiguously, used to signal all possible change. In his opening words to 'An Introduction to Modern Architecture' (1940) the British critic J. M. Richards expressed what most architects expected from this architecture as it gathered pace in the late 1920s and '30s. The ideal, the expectation and the enthusiasm were all – eventually – shared, though at different moments, with differing intensity:

> The words 'modern architecture' are used here to mean something more particular than contemporary architecture. They are used to mean the new kind of architecture that is growing up with this century as this century's own contribution to the art of architecture; the work of those people, whose number is happily increasing, who understand that architecture is a social art related to the life of the people it serves, not an academic exercise in applied ornament.[3]

For small countries, for poor countries, for many who had little, such thinking associated with architecture could not fail to offer improvement over the traditional, 'backward' way of life. The extent to which Finland was seduced by an agenda embedded in a careful and controlled interpretation of this Modern Movement and how this allowed the profession to resist other excesses will form part of our enquiry.

To explore the history of modern architecture and the shape of Modernism is difficult in a country like Finland. Small, partisan and polemic institutions that should open up critically have in fact often closed up and resisted scrutiny; these institutions may have repressed and distorted the very history we attempt to unravel. The Museum of Finnish Architecture (founded in 1956), an extremely important institute in the construction of the legend of Finnish architecture, has, for much of the latter half of the twentieth century, acted as a kind of advertising agency. The Finnish architectural profession (known by its initials SAFA) has also collaborated in steering and narrowing selected architecture to perform with a much admired solidarity and nationalistic urge. The prestigious school of architecture on the Otaniemi campus, a little

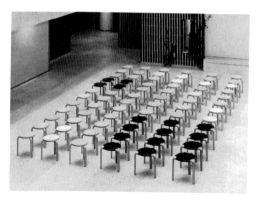

Internationally recognized design: stools by Alvar Aalto, produced by Artek.

outside Helsinki, has over the years been the hotbed of a modern architecture. Keen to resist change, it has inevitably also been influenced by, and filtered, most new trends, ideas and fashions. Pedagogical models have often consisted of 'follow the leader' strategies. The much-loved Finnish restraint has become a double-edged sword; a resistance to theory and conceptual adventure can celebrate the pragmatic and practical, but struggles to filter out the cynical agenda of control. Many histories of Finnish architecture over recent years have chosen to follow the 'heroic' narrative.[4] Individual architects embodied – or like Alvar Aalto were thought to embody in their own person and work – the fate and national destiny of the young republic. With more recent critical developments emphasizing Aalto's singular role in the modern architecture movement of the twentieth century, it has become important to reassess the role of Modernism in Finnish architecture: the power games, the need for recognition from abroad, the assimilation, courage and opportunism.

Anyone who knows a little of Finnish society, the Finnish atmosphere and the internal restraints put on the development of architecture, will recognize the need for a reassessment of that history. For any researcher, this proves a difficult venture. Yet it is incumbent on us to unravel an established narrative at the same time as we acknowledge the immense contribution made by Finland to modern architecture, an achievement unsurpassed even by many larger countries. As a history of a modern architecture, and the shape of the Modernism that influenced that movement, our enquiry must attempt to read between the lines of an already accepted, constructed view of modern Finnish architecture. Taking in the familiar achievements of the well-known heroes of Finnish architecture (Saarinen, Aalto, Pietilä, Leiviskä et al.), we must not only explore the shape of Modernism as Finland emerged as an independent country in 1917 but also attempt to discover how the 'agenda' implied in the Modern Movement became, first, a blueprint to advance the society; second, a visual index for architectural correctness; and third, eventually, a redefinition of Finland's identity. Keeping this narrative in mind, it has also been worth attempting to analyse the dreams and poetry of an architecture that appears, especially to many outsiders, to have answered the modern call. To do this, the cultural agenda implied in 'Modernism' and the social agenda implied in the modern architecture movement have been used as a way to retrace the twentieth century.

'Must the Housing Milieu be Ugly?' Protest installation, 1971, by E. Valovirta, J. Kautto, Pekka Manner and Tapani Launis.

The oscillation between politics and culture enables us to revisit the events and movements that have influenced and shaped architecture.

If we accept the Finnish tendency to see itself as a gateway between the East and the West, it might be reasonable to consider what effect this location may have had on Finland's reception and negotiation with Modernism. In anthropological and political terms, Finland can be seen as a *liminal* space. Some 10,000 years ago, after the retreat of the continental ice sheet, 'the first scattered settlements began to appear on the broad expanse of land, covered with lakes and forests, between the Gulf of Finland, the Gulf of Bothnia and Lake Ladoga'.[5] This area became a kind of transit zone, a country of fens, marshes and lakes belonging racially and linguistically to the Finno-Ugrian peoples, before the Finns reached the country from the Gulf of Finland and gave their name to the land. Its position between Sweden and Novgorod (the north-west region of Russia) meant that Finland would always be a geographical corridor that travellers, adventurers, anthropologists, scientists, architects and others have experienced as a rite of passage.

Historically, Finland has always been a divide between two religions, two cultures. A religious and political wilderness, in the thirteenth century there was a loosely defined border dividing Swedish and Novgorod interests; there has always existed a difference between the inland and coastal areas, still detected today in the way of life and the different racial and cultural traditions within the country. After the Swedes' First Crusade in 1155, the Second Crusade in 1238 took them far inland to the region of Häme. By 1293 and the Third Crusade, Sweden reached the Gulf of Finland and built the fortress at Viipuri (Viborg). Under Sweden Finns had some say in their own affairs and in 1362 were granted the right to take part in the election of the king. At the end of the fifteenth century Finland had a population of around 300,000. The Treaty of Pähkinäsaari established the border between Sweden and Novgorod, leaving the eastern Karelians part of Novgorod. These Karelians fated to be east of the border naturally formed close ties with Novgorod and the Orthodox Church. North Karelia, Käkisalmi and the

US Vice President Lyndon B. Johnson, 'Lady Bird' Johnson and their daughter Lynda in Aleksanterinkatu, Helsinki, 7 September 1963.

Karelian isthmus were annexed to the Kingdom of Sweden (1323–1809), only to become part of the Russian Grand Duchy from 1809 until independence in 1917. Later these same areas were part of bitter spoils and struggles during the Second World War. Some 400,000 Karelian Finn evacuees from this region, which was ceded to the Soviet Union, would cause an intense need for housing and relocation during the 1940s.

Politically, Finland has operated as a kind of buffer zone, and would do so increasingly during the twentieth century. For those coming from Sweden and the West during the Cold War, Helsinki offered a pause before going East. For citizens of the USSR, Helsinki was western enough to be attractive, but eastern enough to be welcoming. In a similar way it is quite possible that the ideals and agendas of Modernism have not only been tempered in this zone, but their excesses have had something other to restrain them. A chance to pursue this idea might allow us to consider the restraints that the proximity of Novgorod put on the culture of Modernism. There is, in the geopolitical mind set, in the psyche of the Finns, a propensity for restraint; it is a culture that sees in the modest understated expression a creative stubbornness and strength. Modernism would prove to be both an adventure and a restraining influence, as Modernist experiments would respond to an Orthodox ritual with a constructive mystery and utilitarian sense. For a country like Finland, however, Modernism, and especially modern architecture, appeared to offer so much more. Not only did it arrive at about the right time for a newly emerging nation (if there is a 'right time' outside history books), it appeared with such force and promise that it soon became, unmistakably and unquestionably, the movement that could define the nation's identity. It still does. Yet in what was a period of 'modernizing' throughout almost all Europe – the first two decades of the twentieth century – Finland as we speak of it today did not exist. Ever since the first Finnish-language newspaper was founded in 1776, industrialization, national and social development would always be ambiguous as the country struggled between a 600-year centralizing rule from

Gesellius, Lindgren and Saarinen, Finnish Pavilion, Paris World Fair, 1900.

into the Russian army. This period of renewed oppression came to an end in 1904 with the assassination of Bobrikov. A general strike followed in autumn 1905 and, with Russian losing the Russo–Japanese War that year, the First Oppression ended. In 1906 a single-chamber parliament was established and 'at a stroke Finland changed over from the oldest parliamentary system in Europe to the most modern'.[18]

Inspired by the internationalism of Art Nouveau, the interior of the Pavilion, the Iris Room, was also designed by Gallen-Kallela whilst the furniture was made under the supervision of a Swedish count, Louis Sparre.[19] Although the Finnish Pavilion in Paris was neither a copy of an existing building in the Grand Duchy nor did it belong to any existing construction, it was considered to conform to a national style. But the

Gesellius, Lindgren
and Saarinen, Finnish
Pavilion, Paris World
Fair, 1900.

source for this work was wide: the Arts and Crafts movement, the influence of Scotland and England, Art Nouveau, the solidity of American
natural stone architecture, plus early industrialization in Germany and
Austria, all helped to approximate an architectural form. Those aware
of the intense eclecticism within Finnish building history would know
well enough that the papier-mâché humour of the building was ironic,
possibly even a touch off colour. In the context of a Russian empire the
irony must have been unmissable, even 'politically' dangerous.

Those detached from the 'nationalist' context, however, saw the
Finnish Pavilion 'exotically'. This also was an approximate but legitimate
reading. It was 'Finnish' because it had obvious natural features. It was

Finnish Pavilion, Paris
World Fair.

'international' because it was in Paris. It was 'new' because it was not
quoting or parodying nineteenth-century architectural styles and motifs.
But the achievement of the young architects Gesellius, Lindgren and
Saarinen was also translated thinly and patronizingly. The little country
'Finland' was naturally praised for doing its Art Nouveau versions as
well as anyone else, if not better. As everyone was doing this at the time,
this was not serious praise. But what the Pavilion did brilliantly, the
critics thought, were its dancing elves and frolicsome frescos. The exotic
was what interested the world; the international world responded by
being seduced by folkiness. The sensation was its 'bizarre mixture of styles
taken from the Finnish rural vernacular and from the various avant-

garde movements'.[20] The mythological and propagandistic potential within architecture was established. As a cultural *and* political image the Pavilion stood in for that distinctive Finnish character that would eventually lead to the achievement of Finnish Independence in 1917.

Hermeneutically, depending on connotation sought and context used, the Finnish Pavilion can be seen as an open *and* a closed work, just as many of the subsequent and significant World Fair Finnish Pavilions would be throughout the twentieth century. Despite this fluctuation in meaning, the epithet 'national' stuck awkwardly. Neither a bank nor strictly a museum, the Pavilion represented a strange repertoire. Some called it the 'new spirit of the time', which was also emerging in museum and commercial buildings in central Helsinki. No sooner, though, would this 'national romanticism' be accepted, it would be changed by its detractors and critics back home. The debate that this and other buildings around 1900 caused would lead to the consistent tension between the borrowed forms of an 'internationalism' and the assimilated forms of a poetic and 'national' (not nationalist) architecture. This was a debate with enormous consequences to the way that Modernism and modern architecture were continually received and reshaped. One need only compare, for example, the Lundqvist Commercial Building (1900) by Selim Lindqvist with the frolicsomely decorated Pohjola Insurance Building (1901) by the architects of the Pavilion, Gesellius, Lindgren and Saarinen, to identify this tension. Already in Selim Lindqvist's work, the steel and concrete frame, the large windows with few partition walls, despite its neo-Gothic exterior, would represent the Continental direction. Influenced by nineteenth-century German department stores, there was already that pull towards a simplified, functional appearance.

The Finnish Pavilion of 1900 brought Finland to world attention. A similar seduction, folkiness and the exotic, in varying degrees, would be repeated throughout the twentieth century as the modern agenda negotiated Functionalism, Internationalism and later Postmodernism.[21] And if we accept that the Finnish Pavilion was an image politics in the making, then the consequence for the twentieth century is clear. A sort of *image-truth* of poetic nature and folkiness would always threaten architecture with similar sentiment. Architects soon realized that whilst the romance of landscape and nature was necessary to be identifiable, the exotic would always need resistance and holding back. The idea of Finnish restraint, modesty and the constant need for less embellishment would produce a tension within architecture so naturally sited, so seductively placed in the landscape. The implied honesty in this restraint would offer the architects a guide to what would be authentic or not in modern architecture. This not only pre-empted the way that building and architecture would shape the nation's identity, it hinted at the programmatic position that architecture could take within the society.

The idea that architecture held a symbolic logic would fuse with the struggle for independence from Russia. Attributing to architecture such a symbolic logic implied, early on in the twentieth century, the act of *reading* architecture. The Finnish Pavilion in Paris would not only identify to others the small country seeking independence, it would introduce early and developing notions about how architecture could nurture and steer the modern development of the country. Social equality and technological progress implied by the 'modern' gesture would keep architecture at the forefront of this development. And the figure of Paavo Ruotsalainen, the notion of *sisu*, the systematic Hegelianism of J. V. Snellman and the romance of the *puukko* would ensure an entirely Finnish approach to what began in Paris and continued in the Bauhaus in Dessau.

chapter one

Pioneering Finnish Modernism

In truth, Finland is utterly charming. Its lakes, its canals, its rivers, its forests are
beautiful, and its customs are interesting. It is primitive and picturesque, and its
people are most kind and hospitable ...
Mrs Alec Tweedie, 1897[1]

The qualified enthusiasm about Finland with which the British traveller
Mrs Alec Tweedie wrote in *Through Finland in Carts* was to pre-empt
the debate on the primitive and the Picturesque. This duality was to parallel the way in which early Modernism began to transform and social-
ize a country not yet independent. Preparations had been put in place
earlier in the nineteenth century as part of the Russian empire. With
unusual autonomy under the Russians – Finland already had its own
Diet (assembly), its own army and its own unit of currency, the *markka*
– such infrastructure could not fail to influence the country's political
and economic life and the process of modernization.[2] That the Russian
empire proved somewhat unpredictable obviously had its advantages;
in 1863 Czar Alexander II had made Finnish an official language of
administration and legal proceedings. Finnish institutions followed. The
Sculpture School, later known as the University of Art and Design, was
founded in 1871. The Vienna World Exhibition occurred in 1873 and the
Finnish Society of Arts and Crafts was founded in 1875. In 1874 the
Swedish-Finnish company Arabia displayed its products for the first
time, and in 1879 The Friends of Finnish Handicraft developed and
exhibited what became recognized as a strongly independent Finnish
style. The base was formed for the *Gesamtkunstwerk*, the total work of
art, which would become so important in Art Nouveau at the turn of the
century.[3] In 1889 the artist Albert Edelfelt depicted the national awakening in a poster showing Mme Paris receiving Finland, a damsel, who
alights with a model of Helsinki Cathedral on her hat; the parcels in the
boat are all marked EU (Exposition Universelle).[4]

Releasing itself from ties to the rouble, during the second half of the
nineteenth century the country showed an increasing awareness of the
possibility of freeing itself from the Russian empire, an awakening that
was helped by the Finnish language. Indirectly the status as a Grand

Eliel Saarinen, Helsinki
Railway Station,
1904–19.

Duchy had helped the strategy of modernizing the Finnish economy, thereby promoting industry and further autonomous developments. Transport and the opening of Western markets increased both imports and exports. Customs autonomy also favoured Finland's industrialization process, particularly important for its emerging paper industry. It is now possible to see how strong this first major period of growth, from the 1870s to the 1920s, was for Finland, since it coincided also with the increased nationalism and eventual Independence.[5]

Poster by Albert Edelfelt for Finland at the Exposition Universelle, Paris, 1889 (Mme Paris receiving the damsel Finland).

The Finnish Architects Club was founded in 1892 within the Swedish-speaking Engineering Society (Tekniska Föreningen). Originally a loose forum for collaboration and discussion, its voluntary basis meant that it operated informally in cafés and restaurants. In this way it resembled many of the writers' or artists' clubs of the time and generally fostered a collegial spirit of some solidarity. It quickly helped to establish the architect as an artist responsible for aesthetic decisions. Most architects were from Swedish-speaking families with connections towards the Nordic countries, Germany and Britain especially. Generally speaking, the questions of language placed no national or social limits on the bilingual educated class. Indeed it would be the Swedish-speaking Finns who carried through the awakening and created the staging ground for independence through art, music and architecture. This bilingual nature would also ensure that Modernism entered early via Sweden, only to be filtered later perhaps by the relatively slower nature of the Eastern tradition.[6] This is paralleled by the shift from country to town and the shape these influences had on the emerging architectural profession. At the beginning of the twentieth century 10 per cent of the population in Finland lived in towns. This had risen only to 20 per cent by the 1930s. Yet by the 1970s more lived in town or urban areas than in the countryside.

In 1903, as a supplement to the engineering publication, the Club published the first issue of *Arkitekten* ('The Architect' in Swedish, the language still in use at the time), and although a degree in architecture was not yet required in educational terms (only in 1908 did architecture begin to be taught at tertiary level when the Polytechnic Institute became the Helsinki University of Technology), the Club soon began to operate as a promotional and influential body not only within architectural circles but within the wider society. By 1914 there were apparently about 111 architects, and although most worked in Helsinki, naturally not all belonged to the Club. Gradually but confidently through the printed form, architects began to affect public opinion and engage in topical issues.

Considering the role of architects in municipal affairs, it was only in 1907 that the duties of the civil engineer were separated from those of the municipal architect, when Karl Hård af Segerstad was appointed Helsinki's first municipal architect. More significantly, considering the pioneering work of early Modernism, Bertel Jung began work as Helsinki's Town Planning architect. In effect the split from the engineers had begun already in the late 1890s. Henceforth, planning was to remain in the hands of the architects. This coincided also with the desire for architects to take over the design of buildings. The creativity of the architect necessitated a change from the position in the nineteenth century, when the architect was often a copyist and orchestrator of previously accepted and defined styles. There was a natural progression, as there had been throughout Europe, to eliminate their role as merely designers of façades only.[7]

The intellectual and polemical environment within the small country cannot be underestimated. The first decade of the century saw a struggle

Selim Lindqvist,
City Bazaar, Helsinki,
1904.

between engineers and architects. Significantly, the engineers would henceforth aid, assist and make the architect's design possible, just as the respected skill of the 'master-builder' would also assist in the construction of buildings. Opposition to regular grid planning in favour of topological exercises appeared. Landscape, form and visuality were filtered into the Finnish scene aided by the work of the Austrian planner Camillo Sitte and examples from the British Garden City movement. The shift of the architect towards design and a so-called free spirit would synchronize with the new movement emerging throughout Europe. Artistic invention would gently replace the engineer's more ponderous position.

Although Finnish architecture would remain mainly 'eclectic' until the 1930s, the move toward Modernism – later interpreted as a cleansing of forms or as a disciplining of (Renaissance) classicism towards a functionalist architecture – had its basis in the events around the turn of the century. To integrate the design of the building with its function and, predictably, to take over planning from the pragmatics of the engineers, implied a more artistic emphasis for planning and urban design. The ideological agenda later implied in the Modern Movement would then ultimately offer less hindrance.

If, however, we wish to understand how 'modernizing' occurred and how architecture began to pick up pace both systematically and ideologically, it is to a painter we must turn. In 1898 the first Finnish arts review *Ateneum* was set up, and Albert Edelfelt, Finland's most eminent artist at the time, wrote a piece called 'The Decline and Rebirth of Decorative Taste'. Edelfelt was the son of the architect Carl Albert Edelfelt, who had moved to Finland from Sweden at the age of 14. In 1867 he had been appointed Director-General of the Supreme Board of Public Buildings. Quite the highest authority on building in the country, Carl Edelfelt must have passed on his interest in travel and Britain to his son, for Albert Edelfelt did what many artists and architects were doing at this time: he travelled extensively, spent long periods away from the Grand Duchy and constantly monitored, assimilated and absorbed the new developments in art and architecture.[8]

Edelfelt expressed a number of observations and objectives that framed the general synthetic mood between art and architecture, but his provocative and clear style set a precedent for architects to shape ideals and visions that would, he thought, live on for centuries. Influenced by the British Arts and Crafts movement, especially the journal *The Studio* (begun in 1893), Edelfelt made a case for the New Art. Lamenting the decline of the applied arts, Edelfelt allows us to glimpse the growing attitudes against historicism. The country was not yet independent, but the vision was eternal. Things might have been happening in Chicago, Stockholm, Paris and London, but Edelfelt felt that it was now time in Finland to replace the imitators. The country needed to identify itself amidst the emerging modernizing tendencies, and architecture as the art of shelter would, according to Edelfelt, necessarily take the lead for any hope in the future. This was a call to stop imitation. Forms were to be creatively assimilated, not copied:

> Concealing a building's or an object's meaning, purpose and mechanical composition by covering it with meaningless triviali-ties has been the fundamental error of the decorative arts period of Babylonian captivity, their 70 deplorable years of decay, and the most frenzied Baroque seems logical in comparison with a great many things that have been produced in our day.[9]

Like many artists, architects and writers, Edelfelt was caught up with the swirling movements coming out of Britain, France, Germany, Denmark, Sweden and Austria. Cast iron and glass were already achieving a 'mod-ern style' spoken about in Britain. This 'shock of the new' would replace the lamentable decline in applied art and the spectacles of sandstone, marble and brick that Edelfelt appeared to loathe. Caution at embellish-ment, at decorative excess or indeed anything monumental would be keyed into the Finnish psyche. In one noteworthy sentence he set the tone and anxiety for the architects to come. This was a mission that would steer their role in the twentieth century. 'Without a profound sense of guilt', Edelfelt wrote, 'improvement is impossible'.[10] Beauty and good sense, beauty for as many people as possible; this was what Edelfelt called the 'New Style'. Sharing a widespread disdain for unnecessary adornment, hinting at the tension between the picturesque and the functional, Edelfelt expressed all this as the 'natural language of cultured artists'. The artist was hinting at how the architect could lead.

It is worth putting this search for beauty and good sense in context. Might we not recognize these objectives also in those scripted at the other end of the twentieth century in the Government Architectural Policy Programme of Finland issued on 17 December 1998? Although there is no longer mention of 'modernism', 'modernizing' or 'modernity', it is clearly the effect of a century's concern with a mission and an agenda formed 100 years earlier:

> The societal, cultural and economic values of architecture are great. It is an important part of our national culture. It provides the means by which to create a good living environment –

which every citizen has the right to enjoy – as well as high
quality architecture. It is the duty of every public body to
realise this right.[11]

How then did 'modernizing' express itself during these years? To
answer this it is impossible to ignore the fascination with the East,
especially those Orthodox traces found in what has remained a liminal

zone between Finland and Russia, Karelia. The awareness of the origins of the Finnish language, the Finno-Ugrian peoples and race, and the growing nationalist movement, meant that, by the 1890s, many painters, architects, writers and ethnologists were inspired to research these origins further by visiting eastern Karelia.[12] Encouraged by the studies in Europe on applied arts and folk building practices, encouraged by the notion of travel, the railways and adventure almost everywhere, there was great enthusiasm to research a 'truly' Finnish origin. Many architects felt that a new Finnish architecture might be found in the architecture and ornament of Karelia.

One of the most important and influential journeys made by architects had already taken place in 1894. Funded by the Finnish Archaeological Society, the architects Yrjö Blomstedt and Victor Sucksdorf travelled to Eastern Karelia. The result, for the time, was impressive: 500 drawings and 150 photographs in the publication written by Yrjö Blomstedt, *Karelian Buildings and Decorative Forms from Central Russian Karelia*. Around the same time (although only published in 1911) the photographer and traveller Into Konrad Inha set off for the area of Viena in Karelia and captured what to this day remains the iconographic record of the region, *From the Songlands of the Kalevala*. Although forgotten for a period, a small version of this, published by the Finnish Literature Society in 1968, would reawaken the romance and offer constant recourse later in the century for those seeking once again a truly Finnish origin.[13]

Photograph by I. K. Inha, of a village in Uhtua, Viena, Karelia, 1894.

The romanticism about origins and Finnishness and the impressive vernacular constructions are unmistakable from any of these trips to Karelia. The picturesque, though, is uppermost. Here is the writer and literary scholar Eino Railo noting from his first trip in 1905:

> Shimmering hills, shady hollows, stony hillocks; the scent of resin and fresh leaves, the sounds and silence of the wilderness, spirited skipping on the branches, there are you, holy Karelia, with your memories, your spirits, your slumbering, sacred secrets, your songs, your enchantments . . . [14]

After travelling to this region in 1901, the architect Jalmari Kekkonen would also capture the limits of the romance, acutely analysing in 1929 how 'this entire enquiry was directed at a very limited area and left unexamined . . . what was offered by places closer by, in Finland itself'. In other words, the architects sought something talismanic and saw in this region building forms that were believed to 'represent something absolutely, originally Finnish'. [15]

'Something absolutely, originally Finnish' will crop up again and again. But any romantic idea of this was soon to be rescripted by the architect Sigurd Frosterus in 1904 as he filtered revolutionary ideas and developments from Europe. What began as Frosterus's call for what he termed an 'iron and brain' style in architecture – trimming down the romance of the national style (represented by Gesellius, Lindgren and Saarinen) – was seen as intrinsically 'modern'. It would eventually represent a mind-set and process that could appropriate and assimilate international developments until they too might possibly represent something absolutely and originally Finnish. [16]

The national awakening led to an increased collaboration between an emerging industry and designers, both architects and artists. The turn of the century saw many commercial and institutional buildings appear and the success of the Art Nouveau-inspired Finnish Pavilion meant increased success at home for Gesellius, Lindgren and Saarinen and the emerging work of the other architect recognized from this time, Lars Sonck. The Finnish National Museum, a marathon project from 1901 to 1910, clearly displays a slow taming of the wilder storytelling of Gesellius, Lindgren and Saarinen and the eventual rupture of their partnership. In 1902 Armas Lindgren was appointed Director of the School of Applied Arts, predictably introducing the Art Nouveau crafts of metalwork, textiles and ceramics to the curriculum. [17] Eclectic features would creep into the architecture along with a revivalist style, and Lars Sonck's work alongside Eliel Saarinen's would represent what is now historically characterized as National Romanticism.[18]

If not direct borrowings, all the National Romantic buildings during this period were assemblages more or less of recognizable features echoing, among others, the Scottish-Viennese Art Nouveau and the neo-Romanticism of the American H. H. Richardson. Stylistically all this is now considered a kind of post-Jugendstil period with other consequences, as the historian Marianne Aav put it: 'the omniscience of architects that was linked to the Jugend idea of the work of art as a whole was called into question. It was believed that the solution to both liberation from imitative styles and the predominance of the architect could be found in specialisation.'[19] This specialization led later to the founding in 1911 of Ornamo, the Association of Finnish Designers, and was seen as an obvious bid to protect those involved in applied arts.

Sometimes buildings were more decorative, even cheekier than others with their ornamental additions. Even the new language in the Pohjola Insurance Building by Gesellius, Lindgren and Saarinen (1901) lies rather concealed. Despite the attention to the functional spatial planning, the use of much metal with elevators imported from Sweden and the nuanced attention to corner-plot planning, the façade was still treated as a separate entity. According to the competition brief, the façades were to be of granite or other Finnish stone. Clearly the richly decorated soapstone Pohjola façade, like many buildings around that time, was designed from within to look as 'modern' as modern then was. However, despite its obvious narrative humour associated with the symbol of the bear as the symbol also of the Pohjola Insurance Company, and though designed by the fashionable architects of the day, its heavy joy and decorative jibes would be open to obvious criticism.

Gesellius, Lindgren and Saarinen, Pohjola Insurance Building, Helsinki, 1901.

Bertel Jung (1872–1946), architect, planner and commentator, would acknowledge the free style attempted in the Pohjola Building whilst condemning its romanticism as a 'primitive, partially crude and untamed force'.[20] This would become familiar. Throughout the century the variety and balance of any expressive form in architecture with strong vibrant texture would come up against the more generalized Finnish desire for restraint. Gesellius, Lindgren and Saarinen went on to design a large number of private houses, among which was their most famous Hvitträsk (1901–3).[21] This 'atelier house' continued the wilderness theme: a set of grouped buildings eclectically commenting on and extending the Arts and Crafts movement in Europe provided the perfect setting for the three architects. Working together, living separately, it was not only art and architecture that became blurred, however; families too. The house, though initially representing the national through the international,

Gesellius, Lindgren and Saarinen, Pohjola Insurance Building, Helsinki, 1901.

became the seminal example of that 'escape' from the city for a more authentic existence.

Bertel Jung's comments on the Pohjola Building were timely, and pre-emptive of a more serious critical challenge. In 1904, however, the most important rebuttal to this (national) 'romanticism' appeared in the form of various texts written by the architects Sigurd Frosterus and Gustaf Strengell. The international mood and spirit of the time appear clearer now than they obviously were then, but we begin to understand why a new movement could be moving Britain forward while in another country it already represented an unwanted romanticism. Frosterus's text, 'London Rhapsody', written a year before, was an assessment of the 'modern' that offered more acute observations on the ambiguity of the changes around than perhaps anyone else. The machine romanticism implied in the rhapsody was to set the tone for seduction and constant vigilance. Frosterus was an essayist, polemicist, poet and cultured being, and his praise came with subtle hints of warning. Swarming and dreadful, at ease amid the clamour of the city, seduced by the murky, smoking flames and the peaceful retreat or sudden jolt of metallic clicking, in writing about London he celebrated loss: 'the sun rarely shines on London's city'.

Although Frosterus confesses to finding in the rat-hole of London added life colour and an untamed freedom, it was – perhaps surprisingly after these words – the 'exceptional order' that appealed to him. In a

Gesellius, Lindgren and Saarinen, Hvitträsk Atelier and Home, Kirkkonummi, 1901–03.

conclusion that indicates the melting pot and the synthesis that made up London at the time, Frosterus answers with a counter blast: 'In vain, our generation seeks to gain fresher shoots from Paris and Japan, from the colonies or the world of the fairy tale, onto this languishing hothouse plant. This counter-reaction is bound to come. Since London is itself and no other, London is London as Paris is Paris.'[22]

Frosterus was speaking about the experience of identity through place. More than architecture, more than design, he was speaking about impatience. If London is London, Paris is Paris, here we have the warning that Helsinki (a rather small city at the time, it must be stressed) would continue to find its identity through grafting on from elsewhere fresher shoots. If we were in doubt as to the influence and the international connections that some of the leading Finnish architects worked in, here are the dynamics that were to make Modernism later such a seductive and vibrant force. Influence from others, outside oneself, outside one's country, might cause anxiety to some, but to Frosterus it was second nature. From the mood and emerging internationalism between 1890 to the outbreak of the First World War, for a small country to continue its own youthful search for identity and nationhood, it would be natural for the Finnish architect to trawl, for want of a better word, the developments on offer elsewhere. But what they did with these – and this is crucial for the way Finnish Modernism remained a vibrant force and still does today – remains very much their own.

At a time when Helsinki was growing from a small town to a pocket metropolis, Finland was emerging as a pioneering country in Europe in the adoption of electricity and telephone technologies. Electricity had been introduced in 1880 and by the turn of the century more than thirty independent electrical plants were in operation in Helsinki alone. Adapting a system to meet local requirement became a prerequisite in the development of the city and the country.[23] Reading between the lines, Frosterus identifies the agenda-to-come: synthesizing Modernism was to become second nature (pun intended) to the Finnish architect.

The coincidence was precise. Independence, cultural and political identity, the bilingual nation could not have had a stauncher alibi and ally in the emerging excitement and revolutionary ideas that would later be critically interpreted as Modernism. Frosterus saw the humanism and the barbarism within the new spirit. Only later would it look as if Frosterus hinted at what the Finnish architect knew all along: the varied strands of an endlessly modernizing architecture (Functionalism, Internationalism, Constructivism, Organicism, Expressionism, even Postmodernism) would find their quintessential representative in Alvar Aalto.

Calling for rationalism and dilettantism, for an 'internationalism' and an 'iron and brain' style, Frosterus's arguments (along with Strengell's own text) were strong enough to affect the outcome of the Helsinki Railway Station competition. Writing in 1904, both Frosterus and Strengell attacked the romantic vision that had seen Saarinen win first prize in the competition. The picturesqueness and the folkiness we noticed so acceptable in 1900 were now questioned. The attack caused Eliel Saarinen to look again at his entry and alter it over the years to an approximated 'modern' style where ornament began to take second place to space and structural expression. The building, finally completed only in 1919, uncannily resembled that of Frosterus's own entry to the competition, which had been itself an adept assimilation of the work of the British Arts and Crafts architect C.F.A. Voysey.[24]

Gustav Strengell wrote differently but no less forcibly. Enraged by the decorative excesses of the National Museum (1901) and the Pohjola Building (1901), he identified the dynamics associated with the architects

Eliel Saarinen, Helsinki Railway Station, 1904–19.

Helsinki Railway
Station.

Esa Piironen, Helsinki
Railway Station roof,
2001.

of these buildings (Gesellius, Lindgren and Saarinen) as pure caricature:
'an ugly and twisted version of something that was in itself an absurdity'.
After a lengthy analysis of fashion, taste and the instability of culture,
Strengell went on to denounce the pastoral romanticism of GLS and
others as a mere stage setting, a superficial backcloth and meaningless

vignette art. Strengell supported instead a direction towards a guiding, clear and rational force. Pre-empting Le Corbusier, Strengell identified the new architecture as likely to emerge from new needs. Communication and hygiene would shape both the construction methods used and the forms applied: 'The future architect has far more to learn from the Atlantic steamer and the electric tram, from the racer and the motor car, from American office interiors and English lavatories than he does from art forms belonging to the past.'[25]

Recalling folk history at a time when Russia was squeezing the autonomy of the country during the Russification periods, and wishing to distance itself from the somewhat contrived grace coming out of Sweden, probably gave a seriousness to the Finnish romanticism that could not in fact last. Strengell appealed for an avant-garde dilettantism with strong stimuli and a burning enthusiasm. It was a call for the lucid, the restrained, yet held within it the ambiguity of reckless urgency and the unknown. It showed once more how the desire for the new spirit was emerging within unusually strong polemical forces. Frosterus and Strengell realigned the development of architecture. The significance of reading architecture was emphasized by the two texts that made up their challenge of 1904. It was a proto-Functionalist manifesto and remains to this day one of the most important documents in twentieth-century Finnish architecture.

But how then did the architects take control of the future of planning, urban and building design at this crucial period? Politically and culturally the period was alive with national urgencies. The elevation of architects in relation to the role that architecture and architects could take on proved irreversible, especially considering the immense significance given at that time to international contacts. Ideas about an early Modernism came to Finland through travel, study trips, work and journals. It is possible that the first use of the term 'modern' appeared in a lecture given by Lars Sonck, who was to become one of Finland's leading architects and ironically later considered rather romantic and eclectic. Entitled 'Modern Vandalism: The Helsinki Town Plan', the 26-year-old Sonck argued in 1898 for a more modern approach to city planning, echoing the ideas of Camillo Sitte.

This encouraged a town planning competition for the Etu-Töölö part of Helsinki in 1899, and by so doing the subsequent plan by Sonck and Gustaf Nyström not only confronted the traditionalists, it confirmed the role of the architect as urban planner. This was the first competition of its kind in Finland and marked the beginning of a confrontation between leading architects. The first stage of the competition saw Jung, Sonck and Valter Thomé placed second. Politics ensured a

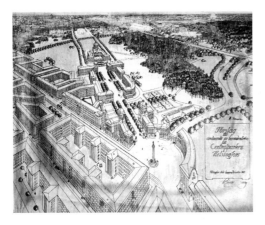

Bertel Jung, plan for Central Park, Helsinki, 1912.

second stage where free assimilations were allowed. In 1900 a kind of compromise solution was submitted by Jung, Sonck and Thomé and others. Developments led to a further scheme drawn up by Nyström and Sonck, which was ratified by the Helsinki City Council in 1903 and passed by the Senate in 1906. Sonck's preference for a medieval intimacy was combined in the final project with Nyström's preference for European circulation patterns.[26]

Considering that there was no education of planners at the Helsinki Polytechnic at that time, the planning role was there for the taking. By 1907, when Sonck drew up a plan for the Kulosaari villa district, the Helsinki City Council appointed a permanent committee for urban planning with Bertel Jung as the first director.[27] Known figures from this period, Nyström, Sonck, Saarinen and Thomé, would all work both as planners and architects. Ideas would soon involve the planning of new residential areas and general development plans; the grand planning works of Eliel Saarinen in the second decade of the twentieth century would be one of the most important results of this shift. As architects took over the planning of larger and larger areas, it became acceptable for them to follow their own inventive and creative design principles. The flourish of this creativity probably culminated in Alvar Aalto's various plans for the Helsinki centre and the intense politics it eventually created in the 1950s and '60s.[28] To this day planning is still in the control of the architects, aided by new alliances with corporations and contractors, as demonstrated by the huge restructuring, currently ongoing, of the Kamppi Bus Station district in central Helsinki.

As this pioneering period developed, the architect Selim A. Lindqvist suggests a fresher picture of the shape that ideas took. If both Saarinen and Sonck have been identified as pioneering the romance and rationalist split, the internal polemics and posturing of the day suggest that things were more experimental and interchangeable. From 1900 onwards Lindqvist appears the undisputed innovator and rationalizer of new structures. How Finland would meet these revolutionary changes surely would also tell us how it would meet Modernism. The historian Asko Salokorpi points out that the neo-Renaissance buildings of the architect Gustaf Nyström (House of Estates, 1891, and The National Archives, 1890) already employed steel framing and hinted at Constructivism.

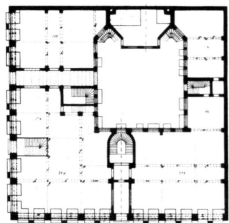

Nyström was an influential teacher at the Technical University and had instructed both Saarinen and Frosterus. According to Salokorpi, Frosterus contrasted Lindqvist's modern commercial buildings with the anachronistic granite palaces of Saarinen and Sonck. Although all architects changed as they met trends, the way that Lindqvist's work changed helps to identify the transition that was to occur so clearly in the 1920s between neo-Renaissance strategies and the emerging Nordic classicism and international Functionalism.

In the Lindqvist Commercial Building on Helsinki's Aleksanterinkatu (1900), Lindqvist wrapped an Art Nouveau-inspired façade around a freestanding super-structure. Large windows offered light, alterable because of the location of the transverse bearing walls. Intermediate floors were supported on slender cast-iron columns, and the effect of lightness compared to GLS's heavy Pohjola Insurance Building opposite was startling for the time. Lindqvist's office in the same building also acted as a meeting place for the internationally minded Euterpe Club.[29] Known as Finland's first real business building, the pillar framework, large display windows and horizontal concrete slab permitted unusual flexibility. Lindqvist went on to explore the possibilities of reinforced concrete. Suvilahti Power Station

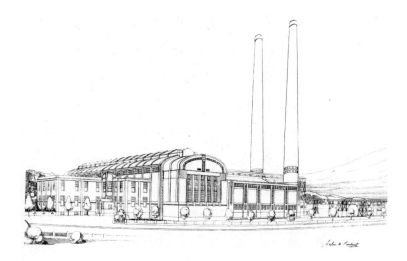

Selim Lindqvist, Suvilahti Power Station, Helsinki, 1908, proposed project.

was completed in 1908 and, it is obvious now, could appear in any text-book of the early days of the Modern Movement, echoing the work of Auguste Perret in France, and pre-empting Walter Gropius.

Contrasted with the emphasized 'primitive' and 'national' in the works of Saarinen and Sonck at the time, Lindqvist's work possessed rather early on the sign of a constructive 'modernity' and a rationalizing tendency more closely associated with Austrian work at the turn of the century. Lindqvist proved to be consistently and modestly Finnish, refined and undemonstrative – a distinctive image of the 'modern' Finnish architect to come. Lindqvist apparently wrote little, explained even less, and, if we follow his work into the 1930s, probably touched on, yet at the same time tamed, almost every stylistic development that we can now recognize during those years.[30]

Accepted histories have interpreted the romance of Saarinen and Sonck as pioneering Finnish identity, establishing the architect's role in society, and helping the cultural drive towards independence whilst responsible for this general National Finnish style. While this is true, these histories may have inadvertently marginalized the significant con-tributions of less recognized architects, such as Lindqvist, who over the decades seem to have laid the ground for the sound, unprovocative and lucid Finnish modern architecture. Equally it may be this rational and reductive approach that in the new millennium proves once more a strategy to face the seduction of international trends while remaining identifiably Finnish and 'isolated'. Although it has not been fashionable to acknowledge isolation and detachment as a necessary creative tension within Finnish architecture, the historian Asko Salokorpi did suggest that it might have been present already in 1900: 'The essential question is whether the rationalists were even more isolated than the romanticists from what was happening in Europe.'[31] Writing this in 1970, a year that was pivotal to the neo-Constructivist period in Finnish architecture, Salokorpi hints at how the century began to unravel as a constant, creative tension between romantics and rationalists.

The challenge of 1904 made by Frosterus and Strengell realigned the architects by voicing the obvious cultural hysteria that built up around any 'Finnish image'. That such imaging was, from some architects' point of view, an unworthy architectural issue held implications for the whole century. The search for the less picturesque in a country considered so 'unspoilt' and 'natural' would question the architect's development. Projects that might have been designed with similar newness, style and some folkiness would be trimmed and restrained after this challenge. The changes were more subtle in emphasis in these Jugendstil-style buildings and in the actual design practices involved. It would be important also to state here that much of Helsinki and some other towns today actually get their tone from this pioneering 'nationalist' period.[32] The somewhat robust decorativism and material symbolism linked to Art Nouveau and European and American architecture, however, would be slowly toned down after 1915. Influence and outside trends, including the developments in Cubism and Futurism in art and architecture, would be trimmed for their own ends, attempting something new.

As different types of contemporary architecture took over the spirit of the age, we are apt to forget that the spirit of the age itself was also transformed. Analysis could be overtaken by change that left an opportunity for each architect to implement their own ideas according to culture, nation and character. And whatever Frosterus and Strengell went on to achieve, compromising and softening Frosterus's own call for an 'iron and brain' style, this challenge outlined a pattern of provocative resistance towards any architecture relying on sensation and scenography. If in 1907 Frosterus declared the British battleship *Dreadnought* to be an aesthetic ideal, he did so also knowing that the modern age would in all likelihood overtake his own machine romanticism, demanding later in life a little more social and global responsibility.

To conclude what is an open and vibrant pioneering period, it might be useful to leave aside Saarinen's later more grand planning schemes for Helsinki,[33] which included separate plans for Helsinki and Munkkiniemi, where the classical would meet the Garden City and expand into a nationalistic vision. Instead, we might go back in time a little to Carl Ludwig

Engel. Engel was born in Berlin in 1778, where he studied architecture with Karl Friedrich Schinkel.[34] Seeking employment abroad, he was appointed City Architect of Tallinn. There he became acquainted with the Empire Style of St Petersburg, the buildings of which he considered 'some of the most beautiful works of modern architecture'. Invited to be the architect of the committee for reconstructing Helsinki when the Russians took over after the war of 1808–9 with Sweden, Engel assumed the responsibility of establishing the ideals and identity of the Russian empire within the autonomous Grand Duchy. Engel would later take exception to Schinkel and others as they moved towards the neo-Gothic, considering it a Napoleonic influence on German architecture. Preferring to remain loyal to a neo-classical style, Engel recognized in such faithful borrowing from antiquity an authenticity appropriate for the time, and in Helsinki he had the advantage of working in a small city with no large factories to muddy the picture. Today, when visitors see the Empire buildings in Helsinki, they can see Engel's miniature version of St Petersburg, in buildings such as Senate Square (1811), the Lutheran Cathedral (1830–40), Senate House (1818–22), the University of Helsinki Library (1836–45) and the University of Helsinki Main Building (1832).

Engel's passion for theory invited an ordered architecture, a less exuberant classical approach; a practical beauty he termed 'high style'. Authenticity and the various ways of adhering to a 'high style' within Modernism were set to become major issues throughout the twentieth century. Engel here seemed to be laying the foundation for what became the constant and creative tension between the function of a building and the forms and ornamentation that also made it that building.

In fact in Engel can we not justly see the modern Finnish architect? Constantly keeping an eye on events and developments elsewhere, modest and restrained where possible, passionate about history but not garrulous about theory, Engel also studied mythology and construction techniques. In a position of responsibility that always demanded loyalty, the freedom to take other directions never presented itself. Classical theory was acceptable because it offered a controllable and authentic expression, while linking Helsinki to the iconography of larger, greater cities.[35]

This pioneering period is undoubtedly one of high international traffic. Yet within this sometimes bewildering cultural traffic was a Finnish way of doing things.[36] That this would become clearer, simple and effective – a brand, even – depended as much on notions such as authority, honesty, integrity and *sisu* as it did on architecture. As the modernizing agenda enters with a fuller force in the 1920s, we will see architects changing tack, altering their ideas to suit the way a post-

Aerial view of Engel's
Senate Square and
Cathedral, Helsinki.

classical, pre-functional or expressive Modernism might solve the
country's and the profession's needs. All of these 'strains', if we can call
them that, as we proceed to the strong 'Internationalism' of the 1930s, are
read now as more or less 'Finnish'.

Finland became independent in 1917. Modernism in the country was
ready for its serious rehearsals. This is where we consider the pioneering
period to have ended. Yet it would be wise to recall the words of the
historian G. M. Trevelyan: 'Unlike dates, periods are not facts. They are
retrospective conceptions that we form about past events, useful to focus
discussion but very often leading historical thought astray.'[37] For a Russian
empire needing to establish some distance from Swedish dominance, we

begin to see the control Engel respected. For a country needing to establish distance after 1917 from the Russian empire, which had then redefined it, we also begin to see how the modern Finnish architect would need similar control, and seek similar authenticity from the modern architecture that Le Corbusier was sketching out, paradoxically using antique as well as modern models – the Parthenon and the aeroplane.

chapter two

Independence: Rehearsals for Modernism

I long for the land that is not
> for everything that is I am weary of craving.
The moon tells me in silver runes
> about the land that is not.
The land where our every wish is wonderfully granted,
> the land where all our chains fall off,
> the land where we cool our torn brow
> in the moon's dew.
My life was a hot illusion.
But one thing I have found and one thing I have really gained –
> the road to the land that is not.
Edith Södergran, *The Land That Is Not*[1]

Towards the end of the First World War, Lenin's own calculation had succeeded in Russia and his government was the first to recognize the independence of Finland on the last day of 1917. A bloody and divisive civil war followed. With some 70,000 Russian troops still in Finland, in January 1918 the 'red guards' of the Finnish working class seized power in Helsinki. General Mannerheim, after having served 30 years in the Czar's army, was appointed by the Finnish government to organize an army of 'whites' to restore order against the Russian-aided rebels. The three-month civil war was short but vicious. Mannerheim won the decisive battle for Tampere at the beginning of April, whilst, upon the invitation of the Finnish Senate, a German force landed in Finland, taking Helsinki and other towns to guarantee the victory of the whites. There had been a plan to make Finland a monarchy with a German king, but the collapse of Germany in November 1918 shifted Finland's necessary allegiances once more to the East. Mannerheim served as regent until the summer of 1919, when Finland's first president, K. J. Ståhlberg, was sworn in. The formal peace treaty with Russia was signed in 1920. The 'reds' were pardoned and the representative of the losing side formed the first left-wing party, the Social Democratic Party, which, as early as 1926, would form the government and get its own taste of power.[2] For a decade before a turn towards the Scandinavian states, the League of Nations became an essential part of Finland's security policy since it pursued cooperation with the Baltic states and Poland.

Sigurd Frosterus,
Stockmann
Department Store,
Helsinki, 1916–30.

Finland may have avoided the resulting ambiguity with the 'revolution' and agitprop strategies that Russians had to go through, but the 1920s meant not only a period of uncertainty but also a tension that would involve Finland henceforth in the spheres of interest of the main powers. The civil war haunted Finns; partisan loyalty would demand unusual favours. Suddenly with its own institutions to form and fund, Finland was also very much left on its own. Between 1917 and 1930 the realities of the new nation could be only pragmatic and to some extent unpredictable. With its own system of representation and administration, elections by universal suffrage, its own civil service and financial institution, its own economy and culture, probably the greatest change in the 1920s politically was the adoption of parliamentary principles.[3]

It is said that the declaration of Finnish Independence in 1917 settled the debate in architecture between the Romantics and the Rationalists. The early years of the new country were a struggle. There was a frenzied, often confused search for new possibilities. Different styles were tried out, but the economic reality of the new country had one huge consequence. The monumentalizing projects of Saarinen, Sonck, Jung and others had succeeded; internationally, Finland was on the map. Although, if the grandeur of any 'national romantic' style had not already run its course, it had by now. Frosterus's words returned: 'We in Finland no longer gain our livelihood from hunting and fishing; thus the planned ornamentation and bears – not to speak of other animals – are hardly suitable symbols for the present time based on the use of steam and electricity.'[4]

However, there were more obvious reasons for this turn towards the utilitarian, efficient, functional response to urgent demands. There was no doubting the momentous task ahead. Finnish independence implied a new relationship to nationhood and existence. Modernism may have been in full swing in France and Germany, but the legacy of war, revolution, poverty and the cautious development in Finland under the Czar needed immense energies spent on production, housing, education, a civic structure and defence. Communities in the rural parts of the country had to re-group; new clusters formed. In response to events and developments beyond architecture, the building tradition turned for a while away from the cities to existing farmhouses and town houses.

Following on from Saarinen's Munkkiniemi-Haaga Town plan in 1915, commissioned by the business concern Stenius Oy, commercial and technical developments had also combined with architecture to demonstrate Helsinki's future possibilities. Proposed by the influential businessman Julius Tallberg, Eliel Saarinen's Pro Helsingfors Master Plan of 1918 drawn up with Bertel Jung, influenced by Ebenezer Howard's Garden City model, had opted for a scattered organic idea: a freely flowing plan

suggesting surprise and the unknown within the expected urban vistas.
Early years after Independence, the scale of such planning ideas began to
represent a 'nationalist' rather than a 'national' architecture. The scale of
its planning and aesthetic style might have echoed and even encouraged
Independence earlier, but it related little to the political and social reality
of the new country. Like much of the pre-war work, its scale, grandeur
and internationalism had boosted national morale, but by the early 1920s
such work had lost its critical edge.

Onne Tarjanne,
Takaharju
Sanatorium,
Punkaharju,
1899–1903.

Traces of Nordic classicism that appeared briefly before the war re-emerged. Further, it was difficult to attribute the necessary progressive and revolutionary connotations – the 'iron and brain' style that Frosterus spoke about in 1904 – to architecture. The mission was more immediate. Frosterus himself revised his own agenda in 1917 and the Stockmann Department Store, won in competition in 1916, was built in stages by 1930. The vertical accentuation and roof-lit central space following the shape of the block and its slight curving steep roof were distinctively controlled. With Germanic echo, it remains one of the iconic buildings of the century. The architectural and planning exercise was instantly more modest, but no less visionary; architecture would now search for a direct response to the new nation's dilemma. The social impacted on architecture, since 'identity' was suddenly secondary to immediate requirements and an increasingly busy city life. And requirements became a responsibility. The newly independent country needed minimal dwelling standards and hygiene. The good sense from the turn of the century would now be reinforced more than ever in the 1920s.

Much has been critically exaggerated in this necessary search for rational solutions. The simplification and clarity that would emerge in the functional requirements of the buildings was precisely the agenda that was also emerging in the strong Functionalism coming out of Germany, especially from 1926 onwards. That these two 'new' directions merged and could play off each other indicates how much Finnish architecture would always oscillate between the 'national' and the 'international'. Critical caution is needed here too. For when we notice a move towards describing Nordic classicism as a restrained and disciplined classicism leading naturally towards Functionalism and Internationalism, it is as much to the East as to the West that we must turn. If we are to understand the tension between two opposing forces, the 'functional' and the 'picturesque', modernity and tradition, we must also recall the early adventures in Karelia that were still to be published during the 1920s. And when we hear the critical distinction made between these oppositions, it is noticeable that the influence of one on the other in relation to Finnish Modernism was constant throughout the century. Although this tension between the rational and the romantic had its basis in the last decade of the nineteenth century, it is in the 1920s that we begin to see the shape of this dualism. In Finnish architecture the utilitarian functional view and the symbolist, more decorative approach by no means exclude each other.

Pick any of the following architects not usually featured in recent critical histories on twentieth-century Finnish architecture: Onni Tarjanne, Wivi Lönn, Uno Ullberg, Martti Välikangas, Elsi Borg, Väino Vähäkallio, Toivo Paatela, Aulis Blomstedt, Lauri Silvennoinen, Erik Adlercreutz, Kaarina Löfström, Jyrki Tasa.[5] Study their trips, their studies, their teaching and diplomas, their professional dreams and their modern design practice and you will discover the shape of Modernism within Finland in the twentieth century. If they were or are women consider how difficult it has been and still is in such a profession. Dig even deeper and you will discover the relationships between tradition and Modernism throughout that century. Go even deeper still and you will discover how the very modern architecture that was to transform society was to become the 'tradition' it now upholds against the contemporary invader. And considered a tradition, the birthright of the nation, we will discover how this modern agenda set itself up as a constant attempt to live in a truth and used architecture to attain that truth. Of these 'unknown' architects, the influence of one in particular became significant: Hilding Ekelund lived – literally – through the whole modern and modernizing period from 1893 to 1984. Italy was always close to Ekelund's heart; it was a land elsewhere brought nearer home. Coinciding with 'Functionalism', this land would eventually become the new home, the new Finland. In a way Ekelund and many other Finnish architects found, through Italy, that 'road to the land that is not'.

It was the work of the Swede Gunnar Asplund among others who primarily opened up the notion of the timeless tradition connected to the Mediterranean. Implied in this fascination was the necessity of good sense, sound planning and a modest and functional response. Study trips abroad to other Nordic countries and Italy had already been a strong part of architects' education, but it was during the 1920s that these would offer influential directions for the architecture to come. Here Ekelund is speaking in the 1960s about the 1920s:

> It seems quite natural that, after the isolation of the war years, young architects should have sought the lands of the south, in particular Italy, and have found their new, inspiring influences – perhaps not so much from monumental classical and renaissance architecture as the simple *architettura minore* of the country-side, which is in certain senses in sympathy with the spirit of the Nordic countries.[6]

Hilding Ekelund,
Töölö Church,
Helsinki, 1930.

You can find any amount of words and phrases uttered later by Finnish architects altering the aims and ideals of the Modern Movement, but Ekelund here captures the underlying shape any modern impulse was to take. Finland would offer itself in a way as a laboratory. It would be Modernism's *architettura minore*.[7] Ekelund as educator, architect, polemicist, editor, planner, administrator and realist worked throughout his six-decade career to prove that the modern age in Finland was one coincidental with Finland's own social and cultural development. Known from the early Helsinki Kunsthalle (1928) and Töölö Church (1930), he went right through the 'functionalist' break to the designs for the Olympic Village and later became well known for his housing projects in Maunula, Helsinki (1951–6), and Munkkivuori (1957–8). Although Alvar Aalto and to a lesser extent Erik Bryggman have become the dominant narrative in Finnish architectural history, it was Ekelund who, along with his peers J. S. Sirén and Martti Välikangas, his followers like Aulis Blomstedt and Aarno Ruusuvuori, and later architects such as Wilhelm Helander and Juha Leiviskä, did much to shape Modernism and ensure the hold its agenda was to take on Finnish architecture. The hold remains to this day.

Directly or indirectly, Ekelund's consistency strengthened the modern agenda into an ideology by collapsing the tradition of Italy's *architettura minore* with the claims and progress implied in the new spirit of Le Corbusier and the Modern Architecture Movement. The conviction and search for authentic architecture defined by Ekelund laid the grounds for a consistent professional application of the new in service of basic, sound, social and functional solutions for the young Republic.

54

It is true that Modernism entered Finland by way of its western neighbour, Sweden. Although we have strong examples in the stripped poetry of Edith Södergran (1892–1923)[8] and the reductive 'modernist' paintings of Hélène Schjerfbeck, at the time their avant-gardism represented more the pioneering of a Finnish-Swedish Modernism. During the 1920s Finland was still very much under Swedish influence, and although the Finnish language had gained much strength, deeper avant-garde practices in Finnish literature, language and art would have to wait for some decades. Although Alvar Aalto was from Alajärvi in Pohjanmaa, a region considered very Finnish, both Aalto and Bryggman were heavily influenced by Swedish culture. Using Finnish and Swedish, Aalto developed into a fine-phrase master. From the outset he was quick to lobby for his own works and would later – charismatically and epigrammatically – shift through Latin, French and Italian. Bryggman and Aalto were young architects beginning their practices in the early 1920s, both naturally drawn to, influenced by, and then eventually able to assimilate the ideas of Modernism and the Modern Movement literally flooding Europe and reaching Finland, primarily via Stockholm and the old Finnish capital Turku. Can we date this invasion more accurately?

The architect Pekka Helin – himself one of today's influential assimilators and shapers of Finnish late Modernism – clearly identifies this momentous turning point (following Hilding Ekelund's suggestion in an interview in 1974) to 21 April 1928: the day that the Swedish architect Sven Markelius lectured on 'rational architecture' at the meeting of the Association of Finnish Architects in Turku.[9] As critically neat as this appears, and as important as the presentation no doubt was, the idea of a single moment for the change towards Functionalism / Modernism is both unrealistic and rather unlikely. Simply, the shifts implied in the Modernism-to-come were already forming in the pre-Modernism that had gone. The route as we enter the crucial first decade of Finnish Independence is somewhat murkier.[10]

During the 1920s, until the Great Depression that began in 1929, Finland would go through an immense development that would define its struggle as an independent country. Housing shortages necessitated invention and thrift.[11] Economic difficulties and a relatively low standard of living were met with an enthusiasm and a social spirit. Successful Finnish sportsmen, the appearance of a new literature in Sweden, and the growing awareness of international ideas through diplomacy and culture, travels and exchange began opening up the country. Fact-finding tours to Scandinavia and beyond became the norm for officials and artists alike.[12]

Modernism, like jazz, steam, electricity and Futurism, was exciting and a touch irresponsible. At the end of the 1920s the Torchbearers were a group of avant-garde Finnish writers that included the influential and charismatic Olavi Paavolainen. The motto of this literary movement became cultural currency: 'windows open to Europe'. Yet it is the accepted superficiality at the same time of some of the language of Mika Waltari's famous novel *Suuri Illusio* (The Grand Illusion) of 1928 that allows us to glimpse the flirtation with the urban and the cosmopolitanism that went along with this excitement of the new.[13] Post civil-war Finnish literature proved useful for therapeutic purposes, idealizing the (Swedish) bourgeoisie and satirizing backwardness.[14] Although there were also signs of a post-Romantic period in poetry with the emergence of Expressionist exercises that would signal a little more contemporary response in the 1930s, as in the poetry of Arvi Kivimaa and his homage to Honegger and the like, the avant-garde Modernist writing remained in Swedish and entered Finnish circles slowly.[15]

The 1920s was all about cross-traffic: in ideas, in influence, in ignorance, in superficiality, in thrill. The Internationalism and Modernism that flourished in Sweden during the 1920s became an influential and inevitable filter to radical movements in France, Spain, America, Germany, the Netherlands and Austria. Finland responded warmly, intuitively, even superficially, to the *Neue Sachlichkeit* movement and the new Dutch architecture. The proximity to Stockholm of the old Swedish capital of Finland, Åbo (Turku), produced a direct, persistent and intense cultural traffic. Although the most important and generalizing models for social buildings were from the Weimar Republic, it was the Stockholm Exhibition of 1930 that appeared to bring the Nordic ideal of Modernism and modern architecture together. As the most celebrated new architect in Sweden, Gunnar Asplund, set out the Nordic possibilities of the new architecture, the Finns were already thinking of how to trim, refine, appropriate and adapt any model they found useful.

It is often pointed out that a Nordic classicism suited the Swedish cultural class who remained very much in control in the newly independent Finland. Its austerity would emphasize the contrasts between the rural Finns and the civil, 'graceful' Swedes. Along with this reading of favoured forms derived from Graeco-Roman antiquity, this influence has been interpreted as architects suddenly re-seeking inspiration from earlier historical periods. This, however, is secondary to the actual architectural exercise, the methodology involved in the light treatment of a 'heavier' form, for it is the inevitably reduced, stripped away, abstracted interpretations of this classicism that are considered to be the true foundation of the Finnish modernist movement.[16]

Although misleading perhaps in emphasis, in the main this argument is true; there are also excellent accounts in more detail of this period.[17] More recently Susanne Salin has helped us to understand the generally accepted shape of this period:

> This 'Swedish Grace' can be seen as an expression of what is called 'light classicism' within Nordic classicism, which was primarily represented by young architects such as Kay Fisker in Denmark, Gunnar Asplund in Sweden and Alvar Aalto, Martti Välikangas and Hilding Ekelund. According to Igor Herler, the style was unconventional, un-academic and characterized by an impression of 'irony and volatility'.[18]

Un-academic, un-heroic; here is that definition again of Finnish restraint. Light classicism implies the existence of a heavier, more academic classicism. If this lightness was to meet Functionalism, to be consistent abstraction and reduction would merely continue known dynamics.

In relation to an emerging modern agenda how then does this period connect itself or differ from the more identifiable movements that had already established a Finnish architecture up to the outbreak of the First World War? And does this period establish the critical exercise in reduction and abstraction often seen as the predominant trait in Finnish Modernism, the way the architects assimilated and redefined Modernism for their own cultural purposes?

Let us return to the pressing national agenda. Aided by the domination of the wood processing industry, Finland grew rapidly. Factories and housing areas were commissioned, and although the decade began with a housing shortage, the period from 1923 until the recession in 1930 saw a rapid growth in housing production. There is no doubt that the general level and design of the built environment in Finland during the 1920s remained one of low-density, modest development and necessarily restrained, careful planning. The Compulsory Education Act (1921) led to an immense effort to build schools. An average of 150 schools per year resulted from this policy, which necessitated a competition in 1921, announced by the National Board of Education, and a manual published the following year: *Architectural Plans for Rural Elementary Schools*.[19] Now often dilapidated, abandoned or reclaimed for artists' ateliers, the presence of these classicist wooden buildings in the Finnish countryside, villages and on the edge of towns is an unmistakable clue to why the simple, strict but logical hierarchy and order in all things classical appealed.

In 1919 a child welfare committee was established; the General Mannerheim League for Children was started in 1920 and the Save the

Children Fund of Finland began in 1922. In 1921 Professor Ylppö, the founder of Finnish maternity and child welfare clinics, launched various service schemes for the training of nurses, activities that also led to the Act on Child Welfare of 1936.[20] The country and towns of independent Finland started filling out with schools, libraries, kindergartens, hospitals, other civic buildings and churches. Functional, clean solutions in housing, hospitals, factories and commercial buildings undoubtedly matched the need for the careful economic development of the Finnish state as it emerged more and more out of its autonomy under the Russian empire. Cleanly rendered surfaces, simple volumes, easily constructed, axial symmetry, logical hierarchy, and simple but adaptable spaces all meant an increase in hygiene and all met fiscal stringency. The un-heroic age had by then its own quiet un-heroic heroes, the architects.

The term 'Modernism', however, was not recognized during this decade. The 'new spirit' resonated with 'older' spirits from the 1890s and with the new movements in Futurism and Cubism. Jazz was modern but frivolous too; the New Architecture had not quite arrived. Lingering Renaissance dreams, classical precision and Italianate fantasies all coexisted in the early 1920s, with the need for simple dwellings and increased production. These all fused into the country's agenda as the early, experimental and sometimes confused years of the decade were to be opened towards the international movement emerging strongly elsewhere.

In 1927 Le Corbusier's pioneering manifesto *Toward a New Architecture* was translated into English. When J. M. Richards described it as 'the great master's dramatically presented ideas about an ideal modern architecture and its relation to modern life' he was probably speaking for the majority of architects who encountered the New Architecture. Many Finnish architects were feeling their way with the new ideas. It is often claimed that the early 'famous' works of Aalto and Bryggman, because of their strong links to the emerging Modern Movement, have historically overshadowed the importance of other architects. This is as true now as it was in the 1920s. And although not all architects created or could create famous works, all used the New Architecture to test their own 'Nordic classical' ideas.

It is with this in mind that I suggest that we consider the influential architect Martti Välikangas, himself a classmate, colleague and friend of Hilding Ekelund. Born and brought up in Savonlinna, eastern Finland, the 'Novgorod' touch might have meant that a romanticism and classicism lingered a touch longer with Välikangas. Yet, even if so, it did not hold him back for long. Välikangas, like countless other Finnish architects over a 40-year span, went in and out of the visual styles that were applied to test the Modern Movement's ideals.

Martti Välikangas,
Käpylä Garden
Suburb, 1920–25.

Käpylä Garden Suburb, for which Välikangas designed the housing, stands out as one of the most important developments in Finnish planning. Completed in 1925, during the late 1960s it was one project considered unworthy in the 'consensus-Modernism' of the time. Today, however, the garden suburb (also known as Puu – 'wood' – Käpylä) remains a vital and relatively unspoilt idyll on the outskirts of Helsinki. Up to Käpylä we might say Finnish planning had been driven by national, visionary ideals – a question of the aesthetics applied, whilst looking over the shoulder to 'civilizing' examples from other countries. The British garden suburb directed energies: Ebenezer Howard's book *Garden Cities of Tomorrow* (1898) was to influence planning way beyond the 1920s. To the planner Otto-Iivari Meurman, Käpylä Garden Suburb offered a timely example of the type of master plan that could offset rigid formalist planning. Meurman drew up the overall plan with Birger Brunila, recreating the intimacy of grouped housing and open spaces. Later, in 1928, when the modern reliance on transport and the regularity of the emerging Functionalist master plan were more apparent, Meurman outlined the benefits of Käpylä. Here, curiously enough, was an antidote to the diagrammatic, utopian nightmares pre-scripted by Functionalism and followed by many Finnish architects in competitions throughout the 1920s. As Asko Salokorpi has written: 'Planning was not regarded merely as an artistic or traffic movement exercise, rather as an attempt to place the main emphasis on social factors, including, of course, matters of economy and hygiene.'[21] Appointed Professor of Planning in Helsinki in 1940, Meurman was to champion a species of forest planning. Later, this would combine with the diversity recognized in Aalto's fan-shaped Sunila Cellulose concept-housing and factory and provide the freer model for the 'forest-town' concept. Throughout his life Meurman remained an important counter-balance to the grander schemes of the Finnish

Martti Välikangas,
Käpylä Garden
Suburb, 1920–25,
aerial view.

Functionalists and Rationalists. His influence can be seen in Tapiola Garden Suburb, the planning of which began in the 1940s and was to include the work of Aulis Blomstedt, Markus Tavio, Aarne Ervi, Viljo Revell, and Heikki and Kaija Sirén.

If Meurman controlled the garden idyll in Käpylä, Välikangas controlled the light classicism. Built to alleviate the housing shortage, the standardized production of the wooden buildings made a large and rapid production of workers' housing possible and social reform acceptable. Välikangas shaped the form and external appearance of the residential area with an elongated and domesticized classicism of high quality. Ekelund's ideals come to mind. Softening the neo-classical influence, the asymmetric formality of the rectangular blocks merged the idea of a modern open plan, light and planting with the beginning of Functional regularity. Architecturally and socially, the area has remained exemplary. It is naturally no longer a workers' housing area but populated by that professional class enthusiastic for activism and prefabrication but who may have just wanted its removal in the late 1960s.

Välikangas faced new challenges and began to negotiate different styles connected with the New Architecture. He felt the ideals of a natural, almost correct, way to design architecture; the approach was always greater than the style, and the ideology where there was one was embedded in

60

the pre-Modern Movement. Like many of his colleagues in the early 1920s, he travelled to Italy. The war and Independence had lessened the desire for a monumental architecture to represent nationalist dreams. Influenced by his own upbringing in eastern Finland, just as J. S. Sirén was influenced by the grandeur and simplicity in north-west Finland in Ostrobothnia, it was again naturally the small-town, anonymous *architettura minore* of Umbria and Tuscany that also appealed to Välikangas.[22] His stretched, somewhat elongated, classicism and simplicity is extended in the Töölö Housing district of Helsinki (1923). The Italianate fantasies and themed motifs disappear and the classical motifs recede along with lingering Art Deco traces. Concrete and reinforced steel offered simplicity, removing the necessity for the play of motifs (as seen in his themed lobby for the Athena – now the Orion – Cinema, in Helsinki, 1927). By 1928 in Helsinki, Välikangas was attempting the ribbon-window, albeit somewhat robust, as were many other architects. In 1932–3 he went on to produce two of his purest examples of Functionalism, the Artturinlinna Apartment Block and Eerikinkatu 33, both in Helsinki.[23]

Brief though this description is, the pattern remains and research is available on many architects who faced similar decisions, who took similar turns and who used their own 'Nordic' palette sensitively in relation to often bewildering foreign developments.[24] A quick visual comparison of the buildings on the turn from Nordic classicism to Functionalism

Martti Välikangas, Eerikinkatu 33 Apartments, Helsinki, 1933 (*left*), and Artturinlinna Apartments, Helsinki, 1932 (*right*).

during this crucial period, 1926–32, will indicate that any critical attempts to juggle history in order to prove that Aalto had adapted pure Functionalism first (in the Turun Sanomat office, 1926, for example) is irrelevant in relation to the general way almost all Finnish architects were responding to the New Architecture. But like Saarinen, Sonck and Selim Lindqvist before him, like countless other Finnish architects such as Ekelund and Erkki Huttunen, and those ahead of him in the future, Välikangas would produce a spirited 'Finnish' architecture in whichever visual style impressed at the time. A Romantic classicism turned into a Nordic classicism. Then a gradual Functionalism was stripped into its 'heroic' stage, later to be softened by a more contextual functional language. This would break out again into the larger scale, post-war heroic Functionalist works, especially Välikangas's bigger commercial and hospital projects of the 1950s.

Because Välikangas is identified mostly with the Käpylä project in the 1920s, his significance and influence in Finnish architectural history tend to remain tied to this period. In relation to the way that modern architecture has shaped and been shaped by figures such as Välikangas, this has led to a distorted view of the history. Yet, just as we suggested with Ekelund's 60-year journey, Välikangas's 40-year career captures the Modernist enterprise within Finland. When Välikangas was completing his own version of the British garden suburb in Käpylä, Selim Lindqvist, with some of his later work, was achieving a Gropius-inspired new architecture, as were Frosterus and Nyström, albeit with more flourish. Aalto, like Bryggman, was younger and, in the mid-1920s, still involved with Italianate fantasies. Perhaps youth allowed Aalto and Bryggman to take to the New Architecture with its functional hints with less resistance, possibly sensing more opportunity. But there is little doubt that Finnish architects were instinctively stripping back anything that hinted at sentiment and hysteria.

A look at Välikangas's building at No. 9 Vuorikatu, Helsinki, will help us to understand both the shape of Modernism and its general pattern among Finnish architects. Completed in 1928, the traces of a restrained but somewhat 'heavy' Nordic classicism remain, the red-brick massing punctuating the regular window rhythm. We need only to see this building in relation to Aalto's Turun Sanomat newspaper building to know the type of conventional stylistic expectations that Välikangas could not abandon in his turn towards Functionalism. This was not yet a fully expressed Functionalism.

By the 1960s the lower two floors of No. 9 Vuorikatu were part of a department store called Pukeva. The first floor had been replaced by plate glass and windows allowing for the emerging new modernity of advertising 'screens'. In the late 1960s and early 1970s, while many older buildings were removed in Helsinki, Välikangas's building of 1928 was demolished. In its place, in 1973, went one of the first glazed wall units in Finnish architecture. This allowed huge-scale images and advertising to cover the building. Screen printing and the modernizing of the advertising industry needed its own 'stage'. Ironically, this pre-empted the huge structural glass boxes that would cover Helsinki some thirty years later. These are the corporate glass buildings being reclaimed as new, if not late, Modernism. Celebrated today as a restrained neo-Internationalism, we begin to recognize the patterns of an applied Internationalism. But by 1956, however, Välikangas, still a practising architect, produced in Paasitalo a huge commercial building (offices and shops): a functional box complete with italic neon signage and a centrally punched-out tower just as he had done in Vuorikatu almost thirty years earlier. Only this time the box became a two-floor shopping plinth as neon also began to identify the city's functional architecture.

This adventure was to repeat itself throughout the century as architects in fashion and power in one decade would move out of fashion the next, and then re-engage their own palette with later fashion. At all times the convicted belief in the agenda, the ideological hold that Modernism took, would see the resulting architecture in Finland adaptable to all these swings. And at all times the architects were designing buildings responding to time and their own culture as they saw their previous buildings go out of time.

Whether we read critically of the heavy Monumentalism of an architect like J. S. Sirén, the White Functionalism of P. E. Blomstedt, the restrained, elegant Functional classicism of Bryggman and Ekelund, the direction in the emerging new architects' work in Finland after the 1920s would always be towards the rational solution. Respecting the natural surroundings (not a particularly difficult exercise in Finland, where there is so much of it) would remain as constant an exercise as resisting excess. The historian Riitta Nikula puts this succinctly, agreeing with the idea that the 'pure cleansing of forms' is already identifiable in the pre-Modern Movement:

> For the first third of the twentieth century in Finland, architecture was still broadly historicist. Formal choices in the 1920s were clearly made to express particular meanings. The range of forms used was large, although the formal language was continually developing in a more ascetic direction and eclecticism, in the combination of forms, becoming more individual. If we focus on the pure cleansing of forms, we clearly see the models of European Modernism.[25]

Martti Välikangas, Vuorikatu 9, Helsinki, from left to right: as originally constructed in 1928; in the 1960s; during the 1980s; and the building today.

The year 1927 is often identified as a turning point, the pivot in international architecture in Finland. The year saw the Weissenhof Siedlung, the major housing exhibition in Stuttgart, which included works by Le Corbusier, Walter Gropius and others, and was widely regarded as a built manifesto of Modern Movement architecture. Le Corbusier's influence and revolutionary 'nerve' were undoubtedly irresistible to a young architect like Aalto. By looking at the immense ambition and constant writings of the time, Alvar Aalto, in his late twenties, clearly assimilated the early thrill of the new 'modern' architecture more urgently than most. Outgoing, often un-Finnish in his eager brashness, Aalto was constantly in Stockholm, in touch with the emerging Gunnar Asplund and, to a lesser degree, Sven Markelius. Although Aalto was known already for his streamlined classicism in the Worker's Club at Jyväskylä in 1924 and the Muurame Church in 1926, by 1927 he was already at work on what became one of his 'modernist' masterpieces, Viipuri Library.

There is no doubt that in this decade the Internationalism of Aalto began to shape Finnish architecture abroad and to tune the response to the modern agenda at home. He seemed able to negotiate the moment more quickly than most. The Viipuri Library, completed in 1936, echoed, assimilated and integrated Asplund's ideas. For many Finnish architects including Aalto, Asplund had been the catalyst; his Stockholm Library

64

(1924) bridged the classical and functional with enviable restraint for the time. Vibrant and ambitious, by 1929 Aalto had absorbed the works of Le Corbusier and Asplund, even Bryggman. Viipuri had been won in competition in 1927, and Paimio Sanatorium – another recognized iconic work – was on the boards for three or four years. Wedged in between the Turku newspaper building, Viipuri offered an immediate exercise in the transfer of ideas from the already disseminated but not necessarily accepted modern architecture. Viipuri coincided with Aalto's clarification within the emerging Functional movement – technological advances in tubular steel and the use of glass led to an increasing plasticity at both the detailed scale and the larger massing of the building. The delay of so many years also enabled Aalto to use the Viipuri Library as a constant work-in-progress; altered as it responded to new works and trends from abroad, it also gains from interventions from other completed buildings. Buildings like Turun Sanomat and Paimio Sanatorium, though built before Viipuri, embody elements worked out in the Library over the years.

Probably no other building is quite so recognizably orthodox in terms of the emerging Functionalism, however, as Aalto's Turun Sanomat newspaper offices in Turku (1930). On the street side, Le Corbusier's five-point planning principles are identifiable: pilotis, rooftop garden,

free floor plan made possible by the frame structure, strip windows and
open façade. To the rear, with its curved forms and window details, it is
quite the complete work. The Turun Sanomat building is recognized as
the first and ultimate example of Le Corbusier's principles in Finland,
yet it also clearly extended them, hinting at Aalto's individuality. Using

Alvar Aalto, Viipuri Library, 1936.

Alvar Aalto holding up a branch at Viipuri Library, 1935.

advances in print technology, the potential of concrete to create the large open spaces necessary for a newspaper factory, and the development of 'clean' detailing made this an ideally suited project for the modern agenda. With its huge street-facing glass wall, the newspaper could display its daily front page to the city; here, modern experiments in advertising, neon and communication were brought together. More importantly, however, this building enabled the Finns to establish clear precedence, even over their long-time influential neighbours, the Swedes. From this time onwards, influence from Sweden would not so much fade as become a contest. Aalto would go on and explore similar divergence from known sources, especially in the functional architecture that soon developed into the 'White Functionalism', replicated, patterned and refined throughout the Finnish countryside.

The timing of Modernism and the profession's constant recourse to an ideological position and response to the Modern Movement invites us to skip years. To understand modern architecture in Finland is to understand why it is now shaped more than ever by Aalto's works, especially those that formed the breakthrough to the New Architecture, and why, for a period that later lasted three decades, there would be a professional rejection of Aalto's works within Finland. For a significant part of the twentieth century, to the profession Aalto signified an engagingly heroic, more reckless, but *less modern* architecture. If these three buildings – Viipuri, Turun Sanomat and Paimio – formed the Internationalism

Viipuri Library,
reading room.

that established Aalto's position, it would be the ways in which he
steered away from the strict vocabulary that would cause such rejection.
Later, his overtly 'romantic' projects, such as Villa Mairea and the New
York Pavilion interior wall, pre-empting the red-brick works of the
1950s, began to betray the simplicity and accepted severity associated

with a Modernism shaped by Hilding Ekelund's *architettura minore*. Although the 1930s would stretch the 'Existenzminimum' of just about everything, Aalto would part from Ekelund's vision.[26] While Finnish architects established their own White Functionalism after Aalto and other international trends, Aalto himself already began to question the subsequent 'ideologizing' of the modern agenda.

Aalto recognized how the white Functionalist buildings at first were a signal of a greater programme and the initial success of the Bauhaus. He also realized how these buildings would stand in metonymically for the Modern Movement itself. There was no mistaking the excitement, but the aspect of social reform and development would be tackled only in the next decade. As the Finnish critic Asko Salokorpi identified in 1970: 'despite all the talk about social responsibility, functionalism in Finland showed little sign of class consciousness.'[27] Establishing and sustaining the authenticity of modern architecture as an ideology would be crucial to Aalto's greater scheme, but it was the inherent structure of Finnishness, and the role that landscape and natural siting played, that defined its pioneering social and cultural potential.

Erik Bryggman's Hospits Betel (1929) was also the culmination of ideas that had filtered through since the mid-1920s. The building includes a clearly delineated hotel block with regular fenestration, deep-cut details and smooth, flowing but strictly controlled interior planning. External details, however, also indicate the tendency towards an expressive massing that was – paradoxically – both heavier and lighter than Aalto's at the time. Here was a hint of the possible expressive turn that Bryggman might have made, which later P. E. Blomstedt demonstrated so briefly in the early 1930s. The deftness of touch that Bryggman brought to the functional expression concentrated less on technical developments and more on a subtle bridging between a Nordic classicism and the emerging colder 'Internationalism' identified initially in Aalto's early works. Aalto would achieve the transfer from an orthodox Internationalism to a deft modern vernacular, while Bryggman retained the Finnish connection to a refined classicism tempered by some unusual solutions and details, as seen in his two, now renowned, chapels. The large, rather austere forms of Bryggman's Parainen Chapel (1930) hint at a slightly reluctant internationalism, while his Resurrection Chapel in Turku (1941) resolves this reluctance with style and vibrancy. The latter, comfortable with an unspeaking mass, a closed form, holds out architecture to the light of material and void. The paradoxical heaviness becomes lighter, yet avoids the 'transparency' of some of Aalto's emerging works.

One event, however, probably did more in the short term than these buildings to disseminate the stricter aesthetic identification and

vocabulary that would become Internationalism and later a locally tran-scribed Functionalism (sometimes referred to in Finland, misleadingly, as the *funkis* design and lifestyle). It was likely on the strength of the constant traffic between Stockholm, Europe and Finland that Erik Bryggman and Alvar Aalto as joint designers, turned, in 1929, the 700th anniversary of the City of Turku from a trade fair exhibition into a functionalist work-shop. Describing the Turku Fair as a manifesto of orthodox Function-alism suggests though that the models presented were already replicas of work elsewhere. In fact to be 'orthodox' these works, of course, had to be recognizable. By all accounts this fair was not only a dry run of the potential canon of modern architecture, it pre-empted Gunnar Asplund's own demonstration in the Stockholm World Fair of 1930 and the eventual Swedish Modernist manifesto *Acceptera* ('Accept!') of 1931.[28]

The Turku Fair was more instant and ad hoc than has been acknow-ledged, but the modernist vocabulary was formed by the rough-and-ready timber structures. Aalto and Bryggman had not only followed the Bauhaus and the important Stuttgart Weissenhofsiedlung, but, like any good contribution, strengthened them. Picking up on Bauhaus typo-graphical detail and applied arts, advertising columns and structures gave the Turku Fair site a distinctive feel. This was instant architecture and instantly modern. Bryggman and Aalto recognized the use of the imper-manent exhibition building as a means of 'imaging' and disseminating the new visual culture within the country. The roughness allowed them to adapt and assimilate the New Style.

The impermanence of the exhibition process would continue throughout the twentieth century. It would increasingly become part of the propaganda process connected to the establishment of the Finland Builds Exhibition and the founding of the Museum of Finnish Archi-tecture in the 1950s. Adapting to and passing on ideas about architecture, through the developing professional body SAFA (an acronym of Suomen Arkkitehtiliitto Finlands Arkitekförbund – the Finnish Association of Architects) and its publication, *Arkkitehti* (Finnish Architectural Review), exhibitions and promotion would also go hand in hand with the unique competition structure set up at the beginning of the century. Aalto too knew how well competitions and exhibitions served the promotion of a local but internationalist architecture. Competitions, especially during the 1920s, would become the arena for testing out the new architec-ture. Besides those known from the time (Aalto, Bryggman, Ekelund, Välikangas), it is remarkable testimony to the innovative competition structure that most well-known Finnish architects in the twentieth century established offices on the strength of winning architectural and planning competitions.[29]

Erik Bryggman,
Hospits Betel,
Turku, 1929

But the effect and power of such an event and set of structures as the Turku Fair of 1929 cannot be underestimated. The white forms, the stark clarity of the assemblage, the steps, the tower and the advertising columns were as flimsy and diagrammatic as they were modern. They were also more than simply different from what went before; significantly, they began to prophesy the future. Just as in 1900 (although for completely different reasons), the new, the modern, the revolutionary future were there for all to see. Ideas were disseminated. The future was graspable, and Finland had little in the sense of a past to prevent it from reaching for the stars. The future also had an agenda: modern architecture. The rehearsal was over, and the real work would now begin.

chapter three

White Functionalism:
The Modern Agenda

Dashing along on engine's buffer
no cap on her head
her hair flying free
heading for new lands:
Pacific!
Listen to the railway's thunderous music
listen to the engine's shrilly whistling:
Here I come
— a   t r a i n
with sides gleaming black
haughty and beautiful
rushing and dashing
and with me is
Honegger
Honegger, Honegger!
Arvi Kivimaa, *Arthur Honegger*[1]

Once it took hold, Modernism was always a movement in a hurry: as Ford Madox Ford wrote as early as 1923, it 'leavens a whole Nation with astonishing rapidity ... its ideas pour through the daily, the weekly and the monthly press with the rapidity of water pouring through interstices'.[2] Dashing along, sometimes this 'modern' rush serves to alter the culture; sometimes it serves to resist further invasion into the culture. As the national drive and the need for a showy monumentalism receded with Independence, the emerging domestic tradition and the requirements of the new country enabled architects to develop their own version of the 'new architecture'.

Initially, the thrust of the new architecture in the 1920s was an unselfconscious rational rather than 'rationalist' approach to Finland's building programme. It was not yet the internationalist Functionalism that was to characterize the 1930s and offer *a priori* assertions. And though 'Functionalism' was seen as the architecture of the first machine age, it would take some years before architects practising during the 1920s actually crystallized the work they had been doing.

'We should create', Ekelund wrote in hindsight in 1950, 'on the basis of the advanced technology and social life of our time, an architecture

Viljo Revell, Niilo Kokko and Heimo Riihimäki, Lasipalatsi (Glass Palace), Helsinki, 1935–6.

J. S. Sirén, Finnish
Parliament House,
Helsinki, 1924–31,
aerial view
looking towards
Töölö, and Parliament
House interior.

which is logically natural, light in construction, human in mood, delicate in spirit, and even humorous.'[3] Although this was the modern
agenda crystallized perfectly, at mid-century, significantly it defined both
the past and the future. In the 1920s the ideal in Finnish architecture had
been rehearsed; in the 1930s it became a 'deep structure';[4] in the subsequent decades this relation with the Modern Movement was to test out
the underlying ideal of Finnish architecture. Eventually, despite the types
of architecture opted for, the deep structure would be claimed a birthright. Functionalism would collectively and retrospectively imply the
ideology befitting Finnish architecture.

The shape of the 1920s should not deceive us, or encourage us to seek
the 'rational' in only those architects who restrained their architecture to
a recognizably pure Functionalism. Some architects were less convinced;
their classical training accepted change in a more reserved manner. If, in
1950, Hilding Ekelund was pre-empting what is now accepted as the
1950s 'golden age', in the early 1930s the Finnish Parliament House –
designed by J. S. Sirén in 1923–4 and eventually won after a phased competition – had just been completed. Ekelund's commentary was again
at hand; it confirmed the end of an era. In the mid-1930s the Finnish

78

Parliament House was an ambiguous if not entirely unwanted 'rational–classical' monument. 'The Parliament House', Ekelund wrote, 'is an anthem to the monumental architecture in which the basic principle has been art for art's sake; aesthetically its creator had a completely free hand and the beauty of its form is an end in itself.'[5]

'Art for art's sake' would dog the Finnish rationalists for years to come. But Ekelund's appreciation of the architectural consistency, technical skill and stylistic control of the architect J. S. Sirén would resonate with words used to describe and legitimate the neo-functional Finnish architecture at the end of the 1990s. When Ekelund concluded that the Parliament Building was 'consciously in contrast to the new, socially motivated attitudes permeating architecture', he would be rehearsing the same argument that would arise whenever variations to a functional 'consensus' to Modernism appeared.

Indeed, the number of terms used to describe this 'new architecture' indicated the restless and exploratory energy of the time. Finnish architects were trying to come to terms with the four main trends floating around: the Bauhaus school; the works and words of Le Corbusier (for example, with his magazine *L'Esprit nouveau*, begun in 1920); the Dutch De Stijl group; and the more ambiguous connection to the Russian Constructivists. The main players in the Finnish architectural profession would all attempt to define the 'new'. In 1928 alone, P. E. Blomstedt spoke of the 'new rationalism', Erik Bryggman referred to a 'rationalism or functionalism' and Aalto had used the term 'new realism'. In 1930 Ekelund would speak of 'neo-rationalism'; the fluctuation between name and agenda would go on throughout the 1930s. The *a priori* assertions that could be applied to the emerging Finnish architecture, however, would remain unchanged; a deeper structure would emerge only slowly.

Following the stock market crash of 1929 the architectural profession was required to continue the production of quick, efficient and hygienic development in housing and public and civic building. It was the younger architects who gained the confidence to turn the new expression into a stylistically identifiable architecture. How and when this turned into a programmatic modern agenda remains unclear, but Finnish architects were undoubtedly helped in this by the proximity to Sweden and the works of colleagues such as Gunnar Asplund discussed earlier, Sigurd Lewerentz and Sven Markelius.[6]

Although the competition brief for the project announced by the state-run National Board of Education in June 1921 had stipulated 'perfect functionalism and extreme economy', it is likely that the Bauhaus connection remained the most important impulse for Finnish architects.

A clue to the favoured economy within the formal language and social programme chosen by Finnish architects was given by the idea of the *Neue Sachlichkeit* ('New Objectivity'), which was interpreted at the time by some, including Ekelund, as a neo-rationalism, and translated into Finnish as *uusasiallisuus*. This began to implicate the notions of 'object' and 'matter' in architectural ideas. Picking up on Le Corbusier's introduction to architecture through art, it entertained and utilized Purism, Cubism and machine-matter. Since *asiallinen* in Finnish also refers to a 'matter of fact-ness' about things, a kind of no-nonsense is also implied in this phrasing, hence a neo-rationalism. The empiricism within the International Movement began to offer local validity and serious ideology. If no clear agreement about the 'Modern Movement' existed in the 1930s, there really did not need to be, such was the spread and seduction of Bauhaus notions of rationalism, simplicity, non-decoration and a socially responsive and committed architecture.

The break with the past was clear, even if ambiguous, in Le Corbusier's 'new architecture'. Cities as small as Helsinki could be ruptured with diagrammatic dreams of a radiant city, as Oiva Kallio's Central Helsinki planning project had shown already in Elsi Borg's drawing of 1927. Architecture suddenly had more than a constructive function; it was simply revolutionary. International contacts for the young republic and the traffic between architects increased, and although ideas and

Elsi Borg drawing, 1927, for architect Oiva Kallio's proposal for the redevelopment of Central Helsinki.

Architects Elsa Arokallio and Elsi Borg photographed in 1928.

aeroplanes crossed boundaries quite smoothly, mentalities often remained untouched. Social and emotional rather than logical forces would drive the new architecture in Finland. The nature of the product, the 'modern cubic building', allowed this new architecture its 'ideological' replication.

Of course, the 1930s cannot be discussed without reference to the immense presence of Alvar Aalto and the significance of the three buildings already mentioned – Viipuri Library, Turun Sanomat and the Paimio Sanatorium – conceived in the 1920s. And with Aalto also promoting his own work in the International Congress for Modern Architecture (CIAM) for the first time in Frankfurt (1929) and Brussels (1930), the energy he applied was influential. Aalto continued to apply his own approach to the Modern Movement with considerable panache throughout the decade, in one way departing from the ideals set out at the turn of the century, in another way responding to those ideals. He was uncomplicated, pragmatic, un-theoretical and risked his own talent. Aalto was not, however, un-heroic; nor was he un-ideological, though his charisma hid it well. It is clear he represented a genuinely new and individual approach to design, retaining dual forms: the classical and the functional, the surface and the underlying, the appearance and the illusion, the picturesque and the functional. This binary play would eventually distinguish Aalto from the pioneers he caught up with. For many years it was this individualism that not only set Aalto apart but eventually isolated him within Finnish architecture, as the profession grappled later with its own less spectacular, utilitarian and national response to international trends. From 1927 to 1931 Aalto, more than Bryggman, and probably more than any other younger Finnish architect, was consciously developing what is now seen as his own 'Nordic' kit-of-parts within the Modern Movement. Aalto's work also coincided with the multi-disciplined approach to the polished Stockholm Exhibition of 1930, which integrated Russian Constructivism in its graphics, architecture and advertising. The modern world beyond Finland – importantly– became the modern world possible at home. Edith Södergran's 'land that is not' once more became the possible destination.

It is difficult to know where to stop with Alvar Aalto, so incomparable has his position and contribution become in the country. Later in the 1950s the young architects around the influential theoretician Aulis Blomstedt were to consider the copyist in Aalto to be, in the phrase thrown around at the time, 'churning butter from Corbu's cream'. Although churlish, this was reasonable for their own impatient desire to establish difference from Aalto's pioneering but, as they thought, reckless spirit. It was unreasonable, though, because it lacked historical and critical insight into Aalto's earlier contribution during the 1930s. The search for a personal form of expression and the eventual stylistic coherence in Aalto's architecture were, of course, respected. But, probably measured against Hilding Ekelund's more restrained elegance, for many Finnish architects Aalto produced an architecture that veered away from the illusion of the social engineering implied in the Modern Movement. Aalto would later be strongly criticized for attempting to humanize the International Modernist agenda while the younger architects began following another Internationalism of their own; this time in the form of a classical, lucid, anti-rhetorical architecture inspired in the main by Mies van der Rohe.[7] Ironically, as we will discover, all this became confused. For in the very individuality of Aalto's architecture lay the germs of the renewed social awareness and critical humanism.

Closer scrutiny suggests that whilst Aalto did indeed attend the CIAM conferences and operate somewhat as a chameleon in world architecture circles during the late 1920s and on into the 1930s, other lesser-known architects such as Oiva Kallio, Jorma Järvi, Väino Vähäkallio and Gunnar Taucher all designed and shaped the intellectual sensibility of the profession, undoubtedly contributing to the process that turned Modernism into a social agenda and a 'unique' sign of Finnishness.[8] By the end of the 1930s, with Villa Mairea (1938–9) and the New York Finnish Pavilion (1939), Aalto's position in the international community was not in doubt. He had a stunning success with his solo exhibition, *Alvar Aalto: Architecture and Furniture*, at the Museum of Modern Art in New York in 1938. Villa Mairea used the duality of forms with some carefully constructed domestic and romantic touches. A carefully assembled house, Mairea was a homage both to the romance of the site and the romance of its client and owners, Maire and Harry Gullichsen. Commissioned by Gullichsen, it has all the traits of a superbly modelled space, shifting as it does from a sensitivity towards art and Cubism to the plasticity of the Naum Gabo Constructivist manifesto of the mid-1930s. The fluidity of its forms, the detail in window, screen and circulation, began to re-script an acceptable, stricter Modernism. A Japanese affinity was underplayed but evident in the smooth touches that Aalto brought to the house. His New York Pavilion won in competition was even more fluid and plastic; with the undulating wall bringing in the splay, the leaning curve and the expressive timber, the work started to question those that had become so satisfied with the accepted Internationalism. Here was Aalto being as

Alvar Aalto, Villa Mairea, Noormarkku, 1938–9.

Alvar Aalto, the
Finnish Pavilion
at the New York
World Fair, 1939.

image-conscious as the architects in 1900; Finland was useful myth and metaphor for a responsive and humane architecture. The work was a huge advertising hoarding. The regional implications – the lake and land imagery – could not but begin identifying Aalto with Finland and Finland with Aalto. Siegfried Giedion, the critic of the Modern Movement, who later befriended Aalto, would announce with some fiat that Aalto carried Finland wherever he went and inserted it into whatever he designed. Suddenly there was to be no separation.

In the 1940s Aalto began to avoid the term 'national' and spoke instead of regionalist ideas such as 'climate, topography, resources'. He would later attempt to use his position to get US money to fund post-war Finnish reconstruction, but in the 1930s he was held in suspicion by many Finnish architects for an emerging indigenous architecture of the type previously condemned in Saarinen, Sonck and other romantics from the first two decades of the century.[9] For many architects, the Finnish Pavilion in New York was not the masterpiece that some critics like Bruno Zevi claimed, who compared the pavilion with Sant'Agnese in Piazza Navona in Rome: 'Aalto compressed the space with a cyclopic corrugated wall in a gesture reminiscent of Michelangelo'.[10] Rather, it was a romantic anthem to the monumental; it alluded to a national romanticism. It was Strengell's 'picturesque silhouette' all over again. Like the Finnish Pavilion in 1900, nature and the 'exotic' were once more dragged into architecture in a literal form. To many its tamed nature compromised the modernizing and civilizing tendency of the young nation. To be modern could not also be traditional or primitive.[11] To be natural was not to be cultural. The stage was set for later debate and the harsh 'rationalist' games of the younger Finnish architects as they wrested Modernism for their own social and political agenda.

So intertwined are the 1930s and so important did they become for Finnish architecture that we might be better served critically if we attempt to approach it from another angle. Hard years immediately after Independence had readied the society for stringency and clarity. Sigurd Frosterus, who was still living and working, had prepared the ground for the seduction of the new age. Gustaf Strengell too had moved on, fallen for the new architecture but age would resist excess. Selim Lindqvist continued his own revisions into a confident functional sign. These voices were still important and undoubtedly part of the professional picture. Architects important in the first decades of the century such as Bertel Jung, were still around too. They sat on committees, adjudicated competitions, retained control and generally dispensed favour and direction.

J. S. Sirén, like Lindqvist, Ekelund and Välikangas, was crucial to the emerging shape that Finnish Modernism would take. Ekelund would work in Sirén's office, Välikangas would be appointed chief editor of *Arkkitehti* in 1929, and Ekelund would be assistant editor, only to take over later himself. Critics have said that Sirén went from Nordic neo-classicism to neo-objectivism to Functionalism, never quite achieving a modern building. If so, then this could also be said of many more Finnish architects who have negotiated trends and visual styles and never quite opted for the full version. Reductionism played a big part; this too might be the restraint and 'virtue' that held and continues to hold Finnish architects back from the excessive, the apocalyptic and the catastrophic.[12]

Glance at the continuing restraint and clarity in the horizontal and vertical, in mass and fenestration detail, of, for example, Sirén's Lassila and Tikanoja Office Building in central Helsinki, and the transition is clear. It is with some irony that in a decade that was supposed to have absorbed the collective Bauhaus spirit, an architect such as J. S. Sirén won a Grand Prix award for this building in 1937 at the Paris Exposition Internationale des Arts et Techniques and the Milan Triennale of 1936. The competition drawings (1934–5) suggest a much leaner, more rational, cleaner building than was actually built. The sunken rhythmic windows of the eventual scheme recall some of Aalto's later work (such as the Pensions Institute and the Academic Bookshop in Helsinki); light framing gives off both verticality and the sweeping horizontal line. Large plate glass windows at the sloping street level give a decidedly modern feel to the building; its disciplined rectilinearity complements the curved cars and radio sets of the 1930s. Perhaps there is a link here to Italian rationalism and the rise of Fascism in Europe, but the building demonstrates the shift Sirén had taken from the neo-classical; shifts that so many architects encountered as they introduced the new architecture into their repertoires.

Sometimes we need to leave aside the niceties and nuance of change and attempt to understand the more general shape. By the mid-1930s the functionalist mode was everywhere; only the response, talent and timing varied from architect to architect. Sirén, just as Erik Bryggman – himself a little older than Aalto – had to make the transition from classicism in quite another way. He brought along more 'baggage', a Beaux-Arts sensibility. Aalto, like Erkki Huttunen, P. E. Blomstedt and many younger architects, differed more in approach and nuance and less in results. Their youth made them appear ready for the 'internationalist' aesthetic. With less of a back catalogue to clear, Functionalism would consolidate everything the young architects believed about the country. Their nation might not be defined by it, but their psyche could be.

It is worth recalling: Finland was then still a young Republic and would remain so throughout the twentieth century. In many ways the architects were closer to the agenda of Modernism than many other modern architects in the world. The Finnish architects were building their own nation; solidarity in the face of the 'enemy' was taken for granted. Finnish literature, film and art all entertained Modernism during the 1930s, but there is little doubt that the architects were building it. Although the architectural results collided to some extent with the new architecture abroad, to succeed 'ideologically' the general result would have to accept the passion of Frosterus with the caution and elegance of Ekelund's scheme. It was to be a modest architecture – a vernacular Modernism – capable of communicating its ideals without fuss or ostentation.

Planning too took care of itself as the notion of a social community would follow guided by the careful (*Existenzminimum*) housing-type research instigated by the likes of Ekelund in 1932. More importantly, the visionary, artistic bent of Finnish architects could be reinforced. The vigour and robustness necessary for the modern agenda could become painterly and non-representational. The design-architect would fight for this position. Reinforced steel and concrete made production more rapid; forms were exciting but not yet sculptural. But overhangs and cantilevers looked more than modern – they looked daring. The lightness of rendered façades and strip windows began to suggest the sleek lines that appeared in North America and throughout Europe. Positioning these white buildings in the Finnish landscape, redefining small wooden towns with clusters and strips of commercial development, was equivalent to introducing the streamlined wireless or, in car manufacturing, the Cadillac.

Reading historians of Finnish architecture today one is struck by the constant attempt to interpret the inter-war years as a romantic period where the new architecture became more relaxed as it became more heroic and anticipated the 'dawn of a new era' with an 'unsurpassed self-evident sureness of form'.[13] In fact, we notice a more complex picture. The self-evident sureness of form possibly more easily associated with Nordic classicism was at first re-created in the larger, noticeable works like Aalto's Paimio Sanatorium. There is no doubt, however, that Finnish Modernism was also shaped in large during the 1930s by the White Functionalism of architects such as P. E. Blomstedt, Niilo Kokko, M. & R. Ypyä, Oiva Kallio, Yrjö Lindegren, Väinö Vähäkallio and Viljo Revell.[14]

Quickly, as it is with a shift in fashions and stylistic emphasis when the breakthrough has been made, talk in the decade was of a 'vernacular' Functionalism (*Kansanfunkis* in Finnish). Economic development, commercial and retail experiments throughout the country led to the possibility of this approach becoming the dominant expression in provincial towns and countryside. Although the ideal form of international architecture – the flat-roofed cubic house – may have popped up throughout the countryside, in the wider vernacular scene, according to the historian Asko Salokorpi, these buildings 'ousted the "traditional" ridge roof only to a very small degree'. Significantly, Salokorpi reminds us of the identifying patterns, perceptions and running tensions that occur when a new -*ism* has arrived and the dominant tradition or convention is

Yrjö Lindegren,
Pielisjärvi Hospital,
1930.

Väinö Vähäkallio,
otk Headquarters,
Hämeentie, Helsinki,
1933.

Väinö Vähäkallio,
Doctor's House,
Enso, 1936.

threatened: 'The argument about functionalism and traditionalism remained bitter on certain points of detail throughout the 1930s and indeed, at a popular level, continues so even today.'[15] It would be a reluctance and confusion that would be repeated. The profession often imagines greater influence, while the public perception of the 'modern' remains somewhat less convinced.

In discussing the 1920s, we suggested that the accepted conventional history may have distorted our understanding of Finnish architecture by emphasizing the more heroic individual figures. We addressed this issue by exploring the un-heroic Martti Välikangas. In the 1930s there is an equal case. Erkki Huttunen was an architect who probably did more than many to shape the perceived Modernism that emerged throughout the country and within the profession. The 1930s would be incomplete without understanding Huttunen's own process and how he navigated the new architecture. It is generally acknowledged that the flat-roofed cubic form appeared in the Finnish countryside in the main due to Huttunen. While this is an exaggerated professional perception, we could illustrate the decade probably better than any amount of generalized research by attending briefly to this phenomenon. By being the architect for the rapidly expanding Central Finnish Co-operative Society (sok), Huttunen designed numerous industrial premises, factories and shop buildings throughout Finland in a visual style that became known as *osuuskauppafunkis* ('Co-op Functionalism'). It became the trademark for all SOK shops in the countryside and in many ways is now recognized as an essential part of early Finnish Modernism; an existing list puts Huttunen's output as 144 assignments between and 1928 and 1939.[16]

Huttunen began his studies in 1921; he might easily have become a painter. Somewhat apolitical like Aalto and many other architects, he also shared with Aalto an earthy humour. Taught by Jussi Paatela and Armas Lindgren, two important figures, and resisting the mathematical, he was like many of the time: artist first, architect second, engineer third. Trained in the Nordic classical tradition like many young colleagues, he knew very well the rules that existed to be broken. Doubtless, Huttunen's own sensibility developed much like others in the 1920s; Aalto, Bryggman and P. E. Blomstedt were already architects. Graduating in 1927 with a specific interest in art history, his openness could not have been more opportune. There was no sign in his early work of the 'functionalist' style, but by 1931 Huttunen in many ways represented the indigenous Modernism to come. As part of SOK he was one of a few architects who would influence the aesthetic choice the profession had. The flat roof, reinforced concrete, white plastered surfaces everywhere led to the later appearance of the metal ribbon window. Cubic forms, all elegantly proportioned with classical sensitivity, plus the hygiene and clarity of shop interiors, combined to represent the Finnish Modernist's kit-of-parts. There was virtually no hint of the expressive, though the flourish – and there were many – existed in the cautious, often exquisite detailing.

Huttunen went to work at the building department of the Finnish Co-operative Society in 1928 and remained until 1939. Between 1925 and 1929 this department had already turned out drawings for 135 new shops, and one of the first buildings Huttunen worked on was the classically inspired Toppila Mill in Oulu in 1928, just before the economic crash of 1929. A visit to Sweden, Norway and continental Europe in 1929 is supposed to have had instant effect on the architect, and by 1930 Huttunen had two projects of immense significance on the board, both to be completed in the next two years. His first modernist project is considered to be the SOK Co-op in Rauma (1931). A classical proportion and vocabulary met national, now Internationalist, ideals. The white stucco walls, a roof terrace, large street-level windows and that dynamic curve in staircase and balcony all became expressive signs of the new architecture. In 1932 he would introduce the grain and silo metaphors referenced by Le Corbusier as a sign of the new spirit into the Finnish landscape.

In Viipuri, Huttunen designed huge silos using for the first time the American slip-form casting technique.[17] Slowly the classical proportion

Erkki Huttunen,
SOK Office Building,
Rauma, 1930–31.

of the early projects would be flattened as the elegance shifted to another plane in the functionalist style. The aesthetic care and classical sensibility remained and was later reinforced by Huttunen's call for the 'right' Functionalism (such as Paimio Sanatorium) as opposed to the wrong one.[18] Huttunen went on to appear to cover Finland's landscape with this Co-op Modernism. The white cubic forms would be recognizable to everyone during that decade and the decades that followed, as the small co-operative shops in the country became a symbol of the nation's new economy and countryside development.

Huttunen's visit abroad in 1929 allows us an insight into what might have happened to many Finnish architects as they assimilated influence

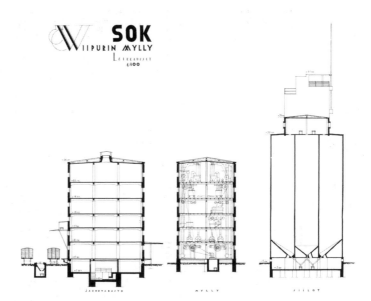

Erkki Huttunen,
Viipuri Mill, 1930–32,
sections and exterior.

and demonstrated the confidence to change. In Sweden Huttunen absorb-ed the Swedish Co-op system and then went on to visit Norway, Prague, Italy, Paris and cities in Germany. The 'must see' modern architecture list at the time was familiar to many: Asplund's Library in Central Stockholm, Villa Garches by Le Corbusier, the cities of Venice and Prague, and Gropius's Bauhaus School in Dessau. On his return, the International Fair in

Stockholm of 1930 no doubt provided the final push. The travel worked just as it had worked for those at the beginning of the century who sought in Europe the future rational aesthetic, and just as it would do for those young students and architects in Finland who in the 1990s travelled to France, Japan and the Netherlands, worked with well-known studios and absorbed and brought back more recent developments.

Clearly, the trip offered Huttunen a window to the new architecture and a way to measure his own classical interest and art history. By spring 1930 he envisaged the clarity of both the Rauma and Viipuri projects. His own office (from 1931) took on projects with a more monumental flavour. Although there is a huge catalogue of works, he is probably best known now for his Sokos Department Store building in central Helsinki diametrically opposite the Glass Palace (Revell, Kokko, Railo, 1936) and across the road from the Helsinki Central Post Office. Begun in 1939, delayed due to the war, Sokos was completed in 1952 in time for the Olympics.[19] This building is now considered one of the first examples of the American department store in Finland and received its shaping and planning after another of Huttunen's influential visits.

In 1937 he left on a tour of North America along with his office colleagues Eero Jokilehto, Pekka Saarema and Bertel Saarnio.[20] They took in New York, Boston, Montreal, Toronto and Washington. America was by then attracting young European architects for developments in building techniques and the artistic potential of the new architecture.[21] In Cranbrook, Huttunen met Eliel Saarinen, who had emigrated from Finland in 1923. They were taken to the Detroit Ford Motor Co. In Philadelphia he became acquainted with the John Wanamaker Department Store. Sokos, completed on return from this trip, is very 'American' in its urban feel, its sensitivity and its programme.[22] An optimist like many Finnish architects of the time, Huttunen adapted to the lean agenda and ideal of a White Functionalism and was instrumental in the way it slowly took over the professional architectural agenda.[23]

Between 1943 and 1953 Huttunen would be director of one of the most significant organizations concerning planning and construction of the Finnish State, the National Board of Public Building. Such a position in a highly centralized society had much power.[24] It enabled Huttunen to continue what he had achieved in the 1930s and direct the development of architecture in Finland during this time and for some years following. A director with such optimism would naturally go on to advance technology and prefabrication, helping the profession to communicate with the building industry. In the early 1950s we see consequences of this in the large experimental 'modernist' works by Viljo Revell, Lauri

Silvennoinen and Aarne Ervi, echoing in housing some of the grander visual expressions that Huttunen had begun in the 1930s.

We can but hint at how the canon of modern architecture spread throughout the country. Journals and publications, travels and study trips brought in the new ideas and have been well documented.[25] Huttunen's case appears more general. The flat roof, white cubic forms, corner windows, curved balcony and balustrading were seen in much of the newer work. The vocabulary was accessible, attractive and reusable, if not repetitive. The restraint, control, economy and finally the modesty that were natural extensions of the architecture of the 1920s merged somewhat elegantly and conveniently with the visual connotations of the new architecture. Industrial and product design in the 1930s also reinforced this refinement of line, although, apart from the work of Arttu Brummer and a few others, much remained somewhat tied to tradition and classical ideas. Glass would be slowly reshaped, and in 1932 the exhibition *Functionalism in Finnish Glass* was held in Riihimäki. In 1930 an exhibition of Finnish design in Taidehalli (Helsinki Kunsthalle) curated by Aalto had indicated the future. Here were the signs of a rationalization of housing and small apartments that enabled the Finnish architects to push ahead with streamlined, economic, space-saving solutions for new housing, along with the new machines emerging from America. There introduced for the first time were the bent and moulded plywood products done with Otto Korhonen that would eventually form the basis of the furniture enterprise called Artek, which Aalto and his wife Aino founded in 1935 along with Maire Gullichsen and Nils-Gustav Hahl.[26] Artek would spearhead the international interest with awards at the Milan Triennale of 1936, at which Aalto was awarded the Milan prize for the Savoy Vase. The work signified the emergence into the country of the softer machine aesthetic and ultimately the burgeoning romance with Modernism. The vase remains today incomparable as a symbol of both the new nation of Finland and its 'wilderness' lake-shaped history.

The influence of Modernism on Finnish design, sculpture and film would be subject enough for another study.[27] But there were parallel issues emerging in the 1930s. Did the developing abstraction and the use of geometric forms in Modernism once more reflect the Finns' constant sensibility towards the humanist dimension? In the silent films of the 1920s, in the realism of the 1930s, it seemed so. Perhaps, as the Polish philosopher Leszek Kolakowski has hinted, we should be studying the history of mentalities, not the history of ideas.[28] Yet of all the arts architecture remained somewhat special. The international events that

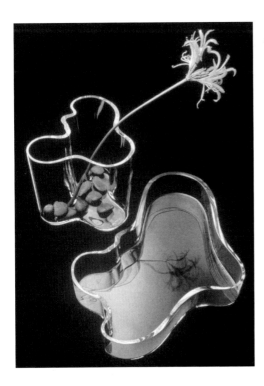

The Aalto Savoy Vase, 1936, produced by Artek.

supported the new architecture throughout Europe offered a more than national agenda. The progressive attributes of machine, progress and the future of man attached an extraordinary claim to the general spirit of the time. While a National Functionalism appeared part of the progressive development within Finland, the Modern Movement was re-grouping and putting forward this expression as an underlying and universalist formal language.

As an architect and constant thinker, and as editor of *Arkkitehti* during the crucial two years at the start of the 1930s, Hilding Ekelund was always in a position to monitor what was happening in Finland. In 1932 he considered that 'the directly structural nature and ascetics of decoration characteristic of older Finnish architecture is what connects it with modern architecture, which both through necessity and for aesthetic reasons has arrived at the same principles'.[29] Ekelund identified the marriage of the architecture of the machine age with the ideals that led towards National Functionalism and the ubiquitous white, flat-roofed, cubic images. Controlled by a steadfast mentality, though it was mostly associated around the word 'functionalism', the implied Modernism was to take over and deepen some of the ideals that had already been in place in Finnish architecture. This response to the modern *Zeitgeist* represented the new dawn.

To close the decade we need again to take another side-stab at the unpredictability of the era. For Modernism was nothing if not avant-garde. By neatly assessing both Ekelund and Huttunen we may have sanitized the fever and political import of the years. Any study of this decade cannot in fact ignore the short-lived and enigmatic life of the man always referred to as P. E. Blomstedt (Pauli E. Blomstedt). His death at 36 years of age in many ways altered what might have been a more expressive, revolutionary and running contest with Modernism itself. Instead of converging on a powerful but reductive tectonic Modernism, a rationalism that began to serve the growing national agenda and Finland's re-awakened need for international representation, Blomstedt's unsteady

P. E. Blomstedt,
Union Bank, Helsinki,
1929.

openness and discipline might have invited wider, some say, wilder
issue. He may have replicated Le Corbusier, but in 1935 and 1936 in
response to alarming planning ideas he would call – surprisingly – for
more sensitivity and a return to 'empire' style planning.[30]

Anachronistic ideas sitting along with the modern were not unusual.
Many architects expressed this ambiguity. Earlier in the decade
Blomstedt would share such wilder ideas with Aalto, and even Ekelund;
the consequences of these if really thought out would have implied
demolition of some of Finland's historical stock. Ideas changed quickly
as they were assimilated and – inevitably – were not always grasped with
any finality, for this was the nature of the decade. Elsewhere in Europe
Fascism threatened and dictatorship loomed. Architecture too was experi-
menting with serious change and the modern agenda; ultimately it would
get tied up with political and social programmes it could not always
support. The little research undertaken has revealed the deep connections
between Finnish architects and the USSR during this period. Although
Russian Constructivism was known through books, and though Hilding
Ekelund is known to have pursued it with some passion, it appeared little in the journals of the time, perhaps for obvious reasons. It is not clear
to what extent the spectre of Communism was present. The Finnish
Communist Party had been founded in the Soviet Union in 1918 but
remained illegal in Finland until 1944. Although in Europe during the
1930s growing Fascism sparred with competing revolutionary agendas,

Finnish history suggests its own particular detached response to this decade. The result by the end of the 1930s, however, was to leave the society looking over the shoulder towards the East. It may also have left smouldering the untidy connection between socially aware ideas in architecture and planning and the more undesirable aspects of a programmed, dogmatic Socialist agenda. Although the Second World War would intervene in this, the spectre and confusion of Communism would again appear in the early 1960s, when the undesirable in a totalitarian post-Hungary Socialism was removed somewhat by an awakened interest in Marxism. The politicization in architecture that threatened to appear in the 1930s (and might have if Blomstedt had lived) I would suggest actually appeared in the 1960s. Architects would find themselves calling on increased sensitivity and social concern through prefabrication and standardization, while at the same time their agenda would imply destruction of existing parts of the city.

By the early 1930s P. E. Blomstedt was already writing to his younger brother Aulis and persuading him to look at Le Corbusier's 'new spirit'. Blomstedt's connections, however, with the Soviet Union and with radicals such as the young filmmaker Joseph Losey and the dramatist Bertolt Brecht meant that his work was nearest to going further, as his Kotka Town Hall competition entry in 1931 suggests. A competition of some scale for the time, many Finnish architects saw it as an opportunity to scale up and attempt the larger 'monolithic Modernist' project. Although won by Erkki Huttunen, the results were an indication of just how far Finnish architects had come in assimilating the reductive elements of a growing Internationalism. Blomstedt, more than most, was tempted to achieve the impossible.

P. E. Blomstedt, Kotka Town Hall Competition Entry, 1931.

Aware of the growing politicization of architecture, having participated in CIAM meetings on the responsibility of the architect with their underlying social-anarchistic thinking, P. E. Blomstedt became the nearest to the radical social-anarchist that Finland had in the twentieth century. Aalto may have had Kropotkin's work by his bedside, but Blomstedt suggested more creative menace with links to and knowledge of the Russian Constructivist avant-garde, the idealistic political radicalism of Mayakovsky and the art of Malevich. Blomstedt put

P. E. Blomstedt,
Pohjanhovi Hotel,
Rovaniemi, 1936.

forward the acceptance that the architect held no right to moralize to his client but could – in the client's interest – propose a radical response to any brief. This was dynamic, even risky, and diametrically opposed to Aalto's own approach, which tended to be the opposite. Blomstedt remained convinced of Le Corbusier's revolutionary importance and the

P. E. Blomstedt,
Finnish Savings
Bank, Kotka, 1935,
and bank interior.

rhetorical power of the architecture he promulgated. Powerful forms, controlled heaviness, measured performance and proportions are present in three of Blomstedt's most important works in the mid-1930s: the Pohjanhovi Hotel, the Aulanko Hotel and the Kotka Bank. The plastic form with the structure enclosed inside gave the buildings a purer and more romantically uncluttered functionalist image than in fact they offered.[31] Tolerance sometimes narrowed with political impatience during the 1930s, but in a short span before his early death, architecture and life proceeded with machine-like precision for P. E. Blomstedt. It would begin to do so, from the end of this decade onwards, for many Finnish architects.

chapter four

War: Standardization and Solidarity

It is not time that alters us,
it is space: the forest that was low as a dark ribbon
round the evening when we were children.
and the water that came up to our feet.

It is the road that is now straightened out,
the trees, the houses, the people the same
looking out of the windows
that are windows in space, not time.
Bo Carpelan, from 'In Dark, in Light Rooms'[1]

The 1940s was a coloured, difficult decade. A passage from the diplomat Henry Bell, the British Consul-General in Finland in 1918–19 writing in 1950, indicates just how misunderstood Finland was, and how situations could be flattened and misread from the outside. 'The German occupation of Finland', Bell writes,

> brought a measure of joy to the Finns because it helped to get rid of the hated Bolsheviks; it also brought industrial Finland much cause for worry. The German officers looked upon Finland, in the early part of their occupation, as a source of loot. They took butter, iron, copper and anything else they considered the Fatherland could do with. They riddled all government service with their own officials: and the Finns suffered much in Entente Countries on account of their so-called German orientation. Finland – let me say this emphatically – was never pro-German.[2]

Bell's misreading from World War I appears awkward and offensive, and warns us against future anecdote and memoir as we find ourselves faced with such generalizations. In World War II, Norway was occupied, as also Demark, but the Germans never occupied Finland regardless of any friendly relationship with them, nor is there any serious record of looting or the misuse of Finnish resources. Finns did, though, help the

The bombed Viipuri Library, September 1941.

Germans hold positions during Operation Barbarossa in 1941 and the Germans did help in the form of material supplies and deliveries as the Finns halted the Soviets at the Kannas Front in the summer of 1944. Yet such distortions in history also redirect us. Finns have necessarily been tested when faced with external political forces. Survival may appear to outweigh reason and odds, but it can ensure security. Stalin's demands for a base on the southern coast of Finland near Helsinki followed Hitler's deals with the Soviet Union. The Soviet sphere in the eastern Baltic was about to grow. The Germans advised the Finns to give in, just as Estonia, Latvia and Lithuania had done. Although the Finns gave up some territory north of Leningrad, they refused the base at Hanko, 65 miles from Helsinki, which Stalin had requested. Talks failed and it is now accepted history that Stalin erred by attacking Finland on 30 November 1939 at the beginning of one of the severest winters of the twentieth century.[3]

The Finns succeeded in stopping the Soviet advance on the Karelian isthmus and held out for a hundred days in what became known as the Winter War. The Finns were suddenly centre-stage. A relatively small incident aided the West's cause for freedom and democracy; Finland was the object of sympathy. The expectation that they would be rescued at any moment might be seen as a necessary but willed deception; yet the effect it had on the nation's collective hope sustained the Finns longer than anyone thought possible. The Winter War had an impact far wider than its military limits.[4] With the Soviets bogged down and forced to reassess the situation, the error was clear for the world to see. By February, war was no option for either party, only negotiation. Although the Finns were forced into the latter, these negotiations had in fact been 'requested' by the Soviet Union. Thereby another small victory for the Finns in defeat. Although Finland expressed a desire to remain neutral, its geo-political position forced the day. It was impossible to prevent the Soviet Union wishing to use Finland to provide greater defence capabilities against an advancing German army. In March 1940 the peace terms far exceeded the initial requests by the Soviets; much land was ceded and frontiers were relocated in favour of the Soviet Union. The treaty was supposed to create 'precise conditions of reciprocal security'. The irony was total; from this point onwards Finland would play a war of nerves with the Soviet Union right up to 1989.

More immediately, Finland found support from Germany as Stalin attempted 'to solve the Finnish question'. Finland was offered the chance to buy arms from Germany if it permitted German troops to pass through Finland to Norway – a cover, of course, to allow Germany to attack the Soviet Union. On 22 June 1941 Germany invaded the Soviet Union and

Helsinki University
in flames, 1944.

Hitler announced a joint action with Finnish troops. Finnish neutrality
under such conditions proved impossible; three days later, on 25 June,
the Soviet Union attacked Finland. By evening the Finnish government
declared that it was at war with the Soviet Union.

The Continuation War began and the subtle defence of the Finns was
lost, as was much of the sympathy felt during the Winter War: the concerns of the greater powers were taken up elsewhere as the Second World
War intensified. The defeat of the Germans at Stalingrad in January 1943
moreover forced the Finns to look for a way out of their own war with
the Soviet Union. Finally, on 19 September 1944, an armistice was signed
with Moscow. A base nearer to Helsinki in Porkkala was created for the
Soviets, huge indemnities were to be paid, and all German assets handed
over to the Soviets. Since Finland also had to drive out 200,000 Germans
from Lapland, the devastation brought on the entire province of Lapland
was seen by the Germans as revenge for what they saw as treachery.
Finland had to give up the Petsamo corridor, its link to the Arctic Ocean,
and eventually some 420,000 Finns living in the Karelian area would be
relocated within Finland rather than live under Soviet rule.

Important in all this, the Finnish Communist party was legalized in
1944 and would gain strength through the suffering caused by the war.
Stalin would seek to shore up the Soviet sphere of influence, thereby
creating further defence against future German aggression. The terms of
the truce were eventually agreed in the Treaty of Paris, which obliged
Finland to pay the Soviet Union $300 million in war reparations.[5]

Recognizing the difficulty of their position during the Second World War, the Finns responded promptly, if reluctantly, to Soviet overtures declaring that concessions must stop short only of sacrifice of Finnish independence. But since the obliteration of Finnish independence, as of that of all Russia's neighbours, had become the ultimate aim of the Kremlin, the Finnish attitude, however accommodating, was characteristically renounced by Moscow as 'obdurate', 'insulting' and even 'aggressive'.[6]

The subtext of this was a possible Soviet takeover of Finland. After signing similar pacts with Hungary, Romania and Bulgaria, on 6 April 1948 the Soviets signed the Paris treaty with Finland. Towards the end of the war Marshall Mannerheim had been elected President, to be succeeded in 1946 by Juho Kusti Paasikivi. The friendly relationship and eventual strong 'neutrality' strategy would begin with the Paasikivi presidency, to be reinforced when President Urho Kekkonen took over in 1956. In 1948 Finland and the Soviet Union signed a Treaty of Friendship, Cooperation and Mutual Assistance, which formed the basis of what became known as the 'Paasikivi Line'. Essentially Finland was to hold onto its own script for the coming decades: according to the treaty, 'Finland had in principle the right to stay neutral in a war between other states.' Finland also became the only country to pay off its war reparations in full, by 1952.

Resistance, stubbornness, ambiguity and guile were qualities necessary for survival as Finland fought a complex and changing war. To be the co-opted enemy of both Germany and the Soviet Union could never turn out well. Compromise may have been hated, but pride held firm as pragmatism dictated the necessary action. Finland lost 87,000 men in the years 1939–45 (2.3 per cent of the population). With the Soviet Union over its shoulder, Finland would demand of itself no small diplomatic and political skill and would see itself existing proudly, for the rest of the century almost, outside the conflicts of interests between the greater powers.

The year 1939 and the onset of the Second World War proved crucial to Modernism and modern architecture. In the year that war broke out, Aalto had designed the interior wall for the Finnish Pavilion in New York, which would confirm his break with the stricter Internationalists. But as if to confirm Aalto's Internationalism, to many Finnish architects it was the classicial Modernism of Erik Bryggman's Burial Chapel in Parainen that had opened the *funkis* decade of the 1930s, and it would again be Bryggman with his Resurrection Chapel in Turku that opened the 1940s. Appearing roughly the same time as the undulating wall of the Finnish Pavilion, one begins to get a hint of the differences that lay

Erik Bryggman,
Parainen Chapel,
1930, exterior,
plan–section and
interior.

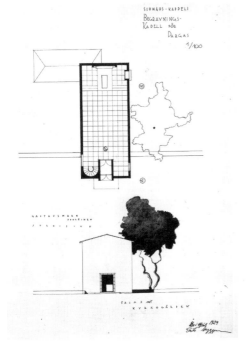

Erik Bryggman,
Resurrection Chapel,
Turku, 1939–41, and
chapel interior.

ahead in the way that Finnish architects would appropriate, adapt and innovate within Modernism. Why this chapel has had more influence on Finnish architects than the New York Pavilion is not hard to see. Bryggman's chapel returns us in many ways to the Italy that had influenced so many in the 1920s. Less original, the Resurrection Chapel was supremely articulated. More than Aalto's venture into decorative, organic shaping, its elegant self-consciousness suited the ideals of many Finnish architects. Bryggman's asymmetric classicism, though uninflected, was bolder; its detailing was weighty, robust and elegant. Bryggman set out the modern-to-come, while Aalto had departed and begun to arrive somewhere else already.[7]

We get a hint of this emerging split in Finnish Modernism by considering how, after the catastrophic environmental consequences of the politicized 1970s, the historian and architect Vilhelm Helander (1987) would link Bryggman's work in the Resurrection Chapel to the 'essential' in Finnish Modernism: 'The space is centrally weighted, and yet its focal point is outside, in the landscape of eternity, where those attending a funeral service may fix their thoughts.'[8] The cliché was unfortunate, but surely everyone by then knew what was meant by 'the landscape of eternity'. This was a phrase, a notion, that had begun to manipulate the constructed image of the Finnish landscape and its expected architectural response. The question at the end of the 1930s, however, was not why but how to respond to the seduction of eternity through architecture. The bifurcations of humanism and materialism, two quite different representational approaches to Modernism in Finnish architecture, lay ahead.

Once again the requirements of an era would do much to script the mission and agenda of the architects. Critical convention has it that, coinciding with the need to distance Finland from both Sweden and Russia after the first two decades of the twentieth century, the Internationalism that emerged during the 1930s from America and Europe not only suited the climate, psyche, temperament and 'idealized' Finnish landscape, it began to reinforce the use of the 'modern agenda' within Finland. Asserting that Finland was tougher and more hard-living than Sweden, the British critic J. M. Richards, writing in 1940, recognized the subtext that would begin to establish Finnish architecture in the eyes of the world. It was an underlying ethic that hinted of the humanistic in Aalto. Frank Lloyd Wright's use of intuition and symbol began to temper the machine aesthetic associated with Le Corbusier. Alvar Aalto was never far behind. The two Aalto pavilions (Paris in 1936/7, New York in 1939) were, to Richards, an 'original and imaginative handling of Finland's traditional raw material, timber'. This, along with the boldness of new methods of construction (reinforced concrete), Richards predicted:

made [Aalto] the man to whom many of the younger European architects looked to show how modern architecture might, without compromising with its principles, achieve the depth and richness and sense of human values also associated with the peculiar genius of Frank Lloyd Wright.[9]

More recent research has allowed a clearer picture of this difficult decade, long considered a vacuum in the history of Finnish architecture.[10] Previously it had been convenient to read the period as a distraction between the *funkis* of the 1930s and the so-called tabula rasa that saw Finnish Modernism take on its heroic, worldwide role in the banquet years of the 1950s. While this distorts the period, it emphasizes the way that history has been shaped and narrowed according to individuals, institutes, visiting critics and historians. The experienced history of the architectural profession, according to the historian Liisa Häyrynen, in all likelihood stresses singular achievements at the expense of factors that shape a more collective spirit. 'History is the profession's own tale of its birth, breakthroughs, successes, diasporas, and difficulties, in other words, the varied transformations of its field.'[11]

The 1930s had seen such transformations close up. The decade had offered a fertile ground for the assimilation of the 'White Functionalism' championed by Aalto, Bryggman, Ekelund, P. E. Blomstedt, Huttunen and others. But the Winter War that began in 1939 halted much construction work and planned projects. When the Winter War peace was agreed in 1940 the evacuation of more than 400,000 refugees began as they fled from areas ceded to the Soviet Union. In the process one of Finland's important developing cities, Viipuri, was lost, along with the library that Aalto had designed and which had been completed in 1936.[12]

Fragmented as the war had been for the Finns, solidarity and new structures were urgent. Although it is partly true that the war and these conditions led to a more modest approach to themes and activities than in the previous decade, it has already been recognized critically that the Nordic version of Modernism would always tend to invite a restrained and more modest approach to international concerns. The broader factors important in the decade were immediately defined. With the obvious urgency to house refugees, there was the need to build rapidly at a scale that could redress war damage. The Finns had proved they could always respond well to a restricted framework, and the 1940s confirmed this superbly. After a tendency to monumentalize Functionalism in the 1930s, there is no question that the instant agenda connected with war enabled the Finnish architectural profession to engage in the wider ideals of the modern programme with immediate, smaller-scale, local but hardly modest results.

The Olympic Village would be a useful guide for us here. Designed and built between 1938 and 1940, then rescheduled for 1952 after the cancelled Olympics of 1940, it has been interpreted as 'the first true modernist urban Siedlung in Finland to be built as an overall housing complex'.[13] Stringent war-time and post-war circumstances permitted less of the grand flourish of the *funkis* decade. Gradually a further reductive strategy crept into many buildings. At the same time, however, there was an almost sentimental attraction to carefully added detail. It was as if natural materials could be used to point up the architect's careful response and ethical position as the decade proceeded. The influence from Aalto's innovative use of timber and leather and other examples from Frank Lloyd Wright were evident. There emerged a romantic attraction for textured surfaces and, specifically, the appearance and symbolism of slate for the base and plinths of buildings.

An example of the subtle trimming and varied transformation of the White Functionalism of the 1930s would be the Children's Castle, a hospital in Helsinki begun in 1938 but completed only in 1948. Elsi Borg (1893–1958), a significant architect who worked for the Construction Bureau of the Ministry of Defence in the 1930s, would take over the design of the hospital after the death in 1939 of her elder brother, the architect Kaarlo Borg.[14] Perhaps more than any other building in the decade, the Children's Hospital illustrates the synthesis between the careful systematic planning and rationalizing of Functionalism, the advances in child welfare, nursing and training, and emerging romantic trends. Never really abandoning her classical then functional background, the allusions were subtle and refined. The floor plans are rational, indicating a general clear deployment of volumes and space, while within the hospital there is ornamental plasterwork. Reliefs and sculptures adorn the exterior. Indeed, Elsi Borg would pose the obvious question when she announced later in 1953: 'the architect does not create so much himself or herself; the period itself draws its mark via the architect'.[15] The paradox was stated: the Finnish architect either follows prevailing trends, applies familiar restraint seen as 'originality', or the hero innovates from these and makes new trends for others to follow.[16]

Clearly, too, the non-architectural conditions that war forced on people necessitated architectural changes within the profession. An unheroic time after the monumental 1930s became heroic for other reasons. Bryggman, Ekelund and Huttunen all represented an unspoken professional restraint, a Finnish subtlety and solidarity. Their influence brought a more intellectual distance to architecture. They stressed a refined detailing and – significantly for the future of Finnish architecture – a more controlled interpretation of architecture's relation to nature. To

Elsi Borg, Children's
Castle Hospital,
Helsinki, 1946–8,
and hospital plan.

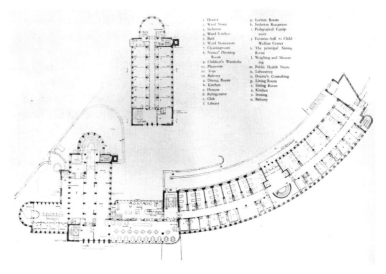

some this began the manipulation and opportunism of an image that would lose control in the 1960s and '70s. Using a modernist shaping of light and form, a careful response to programme and function, during the 1940s this was to be an agenda that could work equally well at the small domestic scale as it could at the larger civic scale.

Pekka Korvenmaa identifies the non-architectural factors that were crucial to the 1940s decade and which had survived the professional assault on the vernacular:

> The ancient basic technique of Finnish building, the solid timber wall, was nevertheless still predominant in the early 1930s. The

adoption of the less craft- and more lumber-based frame construction was hindered by the underdeveloped state of insulation technology: in the severe climate of Finland, a functioning heat economy was of primary importance.[17]

The harsh wartime conditions necessitated stringent measures and the transfer of the energies expected of the architect. In 1940 Aalto had been invited as a Visiting Professor to MIT. He began to monitor the work in America on standardization and prefabrication and how this related to 1930s Functionalism. He was intent on bringing this back to Finland and saw an ideal opportunity to set up Finland during the decade as a laboratory for such experiments. This would not only help the war effort but would allow experiments within the more humane Modernism he envisaged. His own business relationship with the industrialist Harry Gullichsen, whose wife Maire had founded Artek along with the Aaltos, also led the way in developing cheap industrially produced and – significantly for Finnish architects – variable wooden housing types.

Aalto would help to influence the profession as architects began to apply similar site considerations to other work, believing topographic and psychological effects could be achieved at varying scales through innovative standardization. His attempts to obtain money from the USA and his general free role as a roving 'entrepreneur' of Finland's needs, his attempt at a post-war laboratory using architecture and standardization as tools, have recently occasioned renewed assessment of the important civic and innovatory role he played.[18] Intellectually, though, many Finnish architects naturally interpreted Aalto's ability to jump scale as a modern synthesis suiting an agenda of functional control, efficient production lines and a variable but modest modernist statement. This and the war economy had great effect on both architects and the profession since it led to accelerated prefabricated processes and initiatives to develop Finland and extend its social aims and solutions for the single-family dwelling. It would lead to widespread post-war guidelines for the construction industry. Drawing nearer a humanistic programme for the Modern Movement nonetheless also anticipated the modular nightmares to come in the 1960s.

In response to such stringent war conditions, in 1942 a Reconstruction Bureau was established as a central government office, concentrating on the simple but effective design of single-family dwellings. Although Aalto, through his ideological position of leadership within the architectural community, had paved the way for such work, the Bureau with its emphasis on standardization was led by two of his former assistants, Aarne Ervi and Viljo Revell. Connected with this, a highly significant development –

Aarne Ervi, Engineer's House, Pyhäkoski, 1949.

a war-time sensation in hindsight – was the creation of the Building Information File. A continually expandable source, it became abbreviated to the RT system (from *Rakennustietokortisto* – Building Information Card System) and was created by Alvar Aalto with his associates Aarne Ervi, Viljo Revell and Kaj Englund. Although it may have begun as the standardization Aalto had in mind from the swerves made in the 1930s, the beginnings of a 'Dictionary of Building' had been made when the novelist Mika Waltari had rewritten Aalto's abstract ideas into a more practical form in *Architecture and Standards*, which was published in 1942 by the Association of Architects.

Eventually the RT system not only became an everyday tool for architects, builders and contractors during the war, but the essential dictionary of Finnish building, as it remains to this day.[19] Combine this with the ever-growing importance of the architect Aulis Blomstedt, the donation of more than 2,000 prefabricated wooden housing units from Sweden and Aalto's own experiences in America, an American model of using wooden construction elements was interpreted, developed and refined into a remarkable range of architectural expressions.

1940s post-war
building: over 2000
prefabricated houses
given by Sweden,
leading to the
appearance of
'Swedish villages'
throughout Finland.

1940s standardized
houses erected
after the war; here
in Pieksämäki.

There is no doubting the work of the Bureau and the energy in reconstruction at this time. This short reconstruction period demanded enormous strength from those returning from the Front to a normal family life; children followed as did requirements for social health care. A widespread regional system was rethought, as land was reclaimed from swamps to farms. A small plot of land and loans were given along with regulated conditions to build according to standard solutions; the basis for the creation of the Finnish social housing system using prefabrication was laid out, to be picked up in greater scale in the next decade.

Although some architects may have known little about the real needs of the countryside, and although beginning from the needs of the summer house, the adaptability and solidarity of the architects' profession ensured a huge anonymous effort in the administration – the result being some brilliant flexible housing types of one-and-a-half-storeyed dwellings. So successful was this work that the basic building type took the form of the generic energy-efficient, functional Finnish house, with one centralized chimney considered aesthetically appropriate for the Finnish countryside.[20]

The Reconstruction effort could not fail to have an unmistakable impact on the profession and, of course, on Finnish Modernism. Echoing the notion of the 'total work of art' met at the beginning of the century, architecture was shifting its field. By integrating modest, small-scale and careful prefabrication techniques made possible by standardization systems, architecture was approaching the idea of a product. It is possible to argue that the consequences were even greater. Picking up on the reductive versions of Modernism begun in the 1920s and completed in the 1930s, this shift towards the 'product' would not only complement architecture's role in the developing nation's consciousness, it would also see architecture as a marketable, even universal product. Furthermore, it would see a remarkable series of housing and social developments in the 1950s, from the work of Revell, Silvennoinen, Ekelund and Englund, set alongside some of the more recognized heroic Finnish architecture of the decade. The results of this in terms of the cultural propaganda surrounding Finnish architecture will become more obvious as we explore the later decades of the century. For it was not only the wood-processing industry that could increase its own range of products and expand its export potential, it was not only the advances made in the metal industry through industrial goods (paid off as reparations), but the idea of a marketable and controllable product strengthened the emerging approach to, and acceptance of, an ideological industrialism.

In the 1940s the adaptability of the single-family houses also had consequences for planning. The same logic and scalar jumping saw solutions applicable to scattered settlements and industrial areas anywhere. Landscape and siting became non-specific. As a result of this war time solidarity and the professional response of the architects to tighter conditions, Helsinki has now what are considered charming suburban communities made up of wooden housing: Pakila, Paloheinä and Herttoniemi. But it is worth looking a little in the future. This romance would disseminate in the 1950s and see a modern version of an *architettura minore* set within the Finnish landscape. Thereupon, prompted by political and cultural dissent, a more rigid, systematic approach would return to a rational Functionalism; another *serialism* and modular thinking would appear in Finnish architecture in the 1960s, largely influenced by the work of Mies van der Rohe. The students of the early 1960s turned on the flexible and sustainable housing type developed after the war and replicated those single-storey, L-shaped, flat-roof houses that often leaked from the outset and eventually rotted. It is perhaps regrettable now how this rather ideal, ecological, functional and sustainable building type developed during the Reconstruction period was mistreated for so many decades. With this in mind it is also possible to argue that the universal brick and steel, eave-less box architecture, this acknowledged attempt at industrializing the architectural product, was in some way embedded in the architects responsible for the modest war time tests. The irony within the modern agenda that was to develop in Finland during this 'vacuum' period, however, is this: these small-scale, modest, even serial communities, popular for edge-of-city living, opened the way for later, more ambiguous, neutral planning ideas. Resulting mega-box housing districts from the 1970s, like Itä-Pasilä, Jakomäki, Kontula and Koivukylä outside Helsinki, might now be rather forlorn and in need of cosmetic skin treatment, but did they not result from like solidarity, agenda and passion? Catastrophes were quietly systematized; social problems, later blamed on the lack of history, would echo the 1940s and be recalled by some – unfairly – as a 'blank period'.[21]

Although we can identify the solidarity of architects working for the reconstruction of Finland during and after the war, there is little doubt that we also note the constant search for ordering space, the application of a restricted and rigid functional approach, and a regional planning that appears to have strict consequences for the development of Finland as a whole. Here, although the exactitude of it eludes us, is the result of the ideals of a Modernism passed on from Germany and France.

The planning of the humanist Otto I. Meurman, whose ideas made up Tapiola Garden City, begun in the years 1945–7, can be seen as a departure from the increasing trend to rationalize the Finnish town and the consequences we have outlined. Many architects resisted any nature mysticism, though they all operated knowing that their works gained recognition – both internationally and at home – from the natural siting and the landscape that could set them off. The rural population, the conditions of the Finnish countryside and its predominantly agrarian and landscape tradition meant that answers needed to be found for the dispersed planning solutions, for dwellings of both apartment types and individual family units. The 1940s led to a revival of the appreciation of the natural site, and planning in Tapiola was to have the chance for a freer solution. Tapiola became an example to the rest of the world. The meandering, sub-urban scheme envisaged by Meurman began to be seen as the new garden city, left open to development without any overall structure. Groups of buildings were sited within the free-form forest; buildings could be placed on high points, areas of forest left natural and the green fields used for innovative terrace and low-rise housing. In its early stages some of the major Finnish architects all had work in Tapiola as they explored the use of prefabrication in high-rise buildings (such as Revell and Ervi), the low-rise student and housing apartments (including H. & K. Sirén, Tavio), the varied height scheme (R. & R. Pietilä) and the terrace and atelier housing (Sirén, Aulis Blomstedt and others).

Ideologically, within the loose agenda of the Modern Movement, there was a tacit structural move to 'clarify' older communities. Older historical areas of towns and the scale of older wooden housing proved a hindrance to the modernizing programme. This relationship to existing urban fabric and stock is crucial if we are to understand the next 30 years in Finnish architecture. It was not so much that architects wilfully erased whole parts of towns; rather it was the inevitable faith and 'flow' in the new, in the Modern Movement itself. The image and rhetoric of planning schemes, even the image of an imagined landscape within which this architecture worked, from those in the 1920s with aeroplanes, sleek cars and diagrammatic futuristic cities to the visionary boulevards of the 1930s, to the free-forest town developments of the 1950s and '60s, were highly seductive. With Tapiola Finland became a pioneer to rival Sweden in social planning. Later the obvious proximity to nature did not always compensate for the loss of urban factors or feel. The need for cars during the 1970s and '80s would damage the idyll and Tapiola would slowly re-shape, though not always losing the advantages it once had. Tapiola has recently celebrated its 50th anniversary and it is once more the scene of much debate and disagreement.[22] Landscapes and aerial photographs seemed acceptable out in Tapiola, the garden city, but the reality was harder, flintier and dissenting. If older building fabric was to be removed, along with the communities they engendered, it was always done in the belief that something better, something permanent and more democratic would come along.

Suddenly the war decade gave a new meaning to the idea of beginning from zero. Finland was still a small and very young Republic, living next to one of the most ruthless and mysterious 'systems', the Soviet Union. Rural areas had not modernized quite as fast as cities. Women architects had formed their own association in 1942 called Architecta, but it would be another 40 years before women really broke into a profession that remained the male domain of the sexist joke, beer and sauna well into the 1980s.[23] Architects fought in the war, left, studied, graduated at different times. Some retained a connection to classicism, others thought only of grand White Functionalism. Some cared not for the past as knowledge was passed on through different offices, debating Le Corbusier and Mies van der Rohe. Beginning from zero implied less baggage, less history. It also implied the confusion attached to openness: which direction should the society take? If socially improved areas resulted, did this automatically mean the modern age had arrived? It was never quite like that. Model areas, model planning and model buildings all looked good and natural, yet within all this progress there was the stubbornness of the Finnish psyche to contend with, there was a history with Sweden and Russia to negotiate.

Cover of English translation of Tove Jansson's *Comet in Moominland.*

It is no surprise that one of the most popular series of books in the second half of the modernizing century would be – to both children and parents alike around the world – the Moomin series written by Tove Jansson. The series has sold millions of copies and has been translated into 34 languages. Neither is it any coincidence that it began in 1946. With the first in the series, *Comet in Moominland*, there is that sense of impending disaster, always the threat of a comet falling out of the sky, right into the garden of the troll family; and always the solitude and stubborn wit and intelligence of the Finn to cope with such tension. Jansson was to follow this up two years later with *Finn Family Moomintroll*, and these and others remain to this day 'modern' in the way that many of the aspects of an applied Modernism are not. Lest we attempt to diminish coincidence, one of the main critical texts of the time was a small set of essays by Nils Erik Wickberg. Published in the same year, 1946, *Ajatuksia Arkkitehtuurista* ('Thoughts on Architecture') outlined the running dialogue with Le Corbusier. The influence of Wickberg deserves lengthier note; he was editor of *Arkkitehti* three times (for about twelve years in total) and his essay 'Baroque and the Contemporary', published in 1943–4, already began to outline the issues that Aalto's new free-form architecture would invoke in the late 1940s and '50s.[24]

In order to make room for the new, progressive areas, it follows that this tacit modernizing agenda implied the erosion if not the removal of the mixed scale of the low-rise, wooden Finnish town. There is a sneaking feeling that beginning from zero also implied more serious attempts to remove elements of a past – whether connected to Sweden or Russia – seen now as nostalgic. It was this confusion with planning, rationalism and the under-appreciated older building stock that led to a general flattening and erasure of the quality of some of the older Finnish towns. Korvenmaa is again accurate: 'Unlike, for example, in Germany, in Finland towns were destroyed not so much by enemy bombing as by the country's own, voluntary, modernisation.'[25]

While we cannot doubt this assessment we can begin to layer the obvious. Up to that point, at the end of the war and the beginning once more of a new age for Finland, modernization seemed to imply a strategy of restraint along with an agenda for the simple, modest social adaptability that came along with the Modern Movement. Further, professional interest and individualized ideologies implied notions of a wider, far-reaching, even questionable, strategy of retreat. This, as hinted earlier, may help us understand the emerging dissent of the 1960s and '70s. But it can be argued that the 1940s 'in-between' decade led to one of the most effective 'modernizing' decades in Finnish architecture by quietly confirming the 'reductive' mentality and preparing the conditions for Finnish architects to innovate and contribute to the history of modern architecture in the 1950s.[26]

In research on the Finnish architectural profession during the war, Korvenmaa makes a strong case for the consequences of the collegial, militaristic structure of the profession and why 1942 appears a crucial year in defining aims for its membership that would last long into the future. During a meeting in early 1942, the content discussed is revealed: 'all work was to proceed in a spirit of inalienable collegial solidarity, which was regarded as the only way to ensure sufficient influence for architects in their joint activities as a body of professionals'. Militarily, during this decade the architects were mobilized for their collective duty. With hindsight, securing for its members a strong and un-challengeable position during wartime planning and construction would have immense implications for the profession. The events of 1942 show how the Association of Architects, which had just celebrated its 50th anniversary, was able to act with purpose in securing the interest of its members and as a base of specialized professional knowledge. Stringency and the innovative standardization measures laid the foundation for an increasingly controlled profession, and thus, later, a controlled, consensus Modernism. The 1940s, however, had no such worries, so strong was the hold the profession had. It would support conditions for the immense pride of the small nation in organizing and paying off reparations to the Soviet Union. The decade would also lead not only to an intense period of introspection, but would allow the profession to be strengthened by the immense war effort and solidarity.

We now begin to see how a generalized history of Finnish architecture suggests that all this leads naturally to what is often called the Golden Age of Finnish Modernism, the heroic decade of the 1950s. But before we rush into the banquet years, we need to consider whether by creating the necessary conditions for a peace during the war, the architects were also laying the foundations for the later acceptance of what we might term a 'modern serialism'. These are the consistent rational but reductive strategies that would eventually conflate architectural production with minimalism and prefabrication, and – eventually during the 1970s – modern architecture's bad press.

It is worth attempting a summary. International Modernist principles of function, form and space were naturally, and with much commonsense, tempered by the stringency and of course the difficult period of war. Ideas that were perhaps lightly accepted in the 1930s were usefully trimmed and re-tested. Instead of an extended '*funkis*-Modernism', an essential pragmatic 'folkiness' combined with economic stringency in a way took Finland back to the post-Independence times. Developing a nation that has expanded so quickly, a rudimentary standardization and serialized production became inevitable from the combined solidarity of the Reconstruction Bureau. Temporary buildings with only one material, timber, suggested a frame of mind that carried into peacetime and on into the 1960s. Perhaps here the contrary architectural imaginations of 'Modernism' and 'tradition' within the timber buildings during the reconstruction years emphasize once again the essential tensions in Finnish architecture. These too would be conflated. And although Alvar Aalto was among those who showed great enthusiasm for the production issues around standardization, it was only later, in the 1950s, that he and others identified the emerging serial nightmare of standardization.[27]

Korvenmaa's concluding remarks in his fine essay 'War Destroys and Organizes' have a consequence to this frame of mind:

> For architects, the war had brought standardization, types and industrialized methods of construction to the fore in design and planning. This trend remained a permanent and growing part of architecture and construction in Finland . . . In the process of serial construction architects, whom the Finnish authorities and manufacturers relied upon to a considerable degree, were left with the

task of creating a basic type that could be varied. In this respect, the architect's work began to resemble product design, where the designers have no influence on the final locations and use of mass-produced objects. This meant that the construction of houses adopted the rules and norms of manufacturing goods.[28]

The relevance of the last sentence should also be considered in relation to the dilemma that the Finnish architectural profession faces at the beginning of the twenty-first century. Here there is a hint at the *memetic* way in which architecture could be replicated.[29] Locations matter little any more, since much contemporary architecture begins to look as if it offers merely tectonic cleverness to vary a basic type and counter architectural bad faith. Modernizing has become an incomplete hiatus between the promoted universal architectural building 'product' located almost anywhere and the results of a serialization that still has the general public mourning the sterility of a once-famous architectural culture.

Within the new research and material appearing more recently we must also be aware of our own generalizations. Although the 1950s would be critical for the modern image and professional shape that modern architecture took in Finland, although the 1930s introduced Finland to an *applied* International Modernism, it was the 1940s that acted as a kind of 'national' filter and distilling agent of Modernism. Sensitive, simply reduced versions of an internationally accepted visual language were tempered by national concerns, national building technology, localized innovations and materials.

When push came to shove, the Finns altered opinion and direction in order to remain strong and independent. Realpolitik demanded this of them. The state the country was in after ceaseless negotiations, the evacuation of Karelia in 1940 and the ceding of large areas of Karelia and the city of Viipuri to the Soviet Union meant there was only one direction: development. To house the refugees and later to pay off the reparations demanded from the Soviet Union meant that an accelerated production, innovative metal goods and industrial processes, rapid small-scale achievements leading to big-scale prefabrication and the consumption and fetishization of consumer goods. Both expertise and goods became payment, part of the huge bilateral trade with the Soviet Union and eventually to become the international commerce and exchange of know-how, information technology and Nokia.

This decade probably proved more confusing and more experimental than we or the architects may acknowledge. So when did the war end psychologically? And when could modernizing continue and Modernism resume? Or is that irrelevant, when war as well as peace modernizes

Markus Tavio,
Viisikko Housing,
Tapiola, 1954.

Aerial view of Tapiola
Garden City,
masterplan by Otto
Meurman, showing
town centre by
Aarne Ervi, 1954–61.

countries? Undoubtedly, many Finns identify the holding of the Olympic Games in Helsinki in 1952 as the 'real' end of the war. By then the history books consider Finland to have defined itself as a 'modern nation'. Not, that is, by the icons of heroic architecture that would appear soon enough in the 1950s; rather by the strength of its own will, by economic emergence from shortage, hardship and rationing. 'War and reconstruction', according to Korvenmaa, 'were not only a temporary state of emergency, through which pre-war trends could have survived unscathed. The whole country, the work of its architects and architecture in general did not "return" to anything, but proceeded on an essentially new basis'. [30] Is this not why we hear talk of the 1950s as offering a rare tabula rasa? The pragmatics of recovery and reconstruction implied a new beginning – a *zero degree* of the Modern code. The clean break offered a chance at first-hand Modernism.

When talk returns to the unique solidarity within Modernism in the Finnish architectural profession, it is to this period one must turn. The profession took a proactive role. The rigour guided by the likes of Viljo Revell, Heikki Sirén, Aarne Ervi, Aulis Blomstedt and later Aarno Ruusuvuori, in for example their work in Tapiola, was in some way always to be partnered by the individualism that surrounded Aalto's war efforts and the remarkable range of post-war red-brick modernist buildings that established Aalto's overwhelming shadow in the decade.

The 1930s had seen an experimental International style absorbed, assimilated and refitted to suit the Finnish context. The war and the 1940s restrained any expressive or poetic excesses such 'Internationalism' might have encouraged. The 1950s would build on all this. Many towns expanded and Helsinki itself grew with a largely centralizing population. Housing developments demonstrated the importance of the restrained agenda proposed and furthered by Hilding Ekelund and others. Detailed planning, building order, new methods and systematic construction allowed the architects to aim for a wider community structure. [31] 'It is not time that alters us', the poet Bo Carpelan reminds us, 'it is space'. The forest may have encircled the Finns in their youth, but 'it is the road that is now straightened out'. After the 1940s the windows themselves would become space and the forest a backdrop. The road would straighten out.

chapter five

Expressive Modernism: The Banquet Years

This poem intends to be a word-picture
and I want poetry that hasn't much taste,
   and I'm imagining
I'm a thing with the longings of grass;

these lines have very little plausibility, for
this is a journey through known language towards
   the land that is not,
this poem is to be sung standing
   or read alone:
Paavo Haavikko, *The Winter Palace*[1]

We have accepted that it skews the shape of history to consider the 1940s merely an intervening era of 'romanticism' about to be eradicated by a braver, more mature, golden age of Modernism. The stringency and restraint of the 1940s did consolidate an approach to Modernism, function and order, but it did not amputate ideas begun in the 1930s, nor did it erase the turn-of-the-century call for lucidity, simplicity and aesthetic elegance. Architecture would not only contribute to a heroic cultural and social mapping of the nation during the 1950s, it would continue solving 'everyday' post-war needs. Then briefly Finland would have its banquet years.

Clearly the epic resistance that Finland demonstrated in the Winter War (1939–40) brought Finland to the attention of the whole world. Inflicting losses on the Soviet Union way out of proportion to the size of the warring parties invited admiration. Along the eastern border large columns of Russians were annihilated, forcing a complete reorganization of Soviet forces, despite Finland's eventual loss of land. Pride was deserved and Finland would be set apart as a nation of incredible courage, incomprehensible *sisu*. Since Finland was to go on to modernize and to use 'Modernism' to reflect its rebirth as a nation, it became clear, as the historian Matti Klinge points out, that 'despite its relative welfare and success, in Finland the lessons of hard times are remembered as a sort of symbol of the national ego'.[2]

Yrjö Lindegren and Toivo Jäntti, Olympic Stadium Tower, Helsinki, 1940–52.

In 1945 Parliament passed an act creating 142,000 new holdings out of 2.8 million hectares to aid the resettlement of the Karelians. While the burden on the Finnish economy was immense, Finland was the only OECD country that increased its farm population after the Second World War. The Child Benefit Act of 1948 acted as an incentive for having children, and by 1949 welfare expenditure had reached the average Nordic level. By the 1970s, however, the proportion maintaining their living by farming had dropped to 18 per cent, only to drop further to 8 per cent in the 1990s. Although the government-controlled Finnish Broadcasting Company (Yleisradio; YLE) was formed in 1934, it was only in 1955 when students of the Helsinki University of Technology set up their own private television company (Tesvisio) for current affairs and news that a year later YLE began televised broadcasts. By 1998 YLE operated two national channels with two other private channels operating, MTV3 and Channel 4. Finnish broadcasting technology was to pioneer and anticipate the impressive rise of the Nokia Company during the 1990s. Significantly, since the introduction of television during the 1950s, the number of newspapers, books and periodicals has increased, as has readership. If by adapting to rapid change, innovation and social justice the Finnish society had already modernized itself to some degree, the 1950s was to see a 'quantum leap'. Often called the heroic age, more recently identified as a period of 'humane rationalism', it sometimes proves difficult to reassess an era that has contributed so much to International architecture.[3]

In the process of reconstructing Finland in the immediate post-war years, architects had redefined their professional position and authority. Forced to restructure its industry once again, architects who had cut their teeth during wartime would occupy positions of greater cultural significance. The demands for a huge housing programme, schools, hospitals, civic buildings, universities, churches and sports halls would ask of the architects a heroic mission.[4] Although resonating with models from Denmark and Sweden, the Finnish response, encouraged by its unique war struggle, would be unlike any other country in post-war Europe.

In 1950 the signs of a developing country were still present. Almost half the population was still supported by farming and forestry; the reliance on pulp and paper kept the economy tied to the international timber market. Uninterested in timber, Stalin had requested reparations paid off by ships, machinery and engineering products. For a country not used to such production, the Finnish task was immense. Public and private enterprise built up the necessary industries, bringing about huge changes in the industrial structure with consequences for foreign trade.

Once the reparations had been paid off, in 1952, the Soviet Union continued to trade with Finland. In 1955 the Porkkala base was relinquished by the Soviets, enabling Finland to operate in full sovereignty. Wartime and post-war loans from the USA and Sweden were used mostly to modernize industry and develop export markets; prefabricated housing delivered from Sweden in the previous decade began to see immediate results in clustered communities.

The former British Consul-General Henry Bell, writing in 1950, again offers us some idea of the patronizing image of Finland over the years. A growing, general perception of modernity was appearing:

> Finland is a country of western habits, and most newcomers are greatly impressed by her modernness. The towns are small, but up to date and clean. Even in remote parts of the country – which has retained the immaculate appearance of a virgin – electric lighting, telephones and automobiles are the rule rather than the exception . . . above all, there is to be found in Finland 'a feeling of unspoiled nature, of un-breathed air, of freshness and purity lacking in most European countries'.[5]

The unspoilt nature, the freshness and purity; here the echoes of Ekelund's programme start to offer the exotic menu. And although the 1950s have been idealized since by just about every visitor, journalist and critic, it is worth noting that the accepted general shape of the decade is still seen as somehow magic, even as a 'miracle'.[6] Progress and experiment collided as architects began to make poetry from disparate sources. The Modern Movement was ready for a regional reinvigoration and the poets had begun setting the tone for the decade. As the poet and critic Herbert Lomas put it quite accurately: 'The poets grabbed what they needed from Modernist techniques and created an original and popular way of articulating disjunction, doubt, determination to survive, and aesthetic excitement, in a world not very interested in the individuality of small countries.'[7] Was this not the architects' exercise too?

During the early years of the 1950s, Functionalism was the only 'ism' acceptable; its sacred position went unchallenged. No one yet referred to Modernism, perhaps because it was indisputably contained within the notion of modern architecture. Yet already by the second half of the 1950s, a shift would occur. Architects began to use 'Modernism' (*modernismi*) ambiguously as an agreed collective notion. The word 'Functionalism' as a clear movement connected with Internationalism had been distanced the moment it was catalogued in 1932 in New York at the Museum of Modern Art's *Modern Architecture* international exhibition.[8] Functionalism as a term had become too generic. Critical usage of notions such as Vernacularism, Organic Architecture, Expressionism and Constructivism emerged to redefine the Modern Movement, serving to rupture and pluralize it. The allegiance to 1930s Functionalism was loosened by the work of the three leading figures of the time, Alvar Aalto, Aarne Ervi and Viljo Revell, and 'modern architecture' gained currency by the diverse but internationally modern work of these three practices. And as useful as modern architecture was in Finland to adapt to local conditions, needs and mentality, we need to be aware of just what distinguishes this era in relation to the modern agenda. How much does the decade begin to display and confirm general attributes already identified with the by-now recognized Finnish skill of absorption, adaptation and assimilation?

An influential project presenting technical innovation in this spirit of International Modernism was Aarne Ervi's Porthania University Building in Helsinki. Influences may have come from America, but the Finnish transformations were going to be internationally significant.[9] A compact urban incision, Ervi's Modernism was ahead technologically and set a

Aarne Ervi, Porthania Building, University of Helsinki, 1957.

pattern for further Modernism within the city. Cleverly planned, the off-set entrance was flanked by the students' restaurant, which suggested an urban veranda. A building that has proved popular with students, it remained – along with many of Aalto's urban works – an indication of how Modernism could adapt and use new developments in building material and technology.

Larger buildings and developments were made possible as city block renovation led to the removal of old city and town stock. In the 1940s, as bombed areas were replaced, towns received a newer, smaller-scale in-fill development somewhat still in keeping with the existing two-storey wooden building scale of the city. However, the 1950s seemed to ask for and got larger solutions. The post-war housing programme was strengthened as it collided with issues such as flexibility, transformabil-ity, privacy and cluster planning discussed throughout Europe at the time. Larger communal visions were highly successful, especially in the south around a growing Helsinki (which began to merge with the towns Tapiola and Espoo), avoiding the trap of the diagrammatic, which would come to the fore in the 1960s. Density, siting within the landscape and new clustering ideas led to sensitive, humanist housing develop-ments that would snake and twist; they are pinpointed often, especially in Helsinki, with the emergence of the tower block, like those of the architects Lauri Silvennoinen, Osmo Sipari and Viljo Revell. All this re-emerging, clean, modern architecture in the natural beauty of the Finnish landscape represented a streamlined and, to many Finns in the towns for the first time and other visitors, an enviable environmental development. Yrjö Lindegren's Snake House, to the north of Helsinki, became a much-cited example of the variants possible in housing. A rather conventional housing type is revitalized by its snaking form, lift-ing where necessary to follow the contours of the land. A more severe work than much other housing of the time, it sustained, however, the respect for landscape, siting and the immediate environment, thereby strangely enhancing its 'ordinariness'.

The jump in scale made possible by increased technology and building methods meant also a growing change in the iconic image of the city, especially Helsinki. Kaivotalo, a large commercial building designed by Paulu Salomaa and finished in 1956, led the way; non-load-bearing walls and prefabrication enabled experiments to be made in space, encouraging more and more experiments in open planning. Neon signage added to the modernity of the façade and city. Later this building would be extended as an urban 'strip', literally an extension of the existing Kaivotalo, by Revell's innovative ideas from the 1950s, and finished in 1967 as a mega-block called 'City-kortteli'. Situated

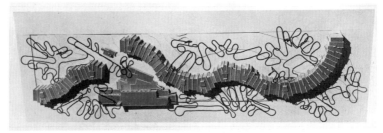

Yrjö Lindegren,
'Snake House'
Housing, and site
plan, Helsinki, 1951.

right opposite Helsinki Railway Station, this massive block resonated
with American models in office building (Huttunen's Sokos Hotel and
Department Store had been finished only in 1952). Nicknamed the
'sausage house' (*makkaratalo*) because of the huge curved concrete
girth to the upper-level car park, the mass is akin to Revell's other
mega-complex 'city quarter' in Central Vaasa.[10] A less known but still
bigger complex having features of the same spirit was designed later in
the decade to cover three city blocks close to West harbour in Helsinki
by Viljo Revell (assistants: Heikki Castren and Matti K. Mäkinen).
Rejected by the cityscape authorities, the project was silently buried
when Revell died in 1964. A row of seven-storey office blocks hovering
above a four-storey platform of parking decks was suspended by steel
bars drawn to the façades from elevator towers. The provocative skyline
with spider-web construction was considered too extreme at the time.

Viljo Revell,
City-kortelli (or city
quarter), Helsinki,
1967 (nicknamed
'sausage house').

Viljo Revell, City Quarter, Vaasa, 1958.

Such a proposal might now be reassessed in relation to the likely emergence of similar mega-blocks in and around Helsinki. For a city without a definite commercial core, these mega-buildings began to redefine Helsinki. Later, this area around the railway station and the bus station would expand on this and become the commercial, communications and shopping node of the inner city.

If Finland is unique in modern architecture, it is not only this decade that made it unique or worked its miracle. It was very much the work and consistency of previous architects that had cleared the way for such courage. Through education and professional guidance, older architects enabled the younger ones to establish their particular and unusual talent.

Erkki Huttunen, Sokos Hotel and Commercial Building, 1952, and Vaakuna restaurant interior.

It sounds more generous than it probably was; but although there was intense competition and envy, there was in the 1950s an extraordinary solidarity among architects.[11] To understand this it is worth remembering those still active from the earlier decades. Besides Aalto, J. S. Sirén, Ekelund, Huttunen, Välikangas, Ervi and Revell among others were all still around and operating to a greater or lesser degree in their professional capacities. It is here that we need to recall the solidity built up over the decades and avoid the danger of isolating the 'miracle' of the 1950s with its heroic modern achievements in the everyday. We could do this best by considering the continuity within the architectural education in Finland and the hints at a consensual Modernism this offers.[12]

Given the to and fro in the small culture, a brief survey of the important professors and teachers of the years around 1900 will enable links to be made to the 1950s and onwards within Finnish architectural circles. Gustaf Nyström, Onni Tarjanne, Usko Nyström, Carolus Lindberg and later Armas Lindgren, all significant architects, feature strongly in the education of the pioneers of Finnish architecture. Gustaf Nyström, as Professor of Public Building at the beginning of the twentieth century, taught Frosterus, Saarinen, Bryggman, Ekelund and, for a brief time, Aalto. Although the bias was naturally towards the Italian Renaissance in the first two decades of the century, the awareness of new building methods in steel and concrete undoubtedly invited students to seek new solutions and design methods. Usko Nyström continued the Beaux-Arts style and Jugend tectonics, emphasizing both style and form, while Onni Tarjanne taught building construction. After Gustaf Nyström, Armas Lindgren took over influencing Aalto with his humanistic approach, tending to prefer the work of Frank Lloyd Wright rather than Le Corbusier. In the 1920s Ekelund carried on the teaching position of Usko Nyström and followed the breakthrough into Functionalism with his own interests in housing, *architettura minore* and the low-cost housing 'Existenzminimum' programme, linked too at the time with his colleague Martti Välikangas and their work at the Finnish *Architectural Review* from 1929 to 1933.

These years would not only influence the next three decades but be mirrored in the way that professional positions were exchanged and the agenda continued. In 1929 the death of Armas Lindgren had opened up the most important professorial position, an appointment that was to have consequences right up until the 1950s and even beyond. Both J. S. Sirén and Aalto applied for the position, and after some time, and not an insignificant amount of power-juggling, Sirén was appointed Professor of Public Building.[13] As accounts go, the selection process led to exaggerated disagreements. Architectural power was centralized, debates were polemical and envy, though gentlemanly, was nevertheless ruthless. The partisan games that had gone on would continue throughout the century; the personal and professional merged, and from the 1950s onwards, with the backlash against Aalto, power and patronage would be crucial to the way Finnish architecture would be interpreted both at home and abroad. The establishment of the Museum of Finnish Architecture in 1956 would not only begin the intense period of promotion of Finnish architecture abroad, it would signal the power lines, political manoeuvring and patronage that would define the remaining decades of the century.

But this selection in 1929 is important. According to the deciding voices and minutes of the meetings in 1929 among Onni Tarjanne, Carolus Lindberg and Sigurd Frosterus, at stake were the rigour, rationalism, elegant restraint and reliability of Sirén against the intuitive energy, unmentioned opportunism and suspect brilliance of the young Aalto. This was a struggle for the 'heart' of Finnish architecture. The schism that developed later in the 1950s between Aalto's softer humanism and the rigorous, rational approach continued by P. E. Blomstedt, and later by Keijo Petäjä and Aarno Ruusuvuori in the 1950s, was one consequence of this struggle and the start of the many misunderstandings of Aalto. The decision to appoint Sirén professor in 1929 and not Aalto shaped Finnish architecture from that point onwards. Up until 1956, Sirén in many ways was considered to have been the most significant educator and 'presence' in Finnish architecture.[14] His own position would become available in 1956 and would later be continued by one of his admirers, Aulis Blomstedt, who took up teaching in 1958. And it is a well-known fact that although Aalto had designed the new red-brick campus in Otaniemi, outside Helsinki in the late 1940s and early '50s, none of his work was available or kept in the architectural library at the time.[15] It is thus impossible to appreciate this 'miracle era' without also understanding the stakes that began to be played out in Finnish architecture in the 1950s.[16]

But what gave this decade its heroic structure? Certainly there was a sense that the successful payment of reparations and the subsequent release from rationing and post-war hardship permitted the society a new opening. Young men were no longer young men after a war experience: they entered architecture school with less than the usual innocence. In a way these architects, many born in the 1920s, were fast-tracked into serving society. By the early 1950s both graduated architects and students were open to almost everything that internationalism could throw at them. The time was right for the 'national' to redefine the 'international' as cultural confidence grew and social planning coincided with technological development. The status the profession had organized during the war with the Reconstruction Bureau meant that architects could go for braver solutions.

The Olympic Stadium designed by Yrjö Lindegren and Toivo Jäntti (originally for 1940) was one of the most important buildings to open the new decade. It bridged the decades, echoed White Functionalism, introduced a romantic longing. Although the functionalist tower was undoubtedly the symbol of the young, vibrant republic, the photograph so often shown taken during the Olympics of 1952 held in Helsinki indicates the stepped timber façade as an extension to the elegant and refined Internationalist first-phase of the stadium. Later extensions to the stadium might have reduced the clarity and effect of the early work, but they hinted at a softer aesthetic response to the accepted modern agenda. By the time that things eased economically and politically in the early 1950s, other architects who had also begun in the 1930s and played important roles in the 1940s began to take control of the profession. Viljo Revell, Aarne Ervi, Aulis Blomstedt, Hilding Ekelund, Otto Meurman the planner and Nils Erik Wickberg the editor and historian all developed to varying degrees a cross-programming of humanism and rationalism.[17]

Yrjö Lindegren and Toivo Jäntti, Olympic Stadium, Helsinki, 1940–52.

The public emergence of the arts was one of the most important developments of the 1950s.[18] The Nordic spirit was about to be redefined as

Finnish. A controlled ascetic display with the back-wall summer landscape at the Finnish exhibition in the Milan Triennale of 1954 set the tone for coded restraint and Nordic serenity. The Association of Finnish Architects began in 1953 what became a series of exhibitions every three years called 'Finland Builds'. Later reinforced by the strong singularizing role of the Museum of Finnish Architecture, exhibitions designed by Blomstedt, Jaatinen, Lappo, Lundsten, Pallasmaa and others would signal the rational-humanist cross-over.[19] The respect for tradition and nature in images of landscape combined with an emerging simplicity went further as the architects believed they were communicating something essentially 'Finnish'. Always controlled, always edging out difference, within the highly selected Finnish design and architecture, it became difficult for anyone to miss the notion of 'Finnishness' so evident was this in the romance and poetry of the rationally controlled and graphic displays of the era.

During the 1950s the call to a modest 'peasant' aesthetic (echoes of Paavo Ruotsalainen) and the fondness for utility objects from the past can be interpreted as nostalgic at the same time as 'modern'. There was a longing for national associations and identity brought along with these exercises. Almost any text by Aulis Blomstedt, who became the major polemicist and theoretician during this decade, indicates the movement towards simplicity and a reinterpretation of classical nature. In 1957 Blomstedt would answer the central problem of the aims of the visual arts and architecture for that moment: 'all the visual arts and architecture are currently undergoing an energetic process of simplification'.[20] The general pattern outlined earlier of restraint re-emerged. Being unheroic, unassuming and un-theoretical took on a quiet, mystical, but calculated authenticity.[21] At the same time this mode of thought was sometimes applied very concretely and interpreted rather naively, as the art historian Harri Kalha describes: 'for example, narrow-necked vases that favoured the ascetic arrangement of single flowers or branches were seen as deriving from the rugged Finnish countryside, in which flowers grew too sparsely to be gathered into a bunch!'[22]

Modernism in Finnish literature, theatre, design, industrial arts, fashion, music and architecture all found echo and relevance and made the 1950s rich and often challenging as the culture shook off the influence of the Swedish model of Modernism. With the death of the Independence and Winter War hero and President, Marshall Mannerheim, in 1951, an era was over. The traditionalists could build on the reinterpretations of the novelist Mika Waltari with his displaced historical fiction, *The Egyptian* (1945). War itself would be fictionalized and worked-through with Väinö Linna's best-selling novel *The Unknown Soldier* (1954), filmed by the master of traditional narrativist Finnish cinema, Edwin

Yrjö Lindegren and Toivo Jäntti, Olympic Stadium, Helsinki, 1940–52.

Martti Mykkanen, Winston cigarette advert of 1956, and Lasse Hietala, 'Koh!', Public Information Campaign poster, Helsinki, 1979.

Laine.[23] Tove Jansson's important Moomin series, mentioned earlier, though begun in the 1940s, would become a strong favourite in the 1950s with its special mix of fear, humour, dread and philosophical asides. It seemed to advocate *sisu*, that inner strength – to go on whatever, whether the comet falls in Moominland or not would be the moral of the story.

The work of poets would be particularly important in relation to Modernism. Writers such as Eeva-Liisa Manner, Mirkka Rekola, Lassi Nummi, Lauri Viita, Pentti Holappa and Paavo Haavikko began to define the era and shape the wider modern agenda. An entirely new mode of expression within the Finnish language emerged, developing earlier work by P. Mustapää and Aaro Hellaakoski; world views were balanced by the ever-present relationship to nature. The poets and artists in the 1950s began looking back at the 1920s. Hellaakoski (1893–1952), influenced by Apollinaire and Cubism, produced an experimental poetry that in many ways was not an exercise matched in architecture, though it might anachronistically echo Sigurd Frosterus's Swedish paean to the machine. Hellaakoski moved onto a more restrained urban Modernism that was to influence and be echoed not only in the Modernism of Paavo Haavikko but what is now considered the postmodernist poetry of the *enfant terrible* of the 1960s, Pentti Saarikoski. This had its effect on architecture and the architects, too. The forest space in a way became a literary contract mediated by the Modernism of Ezra Pound, T. S. Eliot and Ernest Hemingway. Only, in the 1950s, no one quite spoke of it as 'forest space'.

Paavo Haavikko would become Finland's most important poet, using poetry to engage and play with politics and the country at the highest level. The most respected living writer, his diversity would consistently challenge the dogma of Modernism as it emerged after the 1950s.[24] Music itself in Finland cannot be assessed here, so large and so vibrant have been its contemporary developments from the 1950s onwards with the work of Usko Meriläinen, Joonas Kokkonen, Erik Bergman and others.[25] But the achievements of Finnish Modernism are relentless and impressive. If birch-bark wallpaper and greaseproof paper (designed by Greta Skogster-Lehtinen, 1942) had been a symbol of wartime design, then new forms of textile art (the work on the traditional *ryijy* rug) would reach the Victoria and Albert Museum in London. Training in clothing design began in 1948 at the Central School of Applied Arts. Fashion itself immediately absorbed international trends, but manufactured an image of practical, well-balanced, striking clothes. Climate factors forced a nuanced, seasonal detail; the design houses Marimekko and Vuokko were to become famous by the end of the decade. The decade was diagrammed by their graphics.

Poster design (as in the work of Erik Bruun and Björn Landström) became important, picking up on Futurism, Functionalism and Art Deco to provide a kind of fresh youthfulness in colour and form. Social justice began to seep through. A particular brand of public campaign posters and travel posters would use reductive strategies, striking photographic imagery, an effective field-use of colour and a rather diagrammatic approach that became favoured in the advertising and social issues emerging in the 1960s (poverty, pollution, the peace movement, drugs, tobacco, alcohol abuse, etc.).[26]

All this offers clues to the 'miracle' of the decade, and it is impossible to understand the 'heroism' attributed to architects without understanding the inter-disciplinarity of the period. Planning could expand and begin anticipating new lives, new beginnings and modern times for all. Alvar Aalto's implemented reindeer-horn master plan for Rovaniemi (1944) and his elongated 'forest town' Master Plan for Imatra (1947–53) would, along with others, lead the way towards larger schemes of regional development. Very much in the control of central government, planning was steered by individuals. Alongside Aalto's own importance in planning, Otto I. Meurman had been appointed the first Professor of Urban Planning in 1940. Meurman's book *Asemakaavaoppi* ('Urban Planning Manual') became the basic work from which others drew up regional plans, following Meurman's example of his own plans for town, cities and areas.

A freer, more open form, with emphatic residential units located within the landscape, managed to hold back for some time the rapid increase in traffic and the eventual 'modernist' re-scaling of cities and towns ushered in by tower blocks. The romance associated with material in the 1940s was less a romance than refitting a style to local conditions. During the 1950s aluminium, copper and glass were all newly developed and favoured materials, but there were still post-war difficulties in the availability of materials. Technical innovation in concrete and prefabrication quickly began to make possible the reworking of whole city areas, some nearer the city, others outlying in sites of clear natural beauty. Although there was a desire for the 'modern solution' by the late 1950s, the lack of development in oil-based materials like bitumen meant that flat roofs would have to wait until the next decade: a delay mourned by the impatient young techno-modernists of the time.

New commissions such as the Palace Hotel and Industrial Centre by Revell & Petäjä (1952) not only brought two functions together (the hotel and an office) but also architects with interior designers. Product and industrial design emerged more powerfully, and, after Artek's experiments into bent plywood furniture in the 1940s, Ilmari Tapiovaara

Viljo Revell and Keijo Petäjä, Palace Hotel and Centre for Industry, Helsinki, 1952.

Palace Hotel and
Centre for Industry,
interior detail.

would become one of the leading furniture designers of the decade. After his work on dug-outs during the war, his interiors in the Domus Academica Student Dormitory in Helsinki (1946–7) indicated the simplicity and modern elegance that would soon be in every interior in the 1950s. The experiments seemed everywhere: glass and industrial design, experimental music and film, the simple, earthenware works – the Kilta line – of Kaj Franck were put into serial production in 1953.[27] A sign of how extraordinary this decade would be was the Finnish success at the Milan Triennale of 1951, whilst at the same time an important exhibition of modern art from Italy was exhibited in Helsinki. The work of Tapio Wirkkala reached the international stage; ascetic, simple designs were applied to glass, timber and birch-ply as an organic Modernism suddenly found the beginnings of a formal language. It is argued that Wirkkala pre-empted some of the more sculptural works of the end of the decade, albeit with a jump in scale, in the churches by architects such as Reima Pietilä, Revell, Antti Korhonen, E. Elomaa, Timo and Tuomo Suomalainen and Aarno Ruusuvuori. Timo Sarpaneva also came to prominence in the 1950s. By 1967, as designer of the Finnish exhibition at the Montreal

World Expo, he probably recognized more than most the power and importance of cultural promotion, image and marketing for a strong design culture. Exploiting the early White Functionalism of the 1930s, architects would now be seen as importers of an 'expressive' Modernism. Finnish design and architecture was set to become a legend.

The frenzied architectural activity continued throughout the 1950s with a strong housing programme matched by an equally strong civic programme. The 1950s was also the decade when Alvar Aalto became an undisputed international master, confirmed in his 'pioneering' position by Sigfried Giedion (in his *Space Time and Architecture*) as a 'Finnish' architect with that 'inner source of energy which always flows through his work'.[28] Here was the 'regional Modernist' *par excellence* taking, as Giedion maintained, Finland with him wherever he goes.[29]

Aalto's catalogue is well known and impressive. Most of his major red-brick works (perhaps picking up on Vähäkallio's red-brick *funkis*), often considered at the time monumental and even romantic in relation to the Finnish architectural profession's own reductivist agenda, were produced in the 1950s. The list is significant, but Säynätsalo Civic Centre (1949–52) is one project often used to demonstrate the expressive intimacy of Aalto's work at this time. Red-brick, clustered and defying

Alvar Aalto, Säynätsalo Civic Centre, 1952.

Säynätsalo Civic
Centre, door handle
and roof trusses.

the domestic scale, this was the building that bespoke an unwanted
romanticism to the Finnish profession and a redirected Humanistic
Modernism to visitors. The scale of his earlier Villa Mairea (1938–9) was
cleverly shifted to a civic dimension, although the building complex is
actually smaller than the well-known images suggest. It is a building so
well sited in the landscape and so vernacular as to appear modern that
it was later used to redefine Modernism's role, especially by Kenneth
Frampton in his important essay 'Towards a Critical Regionalism'.[30]
Aalto's works clearly set a precedent. His position and power demonstrated the way architecture could be used both as a laboratory and a
mirror during the decade. Material and technical advances permitted
increased experimentation in building method, construction techniques
and treatment. Aalto was not slow to exploit these. But, as if to continue his warning against over-rational, standardizing developments, Aalto's
modern idiom became more expressive. Moving from the binary (sculptural and rational) red-tiled House of Culture in Helsinki (1955–8) to

the freer, white expressionism of Vuoksenniska Church (1956–8) and the Wolfsburg Cultural Centre (1958–63), it was the last in many ways that became a dry run for the more monumental Finlandia Hall (1961–75), which to many architects signalled an Aalto disastrously off course. The softer red-brick humanism had in a way de-humanized; the monument had become Aalto himself. For many in the profession, Aalto's architecture was no longer the modern idiom to represent Finland. The elegant dignity of the everyday, the *architettura minore* of a modest, unassuming but talented nation that had triumphed in the 1950s – like Säynätsalo Civic Centre – had been lost.

The rest of the world began to recognize both the success and the restraint of the Finnish response to the Modern Movement. The 1950s was the time when architects began to pay more attention to critics and what someone else said about their work. The Finland Builds exhibitions along with the International exhibitions of the Museum began an intense promotional exercise. In the *Architectural Review* in the UK (April 1957) Reyner Banham linked Aalto's talent to other Finnish architects. In a move that solidified all Finnish architects into a somewhat questionable mass, Banham considered them to 'have Aalto's ability to be regional without being provincial, to command an international esteem while using a national idiom'.[31] Banham's acuteness, generally shared in the international community, was less clear at home. Aalto had proved an architect able to take on the international trends and answer with a local idiom, but at what cost? Describing his incomparable stature as a practically unique achievement in the twentieth century was not

Alvar Aalto,
Finlandia Hall,
Helsinki, 1961–75.

only true, it was seductive to others. The country had once again shown how ill-fortune and war could be turned to advantage. Heroism could be transferred; other architects could achieve what Aalto had achieved. At least, that is what Banham implied.

Historicism and a nostalgia for the past held less for Finns as they pressed ahead to establish their own difference from both their Swedish and Russian past. Many were in awe of Scandinavian models. Denmark and Sweden too were much in vogue during the 1950s with international architects and critics. The work of the Swedes Sigurd Lewerentz and Peter Celsing was published widely. Gentle unassuming work creeping up in scale could take on an accepted modern dignity. However, the Finns had a trump card. Without the Swedes' compulsive order, embedded social democracy and the respective millstones of monarchy, history and hierarchy, Finland could forge ahead in a freer, more youthful way, brilliantly turning the 'international' idiom of modern architecture inside out. Journals, critics and writers would begin to establish a promotional structure for architecture. Initiated in 1956 by Alvar Aalto and Kyösti Ålander, after many years of discussion (from as early as 1906) the Museum of Finnish Architecture was set up in principle to promote Finnish architecture. Although critical debate has always struggled in the more practical Finnish circles, and was to struggle even more towards the end of the twentieth century, the museum attempted to open architecture up to change. Early exhibitions promoted the work of Finnish architects elegantly – and selectively. As a repository of the photographic archive of the Finnish Architectural Association the 'image' bias of its exercise virtually erased history in favour of the present. It moved into an old timber building in Helsinki's Kaivopuisto, the park once the site of the Industrial Exhibition in the nineteenth century. It would become one of the most important institutes for the dissemination and promotion of Finnish architecture around the world. The photographic pull of the venture, seeing architecture through the lens of selected images linked with the ambiguous notion of 'nature's embrace', enabled the main protagonists (Ålander, Revell, Blomstedt, Ruusuvuori) to map out and present an 'absolute architecture'.[32] The small group connected with the museum shaped, promoted and constructed a legend that ultimately narrowed the notion of Modernism in Finnish architecture. Demands of promotion, however, began to unbalance critical content. Accepted dogma and tacit agreement about the aesthetic of Finnish architecture could and would be innocently reiterated until it became a believable, received opinion. By the end of the first decade of the museum's activity, this controlled and intense self-promotion exercise around international exhibitions was to rebound as the 1960s unfolded into awkward protest

Osmo Sipari,
Herttoniemi Housing,
Helsinki, 1957.

and self-censorship among architects. As Petra Ceferin argues: 'What was, in the late 1950s, offered as the best of Finnish architecture, came to function as a framework within which Finnish architects were expected to operate; the "golden age" of Finnish architecture . . . began to metamorphose into the "golden cage" of Finnish architects.'[33] It is impossible not to follow this metamorphosis while critically noting reluctance among the profession to acknowledge the paradox of this shift.

Meanwhile, in all the architectural achievement and construction of the legend a parallel everydayness was going on. Through mechanization and increased building targets, the 1950s naturally went on to lay the foundation for the push towards greater production. Greater production also invited greater visions. Besides the often-published works of the more humanistic, nature-inspired projects (such as Tapiola Garden City and work by Aalto, Heikki and Kaija Sirén and Aulis Blomstedt's residential housing), the image of the Finnish landscape was being altered by medium to large housing schemes.[34] Regional surroundings and city suburbs merged. Neighbourhood projects were often built on uninhabited areas as Helsinki expanded rapidly. Sipari's Herttoniemi blocks (1957), Esko Korhonen's Roihuvuori Housing in Helsinki (1954), the Ruskeasuo area, these and other large-scale housing developments were all set in process by the work of Revell and Petäjä in Maunula (1949–53), the North Herttoniemi project and Silvennoinen's Pihlajamäki Housing blocks. Stepped-slab blocks, star buildings, point blocks and tower blocks opened up and vigorously assimilated international architecture and the new ideas about high-rise planning.

Besides the forest romance of Tapiola, other suburbs and neighbourhoods suddenly looked sleeker, braver. This was a freshness uninspired by nature but which could use the natural surroundings to contextualize the work. Photographed outwards, every building seemed to have a forest on its doorstep. In relation to other countries with less accessible nature, the planned districts covered by varying-scale functional blocks appeared remarkably sensitive. Combine all this with the emerging individuality and strength of the younger Finnish architects following on but diverging from Aalto and this was, in modern architecture, the way to go.[35] Finland was, suddenly, the country to visit.

If the modern architecture was not always different from other countries in Europe, the landscape was. The march of prefabrication was evident during this decade. Experiments in industrial buildings permitted architects to attempt far-reaching social and planning goals. Technology and the reductive agenda of Modernism offered structural solutions to housing, schooling and industry. The most iconic competition sketch of the time – and replicated model – belongs to Viljo Revell and Eero Eerikäinen for their Housing Reform competition named Blue Ribbon (1953–4). The lack of detail in the drawing would imply an accepted condition and agenda in the profession. This was a tacit space; a consensus emerged. Later, almost echoing this solidarity among architects, many architects would submit competition projects with similar tectonic

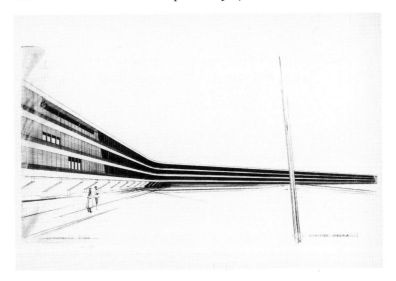

Viljo Revell and Eero Eerikäinen, 'Blue Ribbon' Housing Reform Competition, 1953–4.

minimalism. It was as if by drawing they could indicate a short-cut to a known and expected modern world.[36]

In professional circles it is often mooted that the two pre-war architects Erik Bryggman and Yrjö Lindegren were likely to produce a mature interpretation of the (classical) Functional-Modernism begun in the 1930s. Although both died in the early 1950s, I would suggest that it was their combined sensitivity and those who shared it that set up a resistance to the kind of monumentality Aalto began to propose. Certainly we have identified the importance of the 1950s to Aalto, but again the general 'ethical' shape of the modern agenda was once more steered more influentially by the 'shadow-figures'. Ekelund was still important, as was Sirén as an educator. And besides the influence of Bryggman and Lindegren, two Aalto assistants from the 1930s, Aarne Ervi and Viljo Revell were to achieve prominence. Ervi was the Cary Grant of Finnish architecture – charming, commercially astute, an innovator of existing

Aarne Ervi, Tapiola Administration Tower, 1961.

Aarne Ervi, the 'Cary Grant' of Finnish architecture, in his studio during the 1950s.

trends, his position in Finnish architecture has not really been fully researched. The Tapiola Centre main administration building became not only the iconic core of the centre, but again the place where Ervi developed the use of technology, materials in his planning. Similar somewhat to the interest in new technology of Revell, it was the latter who began to strengthen the 'genre' and imagine more streamlined, massive solutions for the Finnish city, as the projects in Vaasa and Helsinki demonstrate.

Viljo Revell was special. Crucial to the way the 1950s developed, there was professional awe in his presence. The quintessential modern 'functionalist', it is now possible to see how Revell carried on in the 1950s where Aalto had veered away towards Villa Mairea and his 'synthetic' Modernism. Aalto underwent an American period, teaching at MIT, designing and completing the MIT Dormitory in 1946, growing weary somewhat, according to his letters, of the American experience. Not influenced by humanist restraint but seduced by the new methods implied in the 'modern' machine age, Revell reacted differently. He pushed forward, often with associates like Keijo Petäjä. He would explore bigger scale and take on grander, more diagrammatic projects befitting some of the promise of the early Modern Movement. Revell appreciated industrial buildings and studied how better to achieve a more efficient industrial production in the Palace Hotel and Industrial Centre and in apartment blocks like Mäntyviita. Introducing team work and shared concerns – a less hierarchical structure for the profession – Revell encouraged a more open approach to the modern office and design practice. The Revell office would for a period vie with the Aalto office for ideological leadership. In fact these two practices represented the developing struggle between what might be called a Humanist Modernism and the stricter, more abstract, intellectual Rationalism. During this decade the Aalto office would often be accused of succumbing to a romantic Modernism, based on 'national' characteristics. (Aalto has been seen to influence the likes of Aarne Ervi, Erkki Loma, Veli Paatela, Jaakko Kontio, Kaarlo 'Kale' Leppänen and Arto Sipinen, and it was Aarne Ervi who won the Tapiola Garden City Tower competition.)

Revell won the Toronto City Hall Competition in 1958 along with Osmo Sipari and Seppo Valjus, and but for his death seemed set to go on and explore outside Finland a wider repertoire of Modernism. His approach now echoes much of the way that Eero Saarinen worked in the USA in the 1950s, after emigrating there in 1923, and hints at the individuality, plurality and courage of a more recent Finnish architect, Jyrki Tasa. The Revell office was the precursor for the collaborative practice, and his untimely death in 1964 once again deprived Finnish architecture

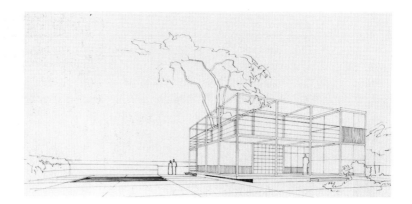

of the chance to balance what at that time appeared a top-heavy archi-tectural culture. Aalto was to occupy, in the 1950s and into the early 1960s, a position of unequalled and unchallenged dominance.

Resistance to Aalto, though, began to re-shape Finnish architecture and return it to the accepted agenda. Significantly for the development of the late 1950s and the '60s, it was Revell who taught – directly or indirectly – many who would become important in the late 1950s and '60s, among them Keijo Petäjä, Reima Pietilä, Aulis Blomstedt and Aarno Ruusuvuori. Combine this with the fact that Blomstedt and Ruusuvuori became influential and powerful professors at the Otaniemi School of

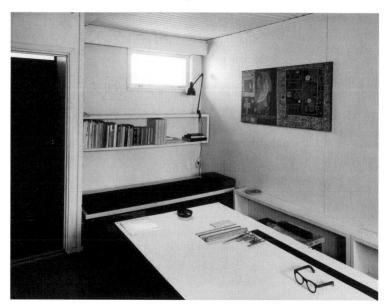

150

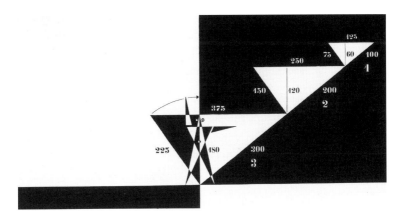

Architecture in Helsinki, and the 'miracle' decade begins to leave its ideological stamp on the coming years.

Theoretically, it was probably Aulis Blomstedt who was the strongest influence on Finnish architecture of the 1950s. Professionally he established and maintained links with CIAM, forming the Finnish chapter PTAH in the early 1950s. Along with Pietilä, Petäjä, Ruusuvuori, Nurmesniemi, Ålander and Andre Schimmerling, he also began the now legendary iconoclastic review of architecture, *Le Carré Bleu* ('The Blue Square'). Importantly, this group would convene in Imatra in 1954 to discuss many issues that would later be echoed in the 1960s.[37] Aulis Blomstedt's appeal to the 'real' pre-empted the essentialist, utilitarian mood of the 1960s. His theoretical and cultural interest pre-empted also the phenomenological props that were to rescue the agenda for Finnish architecture in the 1980s. And although his resort to nature as a model for architectural theory owed possibly more to a numbers mysticism than to Zen, it was no less an alibi for a realness in architecture than Reima Pietilä's 'stranger' morphological and 'forest space' language theories that began appearing in *Le Carré Bleu* in 1957 and 1958; theories that led to an unfinished, unsettled 'anti'-architecture which would cause uproar in the next decade with the Dipoli Students' Centre.

Although much of Blomstedt's own work remained under-achieved, his theories undeveloped, his own thinking, his antipathy to Aalto's architecture, his revised versions of an 'absolute architecture' were all to be continued and re-mastered in various strains by many of the now well-known Finnish architects. His Extension to the Helsinki Workers' Institute, though finished in 1959, remains one of the most iconic projects in Finnish architecture. Modest it may be to anyone who now glances at this work, it is not a slight achievement. Blomstedt built a

Aulis Blomstedt,
Workers' Institute
Extension, Helsinki,
1958.

Heikki and Kaija
Sirén, Otaniemi
Chapel, Tapiola,
1956–7, and drawing,
1954.

quiet manifesto; uncompromising, elegantly controlled and dimensioned, it was plainly in accord with both the classical and contemporary approach to Modernism. The works of serious Finnish architects over the next three decades (Gullichsen, Kairamo, Vuomala, Mäkinen, Leiviskä, Pallasmaa and others)[38] all owe in part a debt to the ideas and theories explored by Blomstedt and exemplified by the Extension to the Worker's Institute.

Do the 1950s then, this 'golden age', illustrate the suggestion made earlier that Ekelund's programme for quiet dignity and good sense would eventually be realized on a grander scale? In a way it does, and although one might be tired of hearing that this or that building is seminal to this agenda there is no escaping it. In Finland during the 1950s Heikki (son of J. S. Sirén) and Kaija Sirén's Otaniemi Chapel is just such an example. Not only for the simplicity it registered, but for the sacredness of site and project linked culturally, this chapel remains singular in Finnish architecture. A sense of calm romance was ushered in with the Otaniemi Chapel; Blomstedt's absolute architecture could be mirrored by the distance it took from nature itself, while being seduced by landscape at the same time.[39] Compared with Sirén's chapel, Aalto's churches can appear bewitching, romantic and labyrinthine. Considering the narrative shape of Modernism even up to the present day, to my mind it is Sirén more than Aalto who achieved the notional authenticity that Finnish architects like Ekelund, Bryggman, Blomstedt and Ruusuvuori attach to the modern. Sirén's reredos at Otaniemi was no longer a wall but a screen to the forest. The competition sketch had signified extreme restraint. This was a serious utopia of surface that let in landscape as much as it let God out. It dematerialized the interior and exterior into 'flow'. This was a 'forest space'[40] that was all that could be modern, yet it used brick, timber and concrete.[41]

At the close of the 1950s there was a spate of sculptural, expressive works. Brutalism also made its appearance. The potential of thin concrete forms saw works – from Aalto, Pietilä, Ruusuvuori, Laapotti, Elomaa, Lappo and Korhonen – that suggest a new creativity. The more 'expressive' projects such as Alvar Aalto's Vuoksenniska Church (1956) and the monumental Kaleva Church (1958–66) by Reima Pietilä (and others by Korhonen and Ruusuvuori) broke with the modest dignity of the everyday. Competition briefs asked for the spectacular; the emphasis on the visual, on the graphic clarity of works, swayed juries. Talk and critical banter started to reach out for an architecture of the modern landscaped soul; instead, the aesthetic weight won the day. And although it was obvious there were new futures in such lucid architecture and such absolute thinking, although the constructed legend of Finnish architecture was well on the way to being established and would continue repeating itself through international exhibitions until 1967, no one at the end of the 1950s was quite sure about the soul.

The decade showed the Finns' new-found confidence in strengthening the modern agenda. The un-heroic modest architects and designers had become heroic. National characteristics were adapted to the international developments in architecture and placed within the natural context. There was some achievement in placing ascetic, stricter cubic forms with suggestively moulded spaces within the forest and asking much from the developing new technology and prefabrication. By the end of the 1950s works were both rational *and* expressive. The plasticity had in some way tamed the more abstract streamlining of modern form and it looked for a moment when the rational and the expressive might live together, just as it had done in some of Bryggman's best works; though for how long remained to be seen. The legend of Finnish architecture was prepared, the exhibitions had been designed and the photographs had been taken. There was one snag: nobody appeared in any of the photographs. Everyday life, the heroism of the ordinary in Finland, was to skip a beat and lose out to the greater agenda represented in the next decade, the years of protest.

chapter six

Fellow Travelling: Militancy, Mies and Constructivism

I live in Helsinki
Helsinki is the capital of Finland.
It's situated by the sea 120 miles west of Leningrad.
Helsinki is an expanding city, and the rents are high.
We sit in the midst of our forests backs to the giant and watch
     his image in a well. He wears a dark suit a white shirt
and
     a silver tie. In his country everything's different,
     there they walk on their heads or without a head.
We sit in the midst of our own forests,
but far in the West there's a land with coastal waters bobbing
     with big eyes, and they can see this far.
Helsinki's being rebuilt after Alvar Aalto's plans.
Pentti Saarikoski, 'What's Going on Really'[1]

The 1960s were to be a struggle for the spirit of architecture in Finland; discipline and geometrically sound works, unassuming tectonic control, concentrated space, the essence of the reduced exercise were not to be found in Alvar Aalto. Or so the era had it. In control of the Finnish state, President Kekkonen presided over a self-censoring period of 'neutrality' during the 1960s and '70s, courting the Soviets and persuading them to trust Finland. Supported for his subtle balancing act between East and West, the consensus surrounding his presidency was rarely challenged except in radical circles. Politically, quietism was the order of the day, and in the Kekkonen age the role of the Finn as mediator was favoured. When John F. Kennedy met Max Jakobson in 1961 his interest slipped out: 'What puzzles us Americans is why the Soviet Union has allowed Finland to retain her independence.'[2] Some considered this a peculiar talent for tolerance and political appropriation; others saw it the necessary act of minding one's own business. Controversies and differences, however, were not necessarily forgotten. When the outside world intervened, when freedom and the right to self-determination were put in doubt, the struggle continued, retreat was legitimized. The society closed in to coexist between the dominant powers that set the wider, global agenda. Later, President Ahtisaari would redefine this in his presidency

Bengt Lundsten and Esko Kahri, Kortepohja Residential Area, Jyväskylä, 1964–9.

during the 1990s as a special talent for adapting to rapid change and a determination to continue building a just society. Finns, he claimed, were experts on social change and transition.

Urho Kekkonen was Finland's longest-serving president (1956–81). He had been a winning athlete from the 1920s and rose to the presidency in 1956, continuing the Paasikivi 'neutrality' line. The multi-party system supported coalition governments, bringing a much-needed post-war stability. The concept of self-censorship arose during the post-war period when Finland was subjected to a strong Stalinist foreign policy. In 1948 the Finnish media were criticized for an inadequate coverage of the death of a Soviet leader. Reactions to the Soviet Union caused increased sensitivity. Once more, forced to re-group in relation to the Soviets, the social reforms and the modernizing of the society after the 1950s produced a convergent solidarity among the Finns. The trade union leader Eero Wuori had already described this attitude in 1940:

> The moment a real danger threatened us like a thundercloud, a mighty wind swept over our nation, erasing even the most deep-seated differences of opinion, and directed the gaze of every citizen to the one all-important matter, namely, the defence of our liberty and independence and the protection of our women and children.[3]

Resulting in much misunderstanding, 'neutrality' and the politics of consensus remain ambiguous to this day. Although in the 1990s preventive censorship applied only to films and videos, the self-censorship culture still exists, including within the architectural community. The historical blunders, for example, in the planning of the late 1960s and '70s have been reluctantly analysed; only now the unknown facts of the Civil War, the shady ambiguities and successes of Kekkonen's presidency, are being unearthed and acknowledged.

To outsiders, during the war, Finland was faced only with a scenario of compromises. But for Finns, as for any nation, war was and remains a matter of life and death. However, it needs noting: not enough credit has been awarded to the small country dependent on the fluctuations of international politics and economics, dependent on developing trends and the winds of cultural and political change. Ironically, as Wuori defined the Finnish attitude as one of stubborn resistance, it would be the welcome extended to external developments that saw younger architects and students from the late 1950s take gradual but seductive steps towards activism. The more formal German-Scandinavian student culture began to break down during the early 1960s. Academic ceremonies and rituals were lightened; the formality of the *te* ('you') form in the Finnish language was replaced by the more intimate *sinä*. A widespread loosening of moral boundaries and other codes followed. Errors of social conduct were challenged. Periodic tensions remained with the USSR. The better Finland managed its relations with the Soviet Union, the more likely were its prospects with the West. The East–West oscillations were continuous while the global seduction in the 1960s opted clearly for change. A redefined Communism, Maoism and Marxist-Leninism, however much diluted in student circles, encouraged a contest with existing order. The 'golden age' of Finnish architecture was no sooner celebrated, pioneered as a new International idiom and image by Revell and others, when it appeared to be under attack.

By the end of the 1960s, as Finland became a member of the Organization for Economic Cooperation and Development in 1968, a revolutionary turn would spread everywhere. There was a call for architects not to put their work in the service of the country; this was now an unwanted nationalism. In autumn 1968 the students hung, above the entrance of the Architectural School in Otaniemi, the now-famous banner 'We'll only build on the ruins of capitalism'. Architects had to appeal to the revolutionary potential in architecture in order to reach a higher social ideal. In many ways this was seen as a higher reality. As important teachers at the School of Architecture in Otaniemi, the rationalist ideas of Blomstedt's 'absolute architecture' and the uncompromising purism of Ruusuvuori began to resonate. Whether these two were directly involved in the revolutionary fervour or not many of the student activists had been taught by Blomstedt and were protégées from the Ruusuvuori practice.

All these are not unconnected factors to the way in which the solidarity of young architects developed in the 1960s and turned polemic. In Finland the 'word' is still binding; loquacity is viewed with suspicion. The reductive exercises demonstrated in architecture – simplification, clarity and lucidity – were those praised also in general speech and in literature. The careful photography of buildings, widely organized and disseminated by the Museum of Finnish Architecture, went unquestioned. This was not the period of unstable meanings.

Social reforms appeared in the 1960s. Old age and disability pensions were set up for the private sector. The Sickness Insurance Act was passed in 1964, and the Housing Production Act in 1966 stimulated the construction of low-interest housing loans. The state and local authorities began managing affairs; the welfare of all citizens was expected to lead to a more equitable distribution of the national income. Finland was being established as a Nordic welfare state. Finnish architects born in the

Leonid Brezhnev with the Finnish President Urho Kekkonen on a visit to Helsinki, 1961.

1930s, evacuated to Sweden and with little direct war-time experience, and those educated in the 1950s, were to rekindle the passion, romance and ambiguity of Sigurd Frosterus. Colliding with protest movements and activism throughout the world, this time in Finnish architecture it was not the machine that was to seduce but the *image* of the machine. Architecture was to take a strange turn; innovation turned to appropriation. Ideas from elsewhere were quickly adapted; short attention turned them into diagrams. Like many around the world, young architects believed things could change for the better and democracy could bring equality and remove injustice. Linked with the Museum of Finnish Architecture and *Arkkitehti*, a ragged group of opportunistic and self-opinionated young architects were to become the group that professionally and pedagogically shaped Modernism in Finland for the next 40 years. A systematic, neutral, democratic architecture born out of collaboration would be anti-individual, anti-subjective and stubborn. Some of these protesters were to become the born-again liberals controlling Finnish architecture at the end of the century.

The post-war debate in Finnish art between Constructivism and Expressionism mirrored the debate between intellectual control and emotional extravagance. Many of the young architects knew of the carefully planned work of artists like Sam Vanni (1908–1993), Juhana Blomstedt (*b.* 1937, son of Aulis Blomstedt) and the graphic dissection of Aimo Kanerva (1909–1991) continued later by the likes of Marika Mäkelä (*b.* 1947).

The Sibelius
Monument, by
Eila Hiltunen,
Helsinki, 1967.

1960s pop culture:
The Finnish group
Eero ja Jussi and The
Boys, 1965 (from the
cover of M-L Ronkko,
*Helsinki in the 6os:
Idyllic and Open
Times*, 1994).

The graphic and visual pull on architects took them closer to artists. An activism influenced by the deceptive diagrammatic ease within the architecture of Mies van der Rohe and the poetry of Constructivism would produce a fellow-travelling modern architecture lasting almost two decades. Don't build anything else but barricades, J. P. Takala wrote in the student's 1968 red issue of *Arkkitehti* complete with a Superman figure on the cover with a big A.[4] To the young students in architecture school at the end of the 1950s and into the early 1960s, the very constructed international success of Finnish architecture prompted a critical over-reach.

The good life, the artistic life, the cultural life, Marimekko and red wine coded the era. There was no doubt about the thrill, the solidarity, the activism and confused militancy of the period. The response was momentarily exciting but ultimately produced a thin version of a neutral architecture. The developments in the 1950s led to an open optimism in economic growth and technology; *elämänmuoto amerikkalaistui*, as the architectural historian Aino Niskanen describes, which translates literally as the 'shape of life americanized'.[5] A special urbanization followed that was not quite the urbanization elsewhere. As Niskanen tells us,

> from 1957 to 1978 a record-breaking over one million new dwelling units were built. The building companies designed and built complete population centres . . . most housing areas were constructed entirely under the conditions of prefabricated building production . . . architects were organized into large design

Good design
for the good life:
advertising images.

Erkki Kairamo and
Raimo Lahtinen,
Marimekko Factory,
Helsinki, 1974.

teams which offered their work to decision-makers and building companies. Many architects became civil servants.[6]

Shopping centres and motorways revised the Finnish landscape while the concepts of 'Finlandization' and 'self-censorship' politicized media and mediation, cultural life and reticence. An education system was renewed with new schools, universities and civic offices. Social reforms such as the introduction of a five-day working week led to more leisure time. Increased wealth, a consequence of the post-war restructuring of industry, expanded tourism. Architects and others opted for summer cottages and, in some cases, a preferred exile; sauna and yachting in the Finnish archipelago.

Architects travelled, just as they had done before the war, in search of the new. Aalto was by now internationally established; Viljo Revell and Aarne Ervi were the two main practices encouraging and directing professional innovation. The first Architects' Association (SAFA) post-war trip to the USA was in March 1960. Ninety architects led by Lauri Silvennoinen took a three-week round trip along the east coast. At Niagara Falls the group met up with Revell, who came from Toronto, where he would eventually supervise the design of Toronto City Hall. In Cranbrook, the group met Loja and Eero Saarinen. Others who received the Finnish group were Mies van der Rohe, Philip Johnson and Louis Kahn.[7]

In the early 1960s Finland presented itself as a rather clear-cut, no-nonsense modern democratic social welfare society. The modern road system, electrification and neon signage, and a dense network of internal air traffic, which had been set up and marketed in the 1950s, increased links in a sparsely populated country, and encouraged movement of the population. The smallholding solution of providing rapid homes and work for the young men returning from war (many countryside boys without wider skills) did not always achieve the required results. Times changed and, along with rapid industrialization, the standard of living in the poor areas of eastern and northern Finland led to a period of migration. In 1966 the Social Democrats became the leading government party and proceeded to rationalize agriculture. Cities, especially Helsinki, became a magnet for young people and parents seeking education and increased opportunities. This resulted in the 'great migration' to the towns of southern Finland and to Sweden. Once again the Finns were faced with a mental challenge to their identity; some left the 'nation' for Sweden, some headed for the cities where new social problems emerged. It is no surprise, prompted by the 'great migration', social democracy, the developing protest movements and left-wing thinking that the children of the 1930s suddenly began to question social and national development.

Meanwhile, the international state-funded promotion and dissemination of Finnish architecture through a series of strong 'imaging' exhibitions was in full swing. *Arquitectura Finlandese*, designed by Martti Jaatinen, went to Barcelona, Madrid, Lisbon and Warsaw in 1960. *Architektur in Finnland*, designed by Juhani Pallasmaa in 1964, went to Prague, Bratislava and Brno. *Arquitectura en Finlandia*, designed by Bengt Lundsten in 1962, travelled until 1967 to Buenos Aires, Mexico City, São Paolo, Rio de Janeiro, Caracas, Lima and Santiago de Chile.[8] This marketing of Finnish architecture would not only reinforce that image-making process identified earlier, from now on it would step up a gear. Finnish architecture would start to perform to an agenda defined by its predominantly seductive, visual impact.

During this decade, despite huge international overtures, it is tempting to speak of a 'collective unconscious' at home in Finland and the contribution that architecture made towards this. This is not to say that there was an aesthetic or social consensus, but the successful planning and architecture of the 1950s had encouraged a public understanding that took for granted the architect's role and expectations. Young architects in the 1960s would exploit this. Events blurred society and art, politics and architecture. Bob Dylan, Nasa's dreams, hippy communities, Pop Art, environmentalism, McLuhan, Marcuse and Marx, *Archigram* and *Rolling Stone* magazine were all irresistible seductions. In fact, there was too much around. The growing protest movement in Europe and the USA would collide with the necessity of the young students and architects establishing once again their own difference with those Finnish architects who had become so quickly recognized in the late 1950s. The Free Art School in Helsinki, with links to Maire Gullichsen (and indirectly to Artek and Aalto), was set up in 1968 by an alternative set of young teachers influenced by French movements rather than the German tradition. There were the copy-cat sit-ins as student protest spread across Scandinavia from 1968 onwards. Some of the militant architects became – briefly – card-carrying members of the Communist Party. Unused to the grand gesture, the inflammatory that protest and politics often required, the quieter Finnish temperaments merely cocooned themselves whilst the activists barricaded and occupied the Otaniemi School of Architecture. In a legendary gesture during an Association meeting on training architects in April 1969, a piglet with 'SAFA' written on it was released, organized by Tapani Launis.[9] The Planning Minister, Jussi Linnamo, held a formal opening speech for the conference as the piglet approached elegantly to listen to him. The battle-lines were drawn.

Attracted by the Miesian aesthetic, as well as early Soviet schemes and functionalist dogma, young architects and students wanted change.

Kirmo Mikkola and
Juhani Pallasmaa,
Villa Relander,
Muurame, 1966.

Fashionable jargon began to give credibility to the changes. It also offered theatricality, as the young appropriators and others temporarily left SAFA during its student attacks. Besides those around Tapani Launis and others from the Ruusuvuori office, the young Juhani Pallasmaa and Kristian Gullichsen (son of Harry and Maire Gullichsen) were considered, mistakenly, the duo responsible for much seduction of the day. Pallasmaa, along with Kirmo Mikkola, would front the challenge to take on the existing established architects. These two ran an office in Huvilakatu, in the Eira part of Helsinki. Mikkola was one of the most important activists of the time, and his influence on later Finnish architecture has been immense, although cleverly unrevealed through the critical attention given to his colleagues and followers. As the son of a university professor who owned much property in Eira, Mikkola for a period operated as a 'godfather' to the young rebels. Fiercely competitive, a historian and intellectual first, Mikkola had a potential in practice that was sadly curtailed; he died in 1980. His was a more natural, intense talent than Pallasmaa's, who, like many of the young protesters from a small country town constantly duelling with the ambiguities of nature and culture, demonstrated a messianic but impressionable immaturity.[10]

In 1967 Mikkola took over and briefly radicalized *Arkkitehti*. It was a powerful but short-lived experiment into architecture as text and manifesto. Appropriated utopias and environmentalism influenced a group of students for years to come. And although the propaganda wars may appear to have ended in 1968 with two or three extremely radical issues, there is little doubt that these events had far reaching consequences for the state of architectural criticism, and the use of balanced discussion and exchange. From 1969 to 1971 a brief editorship by Tapani Eskola resonated with scientific work going on elsewhere. Here mathematical analyses, attempting to deflect the diagrammatic and fashionable thinness all around, were used to explore design methodology linking to early computer use in land form and built studies. During this time, however, the status of architects strangely rebounded; design architects with an accepted wide social agenda would be considered experts beyond architecture.

It is, however, once again impossible to understand the turn that Modernism would take in the 1960s without understanding something of the situation with Alvar Aalto. We are now, since Göran Schildt's extensive writings on Aalto, well aware of the hostility and antagonism shown by the younger generation in the 1960s and '70s towards Aalto, whose work was literally ostracized during this period. The more monumental his work seemed to become, as in Finlandia Hall, or the more far-reaching his plans for the Helsinki Centre, the more Aalto was attacked for his divergence from a stricter Finnish Modernism. In 1962 Aalto completed the Enso-Gutzeit Headquarters in the harbour of Helsinki. The building with Italianate references and an applied marble façade introduced a period when the architect would begin to be attacked for being, among other things, the capitalist's lackey. In 1966 J. M. Richards would also sideline Aalto's later works as if he somehow knew

Alvar Aalto,
Enzo-Gutzeit
Headquarters,
Helsinki, 1962.

166

his influence at the time was slight. He would describe Säynätsalo Civic Centre not as a critical relocation of Modernism (as Kenneth Frampton would do fifteen years later) but as a 'romantic intensification'. It was 'intimate and idiosyncratic', and in relation to a stricter, more refined modern architecture this subjective agenda was problematic.[11]

Doubtless, Aalto's massive contribution to world architecture has now survived all this rhetoric, but the cultural forgetting that narrowed within Finnish architecture in the 1970s remains important. Moreover, it lays the base for the critical desire during the 1980s to bend and even falsify the past to suit the recuperation and restoration of a neo-conservative modern agenda. It is ironic that as architects strengthened their professional and collegial positions during the post-war period, development remained very much tied to persona. The polemical structure and the strong differences between the radical 'expressionist' Reima Pietilä (architect, with partner Raili, of the 'infamous' Dipoli building) and the young neo-Constructivist Pallasmaa, aided by the older Mikkola, polarized the decade. Pietilä was to many an aberrant architect. He began in association with Aulis Blomstedt, produced to many 'stricter modernists' his best work in Suvikumpu Housing in Tapiola Garden City (1967–9),[12] and remained tempted by organic, sculptural free form: slipping and contouring a snaking form within the landscape, Pietilä preserved as much nature as possible. The building stepped down from twelve floors to two, and in many ways was a clever, disciplined functional mix of all the types of housing in Tapiola. The painted green concrete of the balconies also suggested another rhythm alongside the more familiar De Stijl plasticity. Clear, light and adaptable interior planning has made this development one of the most popular housing areas in Tapiola.

Pietilä's stubborn resistance to the rationalist 'rabbit-hutch' architecture (a term he used in 1979) resulted in a committed and creatively searching range of texts, exhibitions and projects. In these Pietilä would consistently challenge the 'rationalists' with his own blend of direct humour, language play and enquiry. Often departing from the work of others, the presence of the Japanese magazine *A+U* (*Architecture + Urbanism*) during the 1970s and '80s, edited by Toshio Nakamura, became an important source for new ideas. Pietilä himself would be an adviser for the magazine during this period. Never one to accept the given, Pietilä would often be found reversing the obvious and challenging the limited and limiting modesty of the neo-Constructivists. These young neo-Constructivists, in direct conflict with the prevailing trends in the achievements of a Finnish architecture recognized abroad, responded and went on the attack. Only later in 1974 did Mikkola recognize the import of Pietilä's dissent and attempt any serious dialogue.[13]

Important in the 1960s was the notion that architecture was inseparable from its relation to the cultural and political community at large. The 'severe assurance' in Functionalism that Ekelund had noted was to veer towards the serious and systematic 'absolute architecture' propounded by Blomstedt. A softer humanism and individualism of phenomenological surprise was suspect as architects opted for a greater socializing agenda. But only diagrammatic architecture could suggest such reach – and in later planning only the diagram would produce such failure.

Influenced by the professors at Otaniemi, Aulis Blomstedt and Arno Ruusuvuori, it was the work of the German emigré Mies van der Rohe that ordered and organized this restatement within Finnish architecture. Mies's work, especially during the 1940s in Chicago with buildings such as Crown Hall and the Minerals and Metals Building at the Illinois Institute of Technology, sharpened a renewed intellectual confidence in Rationalism. Compared with the spectacular iconoclastic Modernism of Le Corbusier's Ronchamp Chapel, the lucidity and classical proportion of Mies's architecture held more resonances for the younger students, though its deeper qualities were rarely studied. The echoes back to an *architettura minore*, to Ekelund, to Välikangas and Sirén, to Huttunen and Revell, could not be missed.[14] And it is the political and professional importance of this 'Helsinki' strand in Finnish architecture that carries this agenda but also distorts the truer picture of the decade.

A more balanced view of the period indicates that Finnish architects continued to pursue a wide range of architectural solutions. During this period, despite the media attention given to the militants, it now transpires that an enormous production of serious, adapted, Modernist architecture still went on (for example, the various works of Airas and Järvinen, Erat, Laiho and Adlercreutz),[15] although many works remained unpublished and un-promoted. A deeper history of this work undoubtedly foregrounded a quietly consistent 'Scandinavian'-, almost 'Nordic-classical'-influenced work; control of scale, domestic to urban, timber elegance and massing puts some of this work in the class of the known Swedish and Danish Modernists. However, the debate hastily closed off, positions polarized into intolerance, and a tacit acceptance of an absolute architecture stood in for the Finnish architectural agenda.

It is here in the 1960s that we see Finnish Modernism diverge; perhaps our understanding of it hinges on the notion of 'appropriation', not 'innovation'. In much of the replicated modern, systematic 'brutalist' and 'structuralist' architecture that would appear in the 1960s deeper preparatory effects were no longer part of the architecture. It is useful to return to the 'unpure' functionalism of the 1930s to understand how a flattening was to take place, and why diagrammatic strategies were so seductive. The difference between J. S. Sirén's rehearsal of functional classicism in the 1930s and the later stricter 'absolute' Modernism supported by Blomstedt and Ruusuvuori can be seen as the loss of secondary spaces. The density of detail and nuanced symbolism in Sirén was flattened; there was a transparency – a matter-of-factness – already suggested in the adoption of an industrial aesthetic and the 'constructive' image. Another new objectivity was sought, *Neue Sachlichkeit* re-emerged. The focal point was shifted from the interior to the surface, a device we see repeated in some of the examples of late twentieth-century buildings such as the Sanoma House and Nokia Headquarters.

The young were angry and getting angrier. Theatre was an area in Finland that took this on directly. Beckett's *Endgame* had been produced in 1957; astonishment quickly spread to the exploration of fear and fragmentation. Vietnam was played out back in Finland. Hanoi was reassessed by writers like Mary McCarthy whilst the Soviet Union stood firm. Few suspected the gulags; and if they did self-censorship skirted the truth. Modernism's radical side finally began to upset the rural idyll and the safety of Finland's middle class. Brecht's work familiarized directors and the acting profession with theatre as politicized debate. Dramatists and poets were extremely active and influential, pushing for new models of communal decision-making. The values of those who fought the Second World War were questioned, strengthening the use of theatre as a critical force for society in general. Those older veterans who had carried the burden of wartime, who fought for 'home, religion and fatherland', felt offended by the brashness and stupidity of the youth. As in many countries in Europe at the time, a radical Leftism led to the formation of many small theatre groups. One of the most important was ком theatre, which began in 1971 and performed political reviews and adapted Brecht and others under the director Kaisa Korhonen and musician Kaj Chydenius. Directors like Kalle Holmberg and Ralf Långbacka began the challenge to institutional theatre, and it would be continued in a more radical way by Jouko Turkka and Arto af Hällstrom.[16]

The poet Pentti Saarikoski, the *enfant terrible* of the day, challenged preceding Modernism and took on a 'Yevtushenko' role within Finland with open, chatty colloquial poems of social and political commentary. The French New Wave cinema spread to Finland as it did elsewhere. The two significant directors of the era were Risto Jarva and Jörn Donner. Jarva would use various genres for his serious social criticism including fantasy (*A Worker's Diary*, 1967; *Time of Roses*, 1969; *Rally*, 1970), and Donner would lift from elsewhere to make replicas of the consummate art films with a Finnish aesthetic (*Black on White*, 1968; *Sixty Nine* and

Portraits of Women, 1970). From the Finnish-Swedish side, Donner would remain an appropriator, occasionally achieving an acute political and personal work. For the real protestors, Jarva remained the singular talent and hero. Mikko Niskanen would continue the national epic film style from the 1950s with films like *The Partisans* (1963) and *Skin, Skin* (1966), and Rauni Mollberg would explore somewhat more intimate, Lappish subjects (*The Earth is a Sinful Song*, 1973).

The radical moves and the seduction of protest were infectious. The inter-disciplinarity in the small centralized society quickly ballooned into a political cul-de-sac. Often forced to take sides, a new solidarity appeared among the younger architects. Architects such as Raili and Reima Pietilä, Kaija and Heikki Sirén, the Suomalainen brothers and Timo Penttilä were, according to the young artists, toying with architectural form and expression. It was felt that serious functionalistic and wider social programmes remained unfulfilled. The intimacy of Tapiola Garden City and other such 'forest-romance' projects began to be questioned. The sketchy project for the Extension of Tapiola (1967, a rudimentary mega-scheme resonating with the British group Archigram and Japanese Metabolism) remains one of the most important indicators of the diagrammatic direction this young group would take. To put its innovation in context, it had none of the scale, interest or wit of Archigram's work. But such mega-schemes have recently reappeared in the new century in Espoo, Vantaa and Helsinki, where they are affordable and luxurious, technically accomplished (social programmes fulfilled) but to many still lacking the poetry and soul that some require from Finnish architecture.

Perhaps hidden from the outside world, Finnish society began a process of social and political questioning that could end only in polemical infighting and meltdown. Though much forgotten, the bohemian brawls not seen perhaps since the 1900s reappeared. Behaving badly collided with the passion for activism and of course freer patterns of behaviour. Architects participated like all the rest. Protest movements disguised much wayward thinking and too easily buried serious intent. If Finnish architecture was marketed and famed abroad for its refined aesthetics, its controlled naivety and regional modernist nuances, a model for the rest of the world, at home there was often mayhem. From the period 1967–74 magazines and journals published this excitement and ambiguity. Projects took on diagrammatic solutions and began to be tempted by an architecture responding to the neutral sign. Form was to be de-emphasized, though not quite de-materialized.

The period went from the elegance of the grand functionalist blocks of Lauri Silvennoinen in Pihlajamäki (1962–5) and Toivo Korhonen's

Element building
on site, 1970.

University of Social Sciences in Tampere (1961) to Koivukylä development, seen as one of the first wider attempts to pull the emerging
Modernism into a comprehensive methodology and on to the Miesian-
inspired Jyväskylä Housing by Lundsten and Kahri (1964–9), which
would be replicated outside Helsinki in Olari.[17] Modular prefabrication
spawned many new housing developments throughout the 1970s. Brave
and socialized at the time, these were seen as awkward and unpoetic a
mere decade on. As the activism spiralled out of control, historical fabric
in cities like Helsinki was no longer relevant to the future vision of the
young architects, who favoured systematic approaches to production,
design and building.[18]

The 1960s were probably the most exciting and impossible time in
Finnish architecture. Their success and effect, however, cannot be measured in the hostility towards a freer form or an expressive Modernism,
nor was its failure inevitable in the eventual collapse of the rationalist
ideology. The industrialism of the huge mega-blocks built in the 1970s
resembling Leningrad suburbs or the blocks built outside Birmingham
in England would be challenged all over the world. Talk later was of the
'banal structuralism' of this period. But only in theatre and literature
have there been serious reviews and reassessment of the thinness of the
time, of the fellow-travelling and runaway dialectics by those artists
involved.[19] Few architects have owned up to the thrill, opportunism and

Domino element
housing system under
construction, 1968.

Myllypuro, Helsinki,
an example of recti-
linear prefabricated
housing from the
1970s.

ignorance; even fewer seem to remember the way the Finnish profession was momentarily trashed as in the 'SAFA' piglet incident. Later in 1973 the oil crisis led to new structures and political alignments; the economy had to fight growing investment greed. The success and failure of the 1960s in Finland are made more apparent by considering the first decade of the new, twenty-first century. The young architect-activists, 30 years on, many of them now mature leaders of the Finnish architectural profession, are filling Helsinki and other cities with what can easily be identified as a restored, rather conservative, Internationalism.

As many architects began exploring the poetics of material and form brought on by new methods of production, especially in reinforced concrete and sculptural concrete, it is important to follow those who would teach and influence the younger architects in the 1960s. Aarno Ruusuvuori taught the poetry of structure favouring the uncomplicated and took on an increasingly important role in how the modern agenda was read in Finland. He clashed often with Aalto. Colleagues compared the ruthless and unruly behaviour of both. Ruusuvuori's sexism was, moreover, legendary; he saw little use for women in the schools of architecture and would announce it to new students even in the early 1980s.[20] Ruusuvuori, like Blomstedt, was an unfulfilled talent; he was an educator, writer, critic, designer, architect, planner, politician, Chairman of the Association of Finnish architects, and Director of the Museum of Finnish Architecture from 1975 to 1978. And, like Blomstedt, Ruusuvuori was also a country boy. Order and security were important in their worlds. Their thinking would steady itself on conditions of safety, order and, ultimately, non-risk. These architects did not talk of the phenomenology of forest space or the geometric morphology of Finnish space or language, as their colleague Pietilä did in this period. Instead they spoke of architecture as a self-contained world, a system that could respond to and build its own logic. Logic was inner-bound outwards, as Ruusuvuori explained in a lecture given in Warsaw in 1960.[21]

Ruusuvuori's Hyvinkää Church is often spoken about at the same time as Pietilä's Kaleva Church. Both from the early 1960s, both monumental and dynamic concrete projects, their logic, however, differs. Pietilä took the metaphorical and imagined the clarity of structure that would be required. His metaphors, a clearing in the forest in section, or a Christian symbol of a fish in plan, were part of Pietilä's operative and hermeneutic games. This was outer-inner logic and allowed Pietilä much play. Ruusuvuori's Hyvinkää Church, however, expressed the inner-outer logic of architectural form and structure and this difference became one of the most important debates in Finnish architecture of the

Reima and Raili Pietilä, Kaleva Church, Tampere 1959–66.

Aarno Ruusuvuori, Hyvinkää Church, 1958–61.

decade. Ruusuvuori used the inner spatial arrangement and structure to provide the frame for the architecture. The church was not seen as an intuitive Gestalt snatch like the image of two hands or any folded-leaf forest. Instead, the dynamics, though expressive, resulted from the careful framing of a tectonic impulse. Ruusuvuori changed from the structural dynamism of Hyvinkää Church to the grain silo of Tapiola Church. Where the former appears a project carried out in successful haste, an instant idea, the latter returns to a diagram, an echo of another, laborious and refined brutal architecture with a quite stunning, tranquil interior garden. Significantly, both Blomstedt's and Ruusuvuori's differences

Aarno Ruusuvuori,
Tapiola Church and
courtyard, Espoo,
1965.

with Aalto became legendary; as the stories go, feelings were mutual, thrown out and banned from each other's offices.

'I modulate all my buildings', Ruusuvuori said in 1991, 'because without a mathematical tuning fork I believe dimensions are difficult to control, especially in the vertical plane.' This cerebral process appealed to many students who wished for more systematic guidance and seriousness. Design emerged when the solution was already thought out. The preparatory work was ultimately of less importance to the result. The consequences of this thinking would stretch over the next three decades. Pekka Pitkänen's Chapel of the Holy Cross in Turku (1967) is one of the more significant projects of the decade. The use of concrete, the floating forms created by careful massing and an understated elegance make this a seminal work. The building's skilful detailing, control of material and aesthetic ritualism bring to mind both Ruusuvuori's and Blomstedt's ideal. But this rather closed thinking would soon encourage a consensus mentality. 'In the sixties', Ruusuvuori noted, 'Miesian designs got out of hand, because they looked so easy, and in the early seventies all successful competitions entries followed Miesian format. The juries supported this trend, although they ought to have made awards to a range of different solutions.'[22] Ruusuvuori was hinting at the diagrammatic. If Modernism itself was beginning to be too loose a concept to contain even the 'modern architecture movement' itself, how then did this activism take hold of Finnish architecture until its fallout in the 1970s?

It is, I would suggest, the influence of Mies to which we must turn to understand this work and the relation of these ideas to Finnish architecture today. Although the Miesian influence on the rational tendencies of the time was explored using concrete and brick, some buildings that used steel indicated the subtext to a future Finnish Modernism. The diagrammatic hint in these projects was a sign of things to come.[23]

In Finland the modern agenda implied in architecture has invariably been taught as an unquestionable notion that could facilitate truth and the ideal. As a more general Marxist-Leninism seeped into all intellectual circles, especially during the years 1966–76, the results were not always an untidy and undirected activism.[24] The 1960s is full of well-researched, well-executed experiments in dimensioning, rationalizing production and 'modular' strategies. Faced with the general popularity and expressive potential of concrete, and the influence of Mies van der Rohe on the rational architecture of the time, the experiments in steel have until recently remained somewhat unexplored. But here, before the larger industrial works crept in during the 1970s, some of the most successful works were achieved.

Kirmo Mikkola and
Juhani Pallasmaa,
Congregational
Centre, Hyrylä, 1967.

The Matilainen Pool in Turku (Esa Piironen and Mikko Pulkkinen, 1967) used a thin, elongated, horizontal, red-steel framing and was as distinctive as it was different from anything achieved with concrete at the time.[25] The Congregational Centre in Hyrylä just outside Helsinki (Mikkola & Pallasmaa, 1967) utilized structural steel, infilled with concrete elements, glazing panels and accessories such as metal stairs. Compared to Finnish churches from the previous decade, the industrial aesthetic and clarity of work were unmistakable. Echoing Alison and Peter Smithson's Hunstanton School in the UK and an 'architecture without rhetoric' (though the Finns never used this phrase), the results were not as minimal, brutal or as 'authentic' in material refinement as might have been imagined.

Were these pre-empting Blomstedtian ideas of infusing rationalism with a tectonic poetry? Probably the clearest and most convincing 'replica' of, yet departure from, 'Miesian' architecture was Ola Laiho's Dance Hall Extension, Valasranta, Yläne (1968). The steel structure is carried inside the building, allowing the simplest of glass façades to hang. This used what became known later as the 'reflective context' – a mirror surface enabling the environment its own presence on the surface of the building, a device, of course, that has since been developed and used throughout the world.[26] There were many other modular experiments in the 1960s and early '70s, including the emerging work of Erkki Kairamo and the Valio Practice, which began to suggest in the 1970s a more robust dynamic in openly using a hi-tech industrial vocabulary.

Valio Practice,
Valio Dairy, Turku,
1966–7.

Architect Reino Kallio Mannila's and engineer Teuvo Koivu's echoed Le Corbusier's Domino housing system and aimed for clarity and a clear construction, while also responding to images that were becoming contemporary in world architecture. Later such housing appeared over-diagrammatic and proved unsuitable for the harsh Finnish climate, eventually leaking and rotting. The pitch roof would rescue the survivors eventually, but the scope of work was only briefly redirected and strangely did not pick up on the work from the war decade. Temporary houses and shelters for catastrophes and other more humanitarian design projects did appear. Pallasmaa and Gullichsen attempted to improve on the instant utopias around, but skeleton systems were favoured for their techno-aesthetic import rather than solving real structural problems or relating to mass production issues.

Many buildings from the time would integrate the Miesian aesthetic into the wooden vernacular, at the same time recalling the affinity to Japanese aesthetics explored by Blomstedt. Clear construction and an implied honesty in structure were linked to the representative image of Finnish architecture, but an open activism and urge for social change became dogmatic and consensual during the 1970s. This categorical overturning of everything was present whether studied in Marxist-Leninist study circles or lifted from the general atmosphere. It defined and expressed opposition to all the successful and well-publicized buildings of the decade. The very way this energy and dissent turned into a fellow-travelling makes it also difficult to describe the real seriousness that Communism and Socialism offered. What such change and radical programme meant to a modern architecture is only now emerging, as powerful architects from the 1960s begin to archive their own history and dogmatic agenda. Witold Gombrowicz, the Polish writer, nailed this dogma to the mast: 'No, communism is not an idea, it is not a truth, it is something that facilitates truth and the idea for man.'[27]

The movement of the young new modern revivalists against Alvar Aalto increased in the early 1970s. The strength and enthusiasm for change ensured, within a small ruling minority clustered around the Museum of Finnish Architecture, Otaniemi and Arkkitehti (the main protagonists operating in all three), a collective consensus of some tyranny. In 1972 Aalto issued a prophetic statement. Though relatively ignored he warned of a formulaic, rationalizing tendency in architecture. Today it is a haunting piece:

> We see this tendency to reduce everything to a formula everywhere, from regional plans to extreme architectural details. It brings together a specified number of people and a specified planning method such that x+z+11+180 will automatically lead to the right result. I have seen it in Helsinki, in Riga, in Vilnius. I have seen it in every town in Scandinavia . . . they are all infected. There's no need to go to Berkeley or Vienna or indeed anywhere else to see it begin with students and see how the professors resist it. It has the danger of transforming pedagogics, of altering the atmosphere in our towns and countryside. Indeed, town and country are almost one already.[28]

The activism spiralled in the 1970s, positions polarized. Architecture was becoming formulaic. Social commitment and the politicization of architecture demanded allegiance. Kirmo Mikkola's editorship of *Arkkitehti* (1966–8) was a strong indication of this short-lived but dynamic flame. Given what Finnish architects had achieved in the 1950s and early '60s no one suspected over-reach. The generalizations that began at the end of the 1960s and into the 1970s led precisely to the possibility of overturning everything. The demolition of the past was on the agenda partly because Finnish intellectuals acknowledged the corrupted history of

their own past, Sweden and the Russian empire, and partly because the mood of the times demanded action.

The nature of the small society, mediation and the continuing development of self-promotion through the Museum of Finnish Architecture meant that architects participated in strongly partisan games. The integrity of Blomstedt, the possibility of the neutral, equalizing façade, the wall of the building as an unspeakable, functional, absolute, neutral zone made it possible to combine the higher architectural ideals of Modernism into a purism. Elsewhere on his own to the side, yet central for a period, the architect Reima Pietilä was to remain for many years the natural successor to Aalto and the maverick in the modern code. His Dipoli Students' Centre (1966) became an expressive work that garnered international praise and put Pietilä into the third generation of pioneers of modern architecture, but caused a furore at home. The building was simply outrageously expressive; Pietilä proved able to take space, puncture it and see it flow against the convention. Sequentially Pietilä was designing a labyrinth; the building's interior was cavernous and the roof contoured to echo the existing typology of the site. Concete, timber and copper were boldly used; tilted and gauged masses and walls could appear overbearing and inviting at the same time. Details and solutions in Dipoli were inventive and spontaneous; although varying in success, the courage and shock of this and later work were undeniable. But Dipoli was considered romantic, nationalistic and awkward; inappropriate to the rational moment. The more famous and international Pietilä became, the more this set the tone in Finland for his work over the next 20 years. Yet the more appreciated Pietilä was abroad, the more ambiguous and resistant was the profession to his architecture. After Dipoli (1966) there was an attempt to suppress Pietilä. Both Kirmo Mikkola and Juhani Pallasmaa would ensure his marginalization well into the 1970s. Although his work would eventually find its way back into the agenda of Finnish Modernism, Pietilä was well aware of this resistance to his work and the 'intermediate zones of Modern architecture' and – unusual in the Finnish circles – he used his position and writings to explore just this estrangement in relation to a lost or unfinished Modernism.

Although there are significant works, not dissimilar to the free spirit of Dipoli, by many other architects in this decade, especially the Suomalainen brothers' Temppeliaukio Church, Helsinki (1961–8), and Timo Penttilä's Helsinki City Theatre (1961–7), Pietilä's polemic outpourings ensured a position for himself on the edge of Finnish Modernism.[29] Talk of an *incomplete Modernism*, of the Third Generation architects who would fill in where the pioneers left off, of phenomenological factors,

Raili and Reima Pietilä, Dipoli Students' Centre, 1966.

Timo and Tuomo
Suomalainen,
Temppeliaukio
Church, Helsinki,
1961–8, as portrayed
on a 1970s postage
stamp and in
aerial view.

were common themes in Pietilä's texts, lectures and exhibitions. Ironically, the current twenty-first century reappearance and appreciation of
architects like Gehry and Libeskind, the 'blob' and 'morphed' architecture, may all invite a new interest in Pietilä's work. Signs are that the new
computer-aided designs will echo if not simulate Pietilä's more personal
and agonizing stubbornness to create such expressive poetry. Yet in
Finland the backlash to such expressive architecture still exists, and,
despite the seductions of the new sensuous architecture, it is the renewed
interest in Ruusuvuori that reveals the architects' seeking once again their
own model of discipline, restraint and the timeless.

While the modern agenda was supposedly taking on a renewed social
commitment to change and solving issues of poverty, injustice and dep-
rivation, the tectonic exercise narrowed. The history of *serialism* from the
1940s and '50s returned to haunt the Finnish agenda. Systematic thinking
was married with the neutrality expected from social equality. There was
a flattening of hierarchical structures and processes. The spatial response
to man's action and psycho-social needs represented a new democracy.
No one was to stand out, and although everyone did stand out, the young
architects did it together. In response to the aesthetics of Modernism
communicated by the Museum of Finnish Architecture in the first ten
years, Finnish architecture post-1967 suddenly became pragmatic, un-
talkative and dull. Professionally it shaped the future; publicly it would
lead to attacks against an architecture of little or no poetry.[30] The propaganda machine was convincing the world of a Finnish architecture of
supreme ethical and aesthetic competence. Yet at home things were going
wrong; the 'revolutionary turn' had quite simply been responsible for an
exquisite, professionally controlled small-scale rational experiment in

Timo Penttilä,
City Theatre Helsinki,
1961–7, and on a post-
card (*above*) *in situ*.

Modernism. Thinking had been extended in the 1970s to a quite brutal
and often banal neo-Constructivism, known as 'Structuralism'.[31] In an
exercise of passion and forgetting, the sensitivity of Bryggman, Ekelund,
Revell, Lindegren and Blomstedt had somehow disappeared. Planning
strategies would explode into myth. By the end of the 1970s Modernism
in Finland had atomized.

183 Fellow Travelling: Militancy, Mies and Constructivism

chapter seven

Deconstruction and Reconstruction

In this park dogs are strictly forbidden
but an alsatian's crouching in the hard snow to shit.
Tail along the ground, like the bottom bough of a spruce,
he's following with his eyes
the industrious municipal tractor
as it impends along the path
    with a fresh douche of snow in its loader.

Now the tractor's passing him, a yard off,
the alsatian turns into a snowdog
but he doesn't pause in his business.
That's how clever he is.
Pentti Saaritsa, 'Hommage au Travail des Chiens.'[1]

Perhaps in line with fellow-travelling everywhere, the more expressive modern architecture was close to being considered an irrelevant art form, a myth of tradition and humanism. Encouraged and misread through social thinking and political texts, this represented a romantic Modernism full of unwanted symbolism unable to respond to wider programmes of social change and democracy.[2] Ironically, the more the architectural world began appreciating Finnish architecture for its regional and humane divergence from a rather dull modular internationalism elsewhere in the world, the young rationalists from the 1960s and '70s who had cried foul had to rethink. Politically, things were about to change in the early 1980s.

Although new political groups and non-aligned movements have sprung up in Finland and can play a role in elections, three main parties have dominated the political scene. After Independence the Social Democratic Party shaped the labour movement towards a Western-style democracy, and following the difficult post-war years held steadfast against Soviet pressure and the emerging Communist bid for power. Backed financially by the large labour unions, the Social Democrats have played out their own power against the Centre Party, which, though once representing rural interests, still maintains to this day a strong presence in Finnish politics. Over the years the third main political

Heikkinen and Komonen, Heureka Science Centre, 1984–8

ARRAK Architects (with E. Helomaa), Valintatalo Supermarket, Espoo 1982 – a modernist makeover.

force, the Conservative National Coalition, developed from its middle-class urban roots towards a nation-wide white-collar workers' party. Today the left-wing Alliance picks up where the Communists left off in the 1980s, and it was only during this period that the Green Party emerged and has begun to play a significant role in Finnish and European politics.

Although it had become difficult for the Soviet Union to see Finland as a neutral country by the end of the 1960s, and into the 1970s, in reality for Finns not a lot changed. Modernizing brought along its progress and paradox. Occasionally difficult, though never really scandalous Finnish–Soviet relations went on in foreign policy circles, while at home the society continued to open up. Formalities were further reduced and student hopes were raised. In 1978 the Stalinist wing of the Finnish Communist party, picking up on the Treaty of 1948 and the possibility of joint defensive action, suggested from a visiting Soviet general, introduced the notion of a joint Finnish–Soviet military exercise. President Kekkonen naturally refused the idea and the authorities played down the episode. With the Soviet Union's invasion of Afghanistan in 1979 political relations with the West were further damaged and Finland slowly distanced itself from its neighbour. On Kekkonen's resignation in 1981, due to ill health, the election of the new President, the Social Democratic candidate Mauno Koivisto, was a triumph for the democratic process. The subsequent rise to power of Mikhail Gorbachev in the early 1980s ensured that internal reform in the Soviet Union would free not only Russia but allow Finland to become – finally – the neutral neighbour.

By 1980 modern architecture almost everywhere was under attack. Attitudes were changing, and texts by Robert Venturi, *Complexity and Contradiction in Architecture* (1966), and Charles Jencks, *Modern Movements in Architecture* (1973), introduced the notion of modern architectures and a continuous play with multiple meanings. Pluralism in fact became the buzz-word that introduced many architects and students to the philosophical ideas within Postmodernism. By 1977 and the publication of Charles Jencks's further volume, *The Language of Postmodernism*, the stricter, reductive agenda of Modernism was being questioned. In 1981 Tom Wolfe brought out perhaps the most accessible reading of this decline, with his book *From Bauhaus to our House*. In spite of its light, almost throwaway tone, it was a book widely read in Finnish architectural circles. The synopsis of the failure of the modern agenda was required reading; the journalistic tone suited the diagrammatic hold on theory and history.

The signs were that Finnish Modernism, to go also by the reaction of the public, was in need of revision. The profession meanwhile had to engage and withstand the semantic trap that Postmodernism encouraged. Architects could entertain new theories in semiotics and the reception of art. Analysing and reading culture and society tempted architects to produce multiple meanings, thereby inviting a new symbolism. Yet if it was to be true to its restraint and simplicity, the Finnish architectural profession needed to redefine architecture as an instrumental representation of the nation. At the same time it had to convince a suspicious public. The rational Modernism of the 1970s had not quite produced the social agenda and progress it had hoped for. While reform was spreading from *Glasnost* in the Soviet Union, Finnish Modernism over the decade was about to be deconstructed and then reconstructed.

To achieve this, in an echo of the early century, those influential in the profession would need to co-opt international ideas and development and once more make of this 'invasion' a natural, contemporary and Finnish idiom. The rational approach would not only echo original 'Modernism', but to dwell within such Modernism – individually and regionally – would very soon be defined as the Finnish nation's birthright. A correct, authentic modern architecture was about to be restored and reinstated as the 'tradition'. But what was this correct, authentic Modernism? To represent the nation, Finnish architecture could no longer be read only within a stricter critical 'reading'. Public disquiet about prefabrication and the failed suburbs outside Helsinki made sure of that. Architecture began to pluralize. The obvious difficulty of any one visual style representing a unified national form encouraged dissent. Or did it really? In the small ruling architectural ideology (centred again on the Museum of Finnish Architecture, Otaniemi, SAFA and *Arkkitehti*), Postmodernism was seen as an invasion, mostly from America. In the wider professional context, however, appropriation became a little more frenetic. Just as books like those of Tessenow and Le Corbusier, Taut and van Doesburg had been scoured for their visual interest and methodological hints during the 1920s and '30s, so too would the new works produced by Stirling, Hollein, Moore, Piano, Foster, Ando, Venturi, Rossi and many others. Encouraged by the writings of Banham, Venturi, Tafuri, Porphyrios, Portoghesi, Jencks and others, positions had to be redefined.[3]

In 1980, as if anticipating the chaos Postmodernism would cause during this decade, an array of architectural stars were invited to the Europe–America Seminar on board a schooner in the Helsinki archipelago. On the agenda was 'The Future of the Modern Movement'. The danger of the postmodern 'fashion' was imminent to the professional leaders; it threatened to destabilize the accepted, albeit damaged, modern agenda. The anxieties that surfaced within Finnish architectural circles once again displayed sensitivity and ambiguity about source and origin. Something 'absolutely Finnish' was slipping away, without anyone really knowing exactly what was 'absolutely Finnish'. Subsequently, on 19 September 1980, the Museum of Finnish Architecture made one of the most important statements of the century. Many of those who had been active students in the 1960s and young 'structuralist' architects in the 1970s co-signed a manifesto. Modernism in Finland, it was asserted, had 'gradually become rooted in the society to build up a firm and genuine

Europe–America Seminar participants on board a schooner, 1980.

tradition'.[4] Would this uncannily repeat Bertel Jung's resistance to Functionalism in 1930: 'What gives this style the right to throw entirely overboard most of the laws that previously determined all architectural creation?'[5] There was no doubting the seriousness of the rear-guard action as it steered Finnish architecture away from the re-emergence of the taboo – decoration and symbolism. Just as Frosterus had redefined his own 'elitism' in 1917, these Finnish architects were re-scripting their own modern agenda. Any architecture called Modernism had to withstand what was considered an inauthentic raid on the privileged code. The signatories were Kristian Gullichsen, Pekka Helin, Markku Komonen, Sakari Laitinen, Matti K. Mäkinen, Juhani Pallasmaa, Timo Penttilä and Jan Söderlund. These signatories became (except Penttilä and Mäkinen), to a large extent, representatives of the born-again Modernism that emerged in the 1990s.

It is crucial to the next 20 years to recognize the importance of these figures. Tracing back these architects to their teachers, their education, their anxieties and their mentors links us back to the Ekelund-Blomstedtian idealism. It is possible to argue that the *formalism* now seen in the plethora of corporate glass and steel architecture of the first decade of the twenty-first century is a direct consequence of this 'revision'. But in 1980, relying once again on professional privilege and a not inconsiderable authoritarian posturing, this rooted-ness within Modernism would need protecting. This not only influenced the future and re-shaped Modernism in Finland, it would also confirm the past agenda. If social progress had been considered an extension of the clarity of thinking, the whole aspect of the meaning and symbolism that had emerged in the 1970s could no longer be avoided. The aestheticizing of the exhibitions coming out of the museum played down the contextual and social siting of architecture, concentrating on singular, isolated 'works of art'. The public understanding and acceptance of modern architecture was low; the achievement of earlier Finnish architecture had somehow drifted and the public did not understand why. There was a loss in environmental and emotional sensitivity. It can be argued that the pluralism that Postmodernism entertained was in a way invited in by the very failure of the 1970s. Marja-Riitta Norri was the editor of *Arkkitehti* for most of the 1980s and then, for most of the 1990s, Director of the Museum of Finnish Architecture; continuing the hegemony of Mikkola and Pallasmaa, she was in a particularly good position to assess the past. Having herself been a young activist during the 1960s and participated in the ambiguous struggle for the higher (ethical) ground in Finnish Modernism, her words have particular resonance to other eager activists from that time. Looking back from the year 2000, Norri describes the resulting grimness:

Such sophisticated planning solutions were not allowed in the housing production of the 1970s. Rectangular urban block designs were dictated by crane tracks. It was not possible to speak of the scalar articulation of the buildings; the grim architecture was accompanied by a half-finished environment, and to crown it all, services were to be found kilometres away.[6]

Grim it was, but not always for the professional reasons offered. The analysis of this period has barely scratched the surface; alibis for a lost Modernism surfaced.

Finland, of course, was not unique in the growing disenchantment with modern architecture, though it would survive this disenchantment better than many other countries. We might put this down to the obvious; by embracing and assimilating the modern agenda so consistently, Finland had less 'historic' resistance to large-scale modern developments. This was still a time, however, when the West really knew little of Finland. To many it was still considered under, if not part of, the Soviet Union. This was to change. Kekkonen's policy of neutrality triumphed in 1975 when 35 countries signed the Helsinki Agreement at the final state of the European Conference on Security and Co-operation in Finlandia Hall. Finland not only opened up a little more internationally but the moral and ideological change in its urban character was beginning to be seen. Having claimed so much for its agenda of social progress and fairness, modern architecture was about to be blamed for just about every failure in the environment.

The promising students and architects from the 1960s and '70s began to react with the same fervour as those at the beginning of the century. Flirting with postmodern symbolism and classicism, gaining from the poetry of structure and tectonic invention, bulky forms, postmodern vocabulary, phenomenology and the twisting and angling form as in later Deconstruction meant that Finnish architecture began to resemble the repertoire of international magazines. There were, of course, successful exceptions. The older 'heroic' architects remained, working abroad sometimes, or their production gradually decreased. Aalto had died in 1976, causing a revision of the anti-hero. The Siréns, the Penttiläs, the Suomalainen brothers and others such as Heikki Castren, Kalle Vaatola, Pekka Salminen and Ola Laiho, would still be building, negotiating Postmodernism, but their professional participation in the imaging agenda naturally lessened. Penttilä, a particularly strong figure in Finnish architecture during the 1960s and '70s, finally left the country to teach in Vienna in the early 1980s, disillusioned after being treated somewhat brusquely by his fellow signatories.[7]

Timo and Tuomo
Suomalainen,
Kivenlahti Church,
Espoo, 1984.

To some, Finnish architecture could only be a 'national' movement
in retreat. Resistance to some fashionable architecture and not others
allowed the professional leaders to set up an *arrière-garde*. While many
architects entertained the openness of Postmodernism, there was in the
south of Finland, especially Helsinki, a strong bohemian disgust at its
historicism, a further tilt towards absolutism supported by the dominant institutions. Not so, however, in other areas of Finnish culture.
Historicism was given more width as culture began to play within and

Scenes from the films of Mika and Aki Kaurismäki.

understand its own history. The protest and general 'revolutionary' atmosphere of the late 1960s and early '70s swept one romance aside for another. In Finnish cinema the 1980s was the breakthrough decade with the works of Mika and Aki Kaurismäki. For a Finnish film to break even it needs an audience of at least 100,000 out of a population of only five million. Film would thus always need government subsidy to survive and in the 1980s it suddenly received this. The auto-didact Aki Kaurismäki produced a remarkable series of *Baltic-noir* films that brought quite another image of Finland to the world stage. Small-scale production with 'New Wave' cheek in a minimalist genre, Kaurismäki began to rewrite the myths of the exotic, the un-talking and uncommunicative Finn. The modern state did not look quite so modern when the under-class of unemployment and poverty – however much tongue-in-cheek – was revealed on film.[8]

Neo-expressionism made its appearance in art in the work of Leena Luostarinen, and Postmodernism released the artists into new directions, away from the stranglehold of non-representational art and earlier Constructivist-inspired canvases. Silja Rantanen and Kari Caven used postmodernist devices – verbal meaning and play suddenly entered as did early installation works and performance art. An entirely new and subtle area of disappearance and dissolution was explored in the installations of Maaria Wirkkala.[9] The photographer Esko Männikkö would take what have been described as Vermeer-like interpretations of the people of the North and, like Aki Kaurismäki, presented a world and a country that were not always in accordance with the neatness and critical schemes imagined to be achieved in contemporary Finnish architecture.

Ecological awareness and ideas about sustainability appeared along with the growing political presence of the Green Party. Renovation also began to present new challenges for architects. A more modest but consistently 'humanized' architecture by Bruno Erat and Erik Adlercreutz,

ARRAK Architects,
Arctic Centre, 1984.

Timo Airas and Kari Järvinen, Georg Grotenfelt, ARRAK Architects, Heikki Saarela, Nurmela, Raimoranta and Tasa and others took on many of these issues in parallel with the propagandizing. Any radical chic was tempered after the students in the 1960s and '70s had taken over institutions in Finland and threatened all-out anti-cultural behaviour. But there was no mistaking the seduction. Egalitarian aims were tested by Postmodernism; the relativism of 'anything goes' reached Finland for the first time in the twentieth century. The somewhat unchallenged position that architects, poets, writers, musicians, designers and filmmakers had cultivated left once again another young generation ready for serious change. The rationalism implied in the 'anti-aesthetic' of the 1960s and '70s had seen too many older buildings and parts of cities like Helsinki torn down and replaced by mediocre corporate city developments. Architectural achievements were disputed, and with Aalto lionized in the mind of the public, nostalgia for symbol, historical precedent and regional, vernacular solutions appeared. In the 1980s housing and planning were ready to be revised accordingly; populism was in the air.

Raili and Reima
Pietilä, Hervanta
Cultural Centre,
Tampere 1975–9.

Few architects resisted the poetry of symbol and detail and Post-modernism became a catalyst for change. The pattern was familiar; the Arts and Crafts movement and Art Nouveau had been such a catalyst in the 1890s, just as Functionalism in the 1930s and a sculptural, freer organic Modernism in the 1950s. One need only look at the work of an architect like Pietilä who registered this change early on, after being marginalized in Finland with his Dipoli Students' Centre in 1966. As a result, his office had little work in Finland and, for much of the 1970s, concentrated on international work in Kuwait, organized through the British architect Sir Leslie Martin. However, Pietilä was able to return to Finland with his projects for the Hervanta Cultural Centre, Tampere (1975–9), and Lieksa Church (1978–82). The red-brick Hervanta complex alluded to the industrial history of Tampere and for many architects this was considered a romanticizing of Pietilä's already romantic image. In the midst of huge housing blocks resembling Leningrad, Pietilä's scheme was inviting and well-liked by the growing local and student population. Lieksa Church began as a more expressionistic project, set aside from the plan of the original Engel Church, which had burnt down. The difficulty with such reflections of the earlier architecture meant that the building took on a more robust form. The low, huddled church echoed the original plan with a squatting domed roof. Inviting the worshippers to view the existing bell-tower outside brought history in and allowed Pietilä to experiment further with resonance and allusion, devices at the time favoured by many postmodern architects. These two buildings, however, were by no means isolated exercises as the postmodern influence spread to many other architects.[10]

From the mid-1970s into the 1980s Postmodernism, though much maligned, was unavoidable as a necessary dynamic within society. But a pluralizing Modern Movement meant to some, however, not richness and diversity, but fragmentation and chaos. The symbolic multivalency within Jencks's thesis implied an operative procedure that relied heavily on reading architecture. Jencks proceeded to interpret architecture for its public reception, for its legibility. All this had been taken for granted in the Finnish architectural profession. New studies appeared and a new awareness of semiotics and phenomenology was absorbed from international writers and sources and simplified for an architectural application.

For a profession that once held clear ideas about architecture's mission and its continuing use within the cultural identity of the country, for a country that was defined by geography as much as geopolitical accident, Postmodernism was useful in another way, not always opportunistic. Postmodernism meant that architecture suddenly could expand to take on the contextual. Site, *genius loci* and symbolic levels became important. No longer was the landscape context taken for granted as a natural consequence of proportion, dimensions and the divine site. For an ideal view of this we need only look at the photographs of Aulis Blomstedt's Extension to the Workers' Institute in Helsinki taken in the 1960s. The neglected response to nature and the romance that came along with such an agenda could now be reintroduced. A reductive agenda controlled the exhibitions; through the superficial use of phenomenological theory, aesthetic theory and *genius loci* a revised Modernism could emerge.[11]

Growing in importance to Finland in all this, somewhat a direct consequence of the selected relationship of the Museum of Finnish Architecture to international journals, critics and universities, was the role of the foreign critic. Around this time, Colin St John Wilson and Kenneth Frampton would in some way take over the role that the Finns had seen in J. M. Richards. For a serious theoretical resistance to Postmodernism, and a useful revisionism for Finnish architecture, Frampton's work was crucial. In his essay 'Towards a Critical Regionalism' Frampton wrote about Aalto as a modern architect who could 'build the site'.[12] In an analysis of Säynätsalo Civic Centre Frampton read the building as an example of the authentic and serious critical work within a relocated critical Modernism. There was no mistaking the point: Aalto's work was not only an example of critical regionalism, it was authentically modern in tectonic and sensual terms.[13]

Frampton's essay was important to a country that had marginalized Aalto up until his death in 1976. Frampton introduced a critical language and freshness not previously used within Finland. Prompted by new publications as diverse as those by the Norwegian critic Christian Norberg-Schulz and the 'new journalism' of Tom Wolfe mentioned earlier, Finnish architecture would learn to speak about itself differently. One of the most important shapers of this decade, who leant heavily on the phenomenological and aesthetic works around at the time, was Juhani Pallasmaa. Having continued to steer the internationalizing of the Museum of Finnish Architecture, and one of the few architects involved in appropriating critical writing from abroad, in what was still a rather repressed environment, his significance increased. His wide-ranging writings would echo and strengthen (though with little reference to) what Blomstedt, Pietilä and company had done in *Le Carré Bleu* in the late 1950s. Heidegger and phenomenology, sensuality and space, tectonics and poetry would continue to muddy the usual untalkative Finnish text with a fake encounter with theory. Pietilä, however, remained a rogue thinker, uncannily closer to more contemporary thinkers than has been acknowledged. Pallasmaa shifted from early convictions that dismissed the individualistic work of Aalto and Pietilä to fluid re-readings of the poetics of architectural meaning. Using aesthetic theory and art, this built up a detailed essentialist defence of Modernism as a critically expedient resistance strategy. Not necessarily un-experimental, this was an informed but safely controlled agenda useful for the pragmatists out to reanimate modern architecture.

Postmodernism helped also to reanimate the 'ideal' within the modern agenda. But for those architects who read not the detail, nor attended to the phenomenological theory, the use of the aesthetics and visual theory of art was once again more pertinent. There is no doubt when we consider our shaping narrative, Pallasmaa continued the singular, guiding role – the absolutist position – that Blomstedt occupied. Although Finnish architects are known for not going into the detail of the theory, this position has been crucial in support of what, during the 1980s, became the work of the Helsinki School. This resistance to theory and the idea of a 'built un-talking discourse' enabled a thinker like Pallasmaa – significant since the debunking of Pietilä in 1967 – to lead the way.[14] Tutored and nurtured by Aulis Blomstedt, he would inherit the mantle of his master. Both wrote and theorized well, but, like Blomstedt, Pallasmaa's own talent in his work would remain somewhat eclectic, contrary and unfulfilled.

In a text from 1993 entitled 'An Architecture of the Seven Senses', Pallasmaa would extend his decade-long revision on a Bachelardian enquiry into a series of phenomenological observations. 'Retinal architecture and loss of plasticity' would be part of a spirited attempt to explore the 'eye candy' factor in contemporary architecture and the real loss of the 'real'. This theorized into how a natural restraint would become a restoration and avoid the excesses of Postmodernism. A saturated media culture, if not controlled, might bring Modernism down. A hypnotic Modernism could answer this loss; a pluralist, phenomenological methodology would reanimate architectural expression while keeping Finnish architecture within its accepted agenda for Modernism. Finnish architecture never comfortable, nor ever quite needing to be with contemporary discourse or theory in architecture, could realign itself.

The teaching of philosophy was gradually introduced into architectural courses. The rhetoric of the student work in most cases followed and often replicated the lines of the master-teachers and professors, all mostly from the leading Helsinki offices, who themselves followed international trends. All assimilated for a quiet, restrained though sometimes spectacular tectonic. Lines and angles tilted, slipped off to one side or skewed, resulting in a tamed, well-controlled expression that merged with recognizable international architectural idioms.

Besides the continued activity of Pietlä and Pallasmaa, the young architect Kai Wartiainen began a timely probe into some of the unspoken issues within Finnish architecture. Using analysis, theory and statistical enquiry, writing in a more operative and provocative mode, Wartiainen resembles the architects of new theory and new urbanism. Following and sparring with international architects such as Rem Koolhaas, Wartiainen, like Pietilä, attempted to push the envelope of the architectural condition and question the very precepts of Finnish Modernism at the same time. But while Pietilä remained the Modernist, Wartiainen attempted to loosen more radically the brief of architecture and urban planning. After an early collaboration with O.-P. Jokela, Wartiainen has gone on to use his own works to test some of these ideas in his Santasalo Gears Factory (1996), Tali Golf Club (1993) and the High-Tech Centre, Ruoholahti, Helsinki (2002). While holding a professorship in the Stockholm KTH School of Architecture, he is unusual among architects in pushing urban developments beyond the confines of an architect's collaborative and on into unknown but potentially new infrastructures for planning and funding new developments, as his recent large urban schemes for Vantaa show. The internationalist deconstructive rhetoric is still present but there are more extreme hints at hyper-radical architecture; a new urbanism may indicate a loosening of the restrained modern code, but, until the rhetoric forgoes stylistic precedent, it is probably too early to tell.

The response to Postmodernism in the 1980s, however, enabled the profession to consider a renewed attention to the poetry of structure,

aided by a kind of decorative minimalism that would humanize a previously 'inhuman' approach. Slowly the agenda of the mentor, professor and moral-shaper Aulis Blomstedt was gradually reformed in the new generation of his students who took up positions of institutional, professional and pedagogic significance.

We have begun to recognize patterns as the twentieth century has proceeded. The extremes of any trend or imported ideas have never been part of the way Finnish architecture has assimilated influence and international trends. Something 'absolutely Finnish' has been redefined, often indirectly, as architects have moved from decade to decade. International contacts and the selection of critics have supported this. The 1980s and '90s would be no exception. Competitions from the early 1980s onwards indicate that almost all architects, including students, began using a flattened postmodern vocabulary. New tectonic repertoires of twist and splay, sheer and slant, were appropriated and mixed in with a heavier, less subtle massing of a postmodern classicism. Any number of competition entries from the time indicate the massing, gridding and square fenestration patterns. The initial competition to completion for the Nokia Headquarters by Pekka Helin and Tuomo Siitonen (1983–97) and the Finnish National Opera House in Helsinki by Hyvämäki, Karhunen, Parkkinen (1975–93) amply demonstrate the journey into the many style trials that occurred in the 1980s. Architecture seemed to mirror the future-to-come. As a refined, structural Modernism had been reclaimed as Finland's birthright in 1980, the parallel project of Deconstruction proved equally productive; its theory less so.

While these style trials continued, the general world recession also affected architects. Soaring unemployment, a bank crisis and the self-crippling welfare system meant that Finland had a serious budget deficit through into the early 1990s. Finland also had one of the highest tax rates; the national income tax is sharply progressive and the marginal tax in the highest brackets is more than 60 per cent.[15] The recession forced architects to compete by putting in an expected bid for work. Often done in cahoots with investment parties and contractors, this led to huge cost-cutting, and works were often accepted quite dubiously on the lowest tender basis. The rather complacent profession suffered shock. Privilege and status dropped dramatically. The dog-eat-dog procedure encouraged larger offices (headed by architects from the 1960s and '70s) to play the tender game and individual architects to hope for a fairer professional competition. The collective nature of Finnish society was breaking up; individualism and opportunism, the necessity to succeed at someone else's expense, made the profession less sure of itself. The Finnish government succeeded in balancing the budget only by the late 1990s. All the more reason, it was felt, for an *arrière-garde* action.

By the beginning of the 1990s more than 50 per cent of architects were unemployed. Designers mourned the loss of a so-recent tradition as if Finnishness was something permanent, nationally protected, a legend now needing only to be replicated. Instead of analysing this loss, protective

Hyvämäki, Karhunen and Parkkinen, Finnish National Opera House, Helsinki, 1975–93.

measures were again taken. Promotion and media management became even more important, replacing innovation. In the late 1980s the whole design industry, including textiles, electronics and paper, had to fight a dissolution brought on by the fall of the Soviet Union. Globalization crept in; surprisingly, the devaluation of the Finnish mark could be affected by and also in turn affect larger currencies. Economic immaturity looked no worse than that of the greater, First World countries.

The 1980s emerged as the most pluralist period in Finnish Modernism.[16] Jyrki Tasa and Kai Wartiainen, professors as well as practitioners, have been, alongside a few others, responsible for a pluralist, deconstructive if you like, counter-Modernism. Their contemporary works now begin to offer an ongoing counter-blast to the recognized rational idiom within Finnish architecture. Tasa, in the earlier elegant Nordic-classically inspired Malmi Post Office (1986) and in the genuinely surprising Be-Pop building in Pori (1988), had taken on the rationalists. A pop-deconstruction with minimalist tectonics, Be-Pop's courage enabled a city like Pori to relocate its own corporate and cultural identity. Here was an answer to the public symbolism missing in much other architecture of the time. This was courage unlikely to be acknowledged easily.[17]

But as with any continuous history explored chronologically we must also not forget the slippage of time. Once more in the 1980s we have architects 'completing' their œuvre while younger architects and offices are setting out on theirs. By the 1980s Reima Pietilä was established as the Academician in architecture, a role he took over from Aalto, and was appointed by the President of the Republic. At this time the President

Jyrki Tasa, Be-Bop
Building, Pori, 1988.

200

Raili and Reima
Pietilä, Official
Residence of the
President of Finland,
Mäntyniemi, Helsinki,
1984–93.

happened to be Mauno Koivisto, coincidentally from the same upbringing, school class and city as Pietilä, Turku. Following his Hervanta Centre and Lieksa Church, Pietilä was able to complete Tampere Library and the Finnish Embassy in Delhi. The library, won in competition in 1979 and sketched out during a late summer holiday on the west coast of Ireland, took its departure from a soft mass, shaped by constant rhythmic sketching. On return to Helsinki, the project was formalized in plan and Pietilä took the unusual step of shaping a building in the image of a capercaillie. The ambiguity of seeing a building's symbol only from the air was professionally derided. However, the robust exterior and sculptural interior, despite the awkward shape for library shelves and filing, have made it one of the oddest and most popular buildings for local people and visitors to the city. The Finnish Embassy in New Delhi was originally a project dating back to 1961, which though awarded first prize was shelved. Later, as Matti K. Mäkinen headed the National Board of Public Building, the project was reintroduced. Pietilä adapted the original design, and although it lost a little of its original daring roofscape, the soaring white concrete structure became a contemporary classic. (Ironically, the New Delhi Finnish Embassy offers a strong clue as to what architecture Pietilä might have achieved had he had more support post-Dipoli.)[18]

Aarno Ruusuvuori
and Reima Pietilä
on the site of the
Mäntyniemi
President's Residence,
late 1980s.

If the early 1980s works flirted with postmodern vocabulary, albeit restrained and picked over, the significant project that signalled a change was Heureka Science Centre (1984–8). Won in competition by Mikko Heikkinen and Markku Komonen, both students out of Otaniemi in the dissenting 1960s, the diagrammatic play of geometric forms and nuanced tectonics was utterly distinctive within Finland. Initially misread as a deconstructive exercise, this was no theoretical project, as the architects claimed. Clear forms – the sphere, the cube, the rectangle and the slanted long rainbow-glass wall facing the railway tracks – were all shaped by an unusual directness and challenging use of material. The building was to

introduce an entirely new tectonic poetry into Finnish architecture, whilst its underlying control echoed the discipline of many of the pioneers.

The work of these two architects, leaning towards the aesthetics of art rather than theory, also confirmed at one and the same time the brilliance and control implied in any 'resistance' strategy and signalled a reanimation of Constructivist-Modernism. Heureka offered other architects a way out of the postmodern dilemma.

The 'birthright of Modernism' announced in 1980 was not, however, shared by those disaffected with the profession's control of Modernism. Neither manifestos, the museum's policies, selected critics nor the friends of *Arkkitehti* could hold back disenchantment with architecture as it slowly fermented into a rampant pluralism. Under Komonen and then Norri, for some time the Finnish professional review *Arkkitehti* had carefully selected acceptable projects for publication. Parallel the activities of these two architects as controlling forces in the Museum of Finnish Architecture and one begins to see how any hints of an exploratory public symbolism in architecture were denied. Those interested in theory and teaching of a more plural kind were often forced to find more reward abroad (including Tapani Launis, Kari Jormakka and Eeva-Liisa Pelkonen, among others).

At the same time there emerged significant opposition during the 1980s. Discontent with the forced Rationalism of the Helsinki School, and the 'intolerance' expressed by the Museum of Finnish Architecture under Ruusuvuori and Pallasmaa (continued later by Komonen and Norri), caused a breakaway movement. The young architects and students connected with the Oulu School of Architecture in the north of Finland were keen to exploit their own difference. Under the leadership of Reijo Niskasaari (who died in 1988) they responded throughout the late 1970s and into the '80s to the vernacularism of Charles Moore and – significantly – to the encouraging plurality and rogue thinking of Reima Pietilä. And although embedded within Postmodern strategies were ideas that could integrate the lost symbolism and regionalism from the north, in fact what these architects sought was quite another idea of 'north'; an approach that would displace and alter the heavily centralized view of Finnish architecture propagated by the 'south'. Both phenomenology and *genius loci* (influenced by Norberg-Schulz's writings and Pietilä's own late 1970s architecture) began to rescript critical theory and reception into a regionalized Postmodernism. A north versus south emerged, since the rational Modernism kept under control by the south was considered by many younger students and architects in the north a 'failed' rather than 'incomplete' Modernism.

Though muted by professional forces, including the by now hegemonic Museum of Finnish Architecture, there is no denying that, for a decade and more, what became known as the Oulu School succeeded in exposing the 'intolerance' of the architects from the south for any deviation from a strict Modernism. Oulunsalo Town Hall, an example often used by both sides, indicates how the architects opted for quite another idea of the 'Modern' within Finnish architecture. Here was a red-brick expressive vernacular that picked up on the pitched roof, the use of timber and other local materials. To some this was a romanticism of no relation to Finnish architecture; to others this was a long overdue return to local poetics. For these architects from Oulu and Vaasa no precedence was given to the south, the Nordic classical tradition or the affected strains of Miesian Modernism. To this day, architects emerging from the Oulu School (practising in Oulu and Vaasa), though still often marginalized by the promotional apparatus of Finnish Modernism controlled in the capital, remain in pursuit of this difference. Many significant, newer organic works have been consistently resisted because they do not conform to the orthodox shaping of Modernism, such as Vihanti Library by V. Heikki Aitoaho (1991), and the technical building Oulaisten Kirkon Huoltorakennus, by Anna and Lauri Louekari (1992).[19]

To close this period, let us return to the south of the country. Perhaps because they were taught by the generation that followed Aulis Blomstedt, these Finnish architects seemed to retain during the 1990s a remarkable sense of their own history and their own legacy. It may be this legacy that helps to temper the rage for instant style and novelty, though it by no means ignored it. It may also be this legacy that both offers opportunities to rescue a type of architecture that might otherwise have gone missing, and yet keep a lid on more extreme contemporary projects. Slowly, as we move towards the 1990s, more than the whiff of nostalgia begins to creep into the shape of Modernism. But things, however, were about to turn once more around 1992, when the recession eased and the Soviet empire had finally run its course.

After 1989, the break up of the Soviet Union and bilateralism with Finland, social, cultural and political structures searched for their own revisions. Left or right, progressive or regressive, there began an oscillating movement as restructuring dominated the early 1990s and Finland became dependent on the fluctuations of international politics, market conditions and, inevitably, cultural trends. The highly regulated and protectionist economy had to be restructured, cartels and bank-run finances replaced, as the money market was liberalized during the 1980s. Coalition governments between the Social Democrats, the Agrarians and smaller parties continued until 1987. The overheated economy meant soaring domestic prices and a loss of markets to the West. At its worst about 20 per cent of the population were unemployed in the early 1990s, although architects as we have noted suffered greater unemployment at the time. Many were forced to close small practices while others began to regroup into free corporate collaborations. The Conservatives formed a coalition with the Social Democrats until 1991, when the Centre Party got back

Monark, Finnish Pavilion, Seville Expo, 1992.

Helvetinkolu, Hell's Gorge, a resonant image for the Finnish Pavilion, Seville.

into power. The electronic, computer-run society was initially resisted, although by the end of the decade the saturation of the media and consumerism brought benefits and pain in equal measure.

In architecture there was an increasing lament for, and at the same time a necessary re-enchantment of, Modernism and the modern agenda. Was it lost, or was it about to be recreated? To some, reconstructing the modern might be nostalgic, but it could also be innovative. This coincided in 1989 with various events, but the award in the competition of 1990 for the Finnish Pavilion at the Seville Expo (1992) to five young students of architecture who called themselves Monark has to be seen as pivotal. To the jury, surrounded by the headache of trends and fashions, this was the only innovative project: mysteriously but recognizably Finnish! The building designed by Monark was eventually realized, at some risk, at some expense, but with much panache. The edge-less abstraction achieved in the construction of the pavilion, the radical minimalism and absence of detail were all significant. To the *manifesto modernists* it became critically obvious that the Finnish Pavilion in Seville gave the revisionism of the modern code clearer emphasis.[20] More importantly, though little more than a diagram of a box and a container, the Finnish Pavilion had what few buildings achieved in the last two decades: lucid aesthetics and accompanying awe.

Importantly, it also photographed well, slipped into the aesthetic mould that the Museum of Finnish Architecture still preferred, and – not insignificant – resisted deeper critical enquiry. Foreign critics either loved it and re-scripted past glory or considered it a sombre architecture suitable for such an activity as slitting the throat. Nothing changes; resonances with the Finnish Pavilion in 1900 are unavoidable. Once again the Finns had attracted world attention, and during an international event their cultural assertion held within it a gentle disquiet. This time it was not an opening to the world, a statement of impending national drive and identity. This time it represented and confirmed a kind of retreat. It also restated the obvious: 'We are Finns,' the young architects said with some *sisu*, 'we do what we do!' As if an unsettled architecture had run its own course, the Finnish Pavilion in Seville slowed down the giddiness of the 1980s. To many it signalled the end of the carnival of Postmodernism and the return to what the profession felt had always been done well: a controlled tectonic flair hinting at innovation.[21]

In this respect the year 1993 was a busy one for Finnish architecture. As the Finnish Association of Architects completed a collegial centenary, there was a feeling that the stylistic-gaming of the Postmodern years were over. In the capital, however, as if to demonstrate just how wrong architecture could go, one project in Helsinki was made the scapegoat of all these style-trials, the Pikku Huopalahti housing scheme. The varying scale and postmodern symbolism attempted to recreate small neighbourhood communities. But identifiable townscape planning features like clusters and courtyards were given little credit. Instead, the relative impossibility of serious exchange and critical hostility shown

Reijo Jallinoja,
Pyramid Housing
Block, Pikku-
Huopalahti,
Helsinki, 1993.

by the orthodox Modernists meant an increase in simplistic 'façade' debates. The architect Reijo Jallinoja's large pyramidal postmodern block in Helsinki's Pikku-Huopalahti district was singled out for hostile reactions. It was considered Finnish Postmodernism at its worst. Jallinoja, a professor now at the Oulu School of Architecture, echoes a history of many Finnish architects. Working in the Helsinki City Planning Office, Jallinoja was also today one of the designers of East-Pasila (Itä-Pasila), the project from the 1970s recognized in Finnish architectural circles as the nightmare of applied Finnish urban mega-structures. Besides the architects from the north, he is also today one of a number of emerging architects who continue to swerve from convention and produce innovative buildings that do not quite conform to 'tradition'.

By 1992 the number of open competitions in the Association's Centenary dropped dramatically to three. The rationalizing strand of Modernism that had for two decades defined the direction of architectural education in the south of the country changed its guard. The enthusiasm in the greater world for architectural theory and philosophy influenced education. Under the brief directorship of Pallasmaa, the merits of an art education and a selected philosophical programme brought a welcome but brief width to the curriculum at the Otaniemi School of Architecture. Meanwhile, more consistently, students' work at Tampere University had succeeded in winning international competitions and the university published the most interesting critical and theoretical papers called *Datutop*.[22] The Oulu School of Architecture continued to explore its difference from the centralized rationalism of the Helsinki School, and by carefully selecting professors (like Jyrki Tasa and Rainer Mahlamäki) and navigating courses students could explore more radical ideas if they so wished.

In 1992 the profession of architects was at its lowest ebb for years, if not since its inception. Generosity and solidarity within the profession had been fragmented, almost lost. This loss in morale was to colour the years through to the next millennium with an increase in aggressive tendering procedures. In many ways the lack of planning initiatives and structures permitted the city of Helsinki, its politicians, planners and investment bankers, to begin dictating the shape of a new architecture to suit the competitive and rapidly expanding European city.

Globalization was even contesting its own 'basics'. This coincided with the mediation of architecture worldwide, the emerging Internet and the ability to be informed of just about everything contemporary while it was 'contemporary'. Suddenly no lag existed. Dutch architecture, Japanese architecture or LA architecture was instant, available and accessible. Models for renewal flooded into the country; much attention was paid to the foreign star architect. The politicians were influenced by their travels and by what they had seen elsewhere. And just as at the beginning of the century, young Finnish students and architects would travel more and more; they would work in offices in Vienna, Berlin, New York, Rotterdam and Boston. Dutch architecture would prove more than attractive to these young students and travellers. The 'fuck-the-context' attitude of an architect like Rem Koolhaas or the trans-programming of Bernard Tschumi would – belatedly – begin to resonate.

Not keen on over-theorizing but inevitably involved in the pitch of architecture itself, the 1990s was all set for another carnival, hinting at but not replicating the 1960s. Modernism could now turn into Pentti Saaritsa's snowdog without pausing in its business. That's how clever it is. And, after 1992, Finland's balance of trade was back in the black.

chapter eight

Late Modernism, Critical Humanism

Just fancy: somehow, through sheer daft youth,
Someone manages a mistake – and is
schooled, intimidated, and shorn of error!

But error's what we're looking for – error to shear
perfection!

Poor you, to learn something here! Look
here is the royal coach of your divinity,
the horse and the driver – all wrong,
so perfectly wrong, no one
but you can adore them, adopt them
and drive away – go, moreover,
wherever you want.

Risto Ahti, 'Mistakes and Intimidations'[1]

Finnish Modernism's most iconographic and elegant late twentieth-century buildings, such as the Sanoma House and Nokia Headquarters, all championed examples of Finland's late Modernism wear their 'heart on their sleeve'. This is Finnish architecture out there: what you see is what you get; fore-fronted technology; structural and tectonic gems. For many, talk now is unnecessary; the same fellow-travelling architects who were so heavily involved in the 1960s and '70s were about to become neo-liberals. The eternal moment of Communism so seductive and thrilling in the 1960s became the eternal moment of late capitalism. Fluidity in society brought in uncertainty; everywhere in the world, it was possible to see ideas and ideologies changed to conform to varying agendas. Notions like the 'left' and the 'right' had broken down. Finland's birthright had now become tradition; if it was Modernism itself, it would be reappropriated once more. To some, however, there is a general lament at the loss of surprise, plasticity and spatial drama. Without deeper poetic dimension and a more humane touch, the public is at a loss. In a world reduced to the diagrammatic, the soul can never be appropriated.

In the last decade of the twentieth century, it looked as if the Finnish economy would be rescued by the generally high standard in education

Jyrki Tasa, Moby Dick House, Espoo, 2003.

Söderlund and Sükala, Sanoma House, Helsinki, 1999.

and the respect shown towards agreements. The smallness of the country, the noted polemical and political intimacy, had its advantages. Corruption remained at a relatively low level and internal security could be controlled.[2] For outsiders, the ability of the Finns to close in, protect their own interests, can be alienating. Despite the massive economic turnaround in the 1990s and its increasing wealth, Finland might not be the coldest country in Europe but it is not always the number one destination. The number of foreigners in the country is among the lowest in Europe. Only a limited number of refugees live in Finland, and the number of persons applying for asylum in 1997 was 973. Too far north to attract a mass tourism or influx, this might also be Finland's joker card.

In the late 1980s the government pioneered its own development to turn the country into a high-tech society. Nokia became the largest producer of cellular phones in the world. Growing from an industrial concern named after its original beginning in the small southern town called Nokia (outside Tampere) dealing in paper, pulp, cables, plastic and rubber boots, Nokia now pioneers the IT world and innovative communication products and strategies. Today its buildings occupy a significant part of the western approach to Helsinki. No doubt encouraged by the rise and rise of the Nokia empire, Finland's R&D input overtook that of the US and reached the Japanese level.

In 1988 about 5 per cent of Finnish exports were high-tech goods; ten years later it had risen to 15 per cent. The 1960s and '70s had seen the workforce employed in farming reduced to a quarter as Finland

Pekka Helin and
Tuomo Siitonen,
Nokia Headquarters,
Espoo, 1997.

industrialized and pulp, paper and timber fuelled a steady market with
the Soviet Union.[3] In 1986 Finland had become a full member of the
European Free Trade Association, and in 1995 the country became a
member of the European Union. Proud of its ability to get things done
in the European Union, by the end of the twentieth century Finland was
no longer a relatively poor, misunderstood agricultural country; it was
an established member-state and one of the most highly developed countries in the EU. Pioneering technologies, Nokia, computers, telecommu-
nications and bio-medicine defied the perception of Finland as one of
the world's coldest places.

Cities also began competing for their own corporate and civic identity. After 1992 an emerging corporate Modernism answered some of
these trends by offering a predominant form within Helsinki and other
major Finnish cities. The result of the aggressive tendering process and
the collaborative alignments among architects, investors and contractors

could be seen in the quick, slick architecture of fast-track investment and building opportunism. The neo-radicals from the 1960s began to circulate architecture as commerce with an altered but mainstream vocabulary, many relying on good, young assistants aware and familiar with new trends and ideas. Increased high-tech luxury and affordability brought relative sophistication, but further increasing the loss of poetic dimensions. In the outlying suburbs of Helsinki, Vantaa and Espoo, advanced images of an airport lifestyle in the malls, offices and secure housing compounds emerged. This was partnered by a worrying remoteness in Finland's small towns and villages.

For the reshaping of the professional agenda the most important project of the closing years of the century was the Museum of Contemporary Art in Helsinki, known in Finland as Kiasma (from *chiasma*, Latin for 'crosspiece' – the architect's pseudonym for his competition entry). Won by the American architect Steven Holl in 1995, for the next four years this project staged an ongoing debate. It both confirmed the oscillations between a convergent minimalism and a kind of divergent poetic expressionism and attempted to bridge technical solutions with phenomenological intention. The significance in Holl's twisting twin-formed museum coated in glass and sheathed in aluminium was immediate and twofold. Holl was the first foreign architect, since C. L. Engel, to design and carry out a building in the Finnish capital. He was also responsible for a building that employed a freer form last seen in the work of Reima Pietilä. Although the details in Kiasma do not carry the clarity of the work, and though Holl never quite gelled within the Finnish context, the question was obviously posed. Was the stricter modern agenda about to be reshaped yet again? Or was this the synthetic Modernism everyone had been waiting for?

The site in Helsinki before the construction of the Kiasma Museum of Contemporary Art.

Steven Holl,
Kiasma Museum of
Contemporary
Art, Helsinki, 1997,
and the statue of
Mannerheim.

The award to Steven Holl's scheme could never merely be an archi-tectural decision, despite the protestations of those who oversee such processes. The professional and ideological impacts were all around, motivated by media games. 'Kiasma' was awarded by a jury that consist-ed of Matti K. Mäkinen, vice-chairman, who consistently promoted a 'national architectural policy' of talented stars, Tuula Arkio (the future Director of the Museum) and two of the stronger opponents to the rigid rational hegemony of Finnish Modernism, Jyrki Tasa and Kaj Wartiainen. The latter two architects, as professional representatives on the jury, were clearly aware of how the future is shaped by the past. However, they were not alone in the mechanics of the decision and it is always difficult to determine individual roles.[4] By awarding the prize to Holl and not to a more recognizably Finnish, rational or even national idiom (and there were many, including the entry by Juha Leiviskä, who was runner up in the competition), the question the jury posed to orthodox Finnish Modernism was simple: was Kiasma a subtle, retooled Modernism, a repatriation of Aalto-esque architecture, or was this the beginning of a series of works simulating a lost or synthetic Modernism?

Steven Holl,
Kiasma Museum
of Contemporary
Art, Helsinki, 1997.

Yet the acknowledgement of Juha Leiviskä's project suggests another agenda. Like Pietilä, Leiviskä has consistently been the odd man out in Finnish architecture of the last 20 years. He had already been identified by Aulis Blomstedt in the early 1970s as an architect to watch. And though his natural inclusion within the normative strain of Finnish architecture is a touch misleading, there is again that talent for assimilation, appropriation and refinement that many Finnish architects have shown. Leiviskä's lyrical expressive rationalism was not a long way from Aalto's critical humanism, whilst his controlled œuvre suited the agenda of a quiet functionalism.[5] In a genuine and unchanging conversation with the modern code itself, projects like St Thomas's Church, Oulu (1975), Myyrmäki Parish Church, Helsinki (1984), and his entry for the Museum of Contemporary Art in Helsinki (1993) confirm Leiviskä's 'modest monumentality' accompanied with a dry, controlled romanticism. Myyrmäki Church holds a controlling linear form off which Leiviskä runs the spaces; resonances to forest light are given by the subtlety of the inflection, material treatment and the changes from space to space. Plasticity echoes Leiviskä's dialogue with elegantly derived sources like De Stijl, Mies van der Rohe and modern art, creating an originality and singularity in relation to Finnish architecture. Leiviskä's subtle architecture converges formalistically; exercises within a narrow theme introduce extraordinary shifts in manneristic elements. It is not unusual to see Leiviskä's work, especially this church, as 'architect's architecture', so careful and musical are its allusions, so lightly does it reference the past.[6]

216

Juha Leiviskä, model
for the Museum
of Contemporary
Art, runner up in
competition.

Juha Leiviskä,
Myyrmäki Church
and Congregational
Centre, Vantaa, 1984.

To go by the omnipresent commentator of Finnish architecture Juhani Pallasmaa, Leiviskä now serves to display the continuity between Aalto and Pietilä; the mutuality being an aspect of 'forest space'. 'In a forest culture', Pallasmaa wrote in 1997, 'built space is not the opposite of nature; instead, the architect reflects the spatial structures of the landscape.'[7] Forest space is rewritten as characteristic of Aalto, Pietilä and now Leiviskä. A clear revisionist line, this re-scripting would always be inevitable as Finnish Modernism proved in need of redefining and restoring itself through a series of verbal and lexical tricks in response to the corporate internationalism of the 1990s. This is also the search for another missing hero, reinforcing the conservative shape and mechanics of Finnish Modernism. Metaphors of the forest, un-geometric space, natural forms and natural rhythm are reinterpreted as the base for a Finnish conception of space. The result, however, and one that has appeared into the new millennium, is, to use a phrase from Bourdieu, a 'subversion oriented towards conservatism or restoration'.[8]

In sharp contrast to the clearly delineated geometry of urbanized European cultures, we cannot fail to notice once more a retreat into the security of known places, the forest and the romance of the late 1890s. It was this retreat that was ironically hammered down in the 1960s; it is this retreat now that defines the modern 'synthesis'. The eminence given this thinking is surely as questionable as the eminence given its defeat in the activist decade. Which is why it is tempting to begin to see this, along with the critical rehabilitation of Alvar Aalto on the centenary of his birth in 1998, as the Finnish architects coming full circle. We are once more – this time dubiously – on the road to the land that is not, Karelia.

However critically attractive and comfortably phenomenological these words about 'forest space' sound, it is not quite confirmed by Finnish architecture today. Instead it elevates once more the individual hero and sidelines the general and strong characteristics that, to this day, many Finnish architects support. If Leiviskä's thinking owes more to a hidden forest morphology, the restraint and modest beauty of his churches surely resonate back to Erik Bryggman, not Aalto, and Hilding Ekelund, not Reima Pietilä. A divergence within a narrow frame suggests that Leiviskä is content in altering an already accepted system. While this may connect to the 'Finnish forest', it is hardly a derailment of hegemonic rationalism, which was part of both Aalto's and Pietilä's exercise and is part of Wartiainen's and Tasa's exercise today. Rarely indulging in hermeneutics and critical analysis, and never resorting to a 'natural' mysticism, Leiviskä became a model talent for an agenda wishing to remain within a narrow range, while exploring the divergence within that range.

Ilmo Valjakka,
Finnish Television
Centre, Helsinki,
1993.

When the Helsinki School rejected Steven Holl's romantic modernist entry, Leiviskä's competition entry was cited as an example of a more 'fitting', even nationalist project.[9] The backlash brought revision to the forefront; birthright could now synthesize Modernism, tradition and change, and by so doing the possibility of Finnish Modernism becoming 'anachronistic' was forestalled but not avoided.

Continuity in Finnish Modernism, though already an accepted domain, remains problematic. The hegemonic order and constant promotion begins to look like a dated model for an architecture trying to repeat itself whilst it can still deny counter-tendencies that remain at present residual. The 1980s, prompted by a Postmodernism that seeped almost universally into architecture, provided short-term investment in a confused public architecture. The Yhtyneet Kuvalehdet building for a large Finnish news and media organization (1987) and the Finnish Television Centre (1993), both by Ilmo Valjakka, in Helsinki's suburbs, are supreme examples of this period. The results of this flirtation have not been short-term. The large double-glass façades in Helsinki replicate a similar yearning for articulation and image in supposedly un-talkative buildings. Huge metallic forms begin to see the public nicknaming this as 'mink-net architecture', as in the new Physicum Building of the University of Helsinki in Outokumpu (2003).[10] A consistent neo-Constructivist repertoire was achieved in its near image-purity by the architect Erkki Kairamo, whose modesty and talent now appear to dwarf many more celebrated architects. Others seem to have continued the pattern, tamed international excess and produced a dynamic, structural poetry.[11]

By joining the European Union in 1995, a sense of creeping infiltration began to intrigue but also worry Finnish society. Innovation had to re-sharpen resistance if Finland was to hold onto some of its revered national virtues. Since the architectural profession was forced to put itself out to tender, by the mid-1990s professional dissatisfaction and public indifference left two clear groups within architecture. One was sincerely concerned about, and sincerely resistant to, radical change in architecture brought on by external and internal social, cultural and

Lahdelma and
Mahlamäki,
Physicum Building,
Helsinki, 2003.

ARK House architects,
Audio Visual School,
Arabianranta,
Helsinki, 2003.

political transformations. To counteract the alleged populism and thinness of Postmodernism and the theories of Deconstruction, retrieval of the modern agenda was, in this group's mind, essential. Anything 'absolutely Finnish', whether anachronistic or not, depended on this. The myth of clarity in detailing, or even the removal of detailing, was to prove useful. A new formalism with an agreed aesthetic and modesty, indebted to earlier figures such J. S. Sirén, Ekelund, Aulis Blomstedt and Ruusuvuori, was now made more possible by the growing strength of Finland in Europe, the advance in new materials, and by the structural elegance given over to detail rather than symbol.

Yet the architecture began to resemble the late modern work appearing all around the world – a *photo-shop* architecture. Advanced visualization systems were used to computer-aid designs, but did little to shift or widen the actual site of architecture, a discourse that was taking place in many of the capitals and schools around the world. Instead, this reanimated architecture was a visual one of polish and aesthetic: the architecture might thankfully no longer claim to save worlds or offer social equality and represent democratic systems, but it would be faultless once more in its architectonic fiat and its accepted retreat into appropriate functional and material response. The result, however, meant that these architects remained once more somewhat isolated and alienated in their own privileged discourse.

The other smaller, less organized group (architects like Jyrki Tasa, Kai Wartiainen, Ulla and Lasse Vahtera, ARRAK, Piironen Adlercreutz and others) was just as concerned about the flirtation with pluralism, Postmodernism and Deconstruction,[12] but their relationship to the modern agenda differed. They saw in multiplicity and contemporary fluidity newer structures, newer counter-moves, as they absorbed international developments and imagined newer ways of thinking through architecture. Long after Charles Jencks had posited plural modern movements, it was necessary to speak of *architectures* in the plural. The consensus Modernism so often controlled by a protective architectural profession and the Museum of Finnish Architecture could, this group felt, be dented if not ruptured. The jury is still out on all this.

Today there are almost as many single-family homes as flats in Finland, accounting for more than 40 per cent of total housing. Other low-rise developments or terraced housing account for 12 per cent. Urbanization accelerated and arrived late, and though a big proportion of Finns long for the peace of the countryside the ambivalent relationships to contemporary urban life remain. There are almost 400,000 second homes in Finland, many of them on the lakesides or on the coast. Life without a sauna for many would be intolerable, perhaps rightly so.

Social and technological progress has indeed been immense, but alcoholism remains the second killer in Finnish society and Finland has the fourth highest suicide rate in the European Union. Fast-food chains spread as elsewhere (and some of the architects attempt to humanize these environments). Chefs adapt, assimilate new ingredients and adjust them, or perhaps innovate them, to Finnish taste. Light-roasted coffee has changed to dark-roasted coffee as tastes have become more sophisticated via Brussels and budget airline travel. The coffee and *pulla* (a type of bun) ritual in Finland still dictates social behaviour, and whether *caffé latte* is served or traditional slow-brewed pan coffee, Finland is a world leader in coffee consumption.

The last decade of the twentieth century cannot be studied without considering the number of trends, theories, fashions and the development of a star-architectural system throughout the world. To every competition jury in Finland fashion has always been something negative, something to avoid. Yet every significant architectural competition has picked up on architecture from both inside and outside the country. Influence is irrelevant under these conditions. It is what one does with the source and ideas that makes of it something special.

Finland's world stars on the rally circuit compete with the international music circuit. The world seems to know of Tommi Mäkinen, Kimi Räikkönen and Mika Häkkinen; and of the conductors Esa-Pekka Salonen, Jukka-Pekka Saraste and Osmo Vänskä. Pianists like Olli Mustonen and the singer Karita Mattila are world-famous too. Contemporary art in Finland takes on all the issues and media of world art. The identifiably Finnish garment and fabric company Marimekko, founded by Armi Ratia (1912–1979), is now part of the myth and reality of Finland. Marimekko's clean lines and boldness actually hid the obvious: the countryside came to the city and then returned slouching back to nature but 'better-dressed'. Today its striking geometric boldness has been revived, echoing two of the original Marimekko designers, Maija Isola (b. 1927) and Vuokko Eskolin-Nurmesniemi (b. 1930), as have many of the heroes of Finnish design – works by Tapio Wirkkala, Timo Sarpaneva, Antti Nurmesniemi and Kaj Franck still sell well. Younger designers often working in collaboration and internationally, like the Snowcrash concern, have taken innovation into the high-tech products and communication industry.

Deconstruction, like Postmodernism, was one of the most important re-shapers of the Finnish architectural repertoire. Its analytical undressing of architectural intent and form suited the methodology of some Finns, but it did not alter the tectonic approach and the disciplined treatment of form; it merely altered the drama and pretence of that form. It seduced just like other movements have seduced and became a visual kit of splayed modernist parts; a neo-modern repertoire appeared first in almost all the schools of architecture. Later, in the last five years of the century, a more sophisticated, slicker, tectonic architecture, aided by advances in material technology, innovations in glass and steel, and the growing uses of advanced visualization systems, modelling software and computer-aided design, would appear. Further experiments in hyper-architecture and morphed space would have to wait until the mid-1990s before other buildings abroad, such as the Bilbao Guggenheim by Frank Gehry and the Berlin Jewish Museum by Daniel Libeskind, suddenly made more acceptable the wavy line, the 'blob' or the emergence of a morphogenetic architecture. Faddish innovation, however, is of course still innovation. In the mid-1990s the breathtaking neo-modernity of the flattened planes, the modular and structural clarity and volumetric subtlety are nowhere better seen than in the best versions of such architecture. The Finnish Embassy in Washington, DC, by Mikko Heikkinen and Markku Komonen (1994) was a 'cube' of undoubted tectonic flourish. It was interpreted as an enrichment of the architectural engagement between building and landscape. The building was elegantly caged with layers of steel meshing, glass and timber; outside the tent-structures added the impression of gaiety while the Constructive logic was well controlled and finished throughout the building. Here poetry was structurally reintegrated into the rational agenda. Following on from their important Heureka Science Centre in 1984, these two Finnish architects were to achieve a blended collage of symbol, form and function that became a model for many.

There are others, however, who hinted at the contract between function and poetry and who, after the 1980s, came into their own in the 1990s. If H. and K. Sirén's Otaniemi Chapel (1956) pre-empted the later formalism in Finnish architecture, then its discipline and discreet phenomenology have been bracketed by the various buildings emerging from the Lahdelma and Mahlamäki practice. Here over a period we see the practice responding to international trends and advances in material technology to produce eclectically, just as Selim Lindqvist did, a range of internationally Finnish buildings.[13] An earlier work of theirs, the Lusto Finnish Forestry Information Centre (1992), probably best fits the appeal to phenomenological echo that was reawakened in Finnish architecture during the 1980s. Sensuality in surface and form is hinted at. *Lusto* is the Finnish word for the growth ring of a tree: the building's symbolic point of departure not only sets out the dynamic programme for the architectural space and function, but also bravely suggests an architecture that can resonate within the natural and cultural. Synthesizing science with

Lahdelma and Mahlamäki, Lusto Finnish Forestry Information Centre, 1990-92.

emotion, movement, control and counterpoint makes Lusto significant. Concrete and wood are set in a continuous dialogue around two main forms, the wood-clad cylinder and the offset rectangle. The olfactory element of the building is strong. The richness of wood, the tamarack, the tar, the pine, all force the visitor to sniff the architecture. Space suggests itself through the senses.

Echo, accentuation, allusion and counterpoint are the qualities within Lusto that became some of the qualities to appear in more and more buildings, especially of younger firms in the 1990s such as ARRAK, JKMM, Quad and others.[14] These buildings begin to overlap space with a subtle density and control. Slowly a complex expression began to creep back into Finnish architecture. Many of the younger architects, often trained in one of the few larger, influential offices, began to take on a new plasticity. Materiality remains thrilling and delicate. Although enhancing the clarity of the tectonics, the work still hangs on to a yearning that echoes the acknowledged high point of architectural Modernism, the 1950s. Yet it spars with more contemporary scale, finish and sophistication. The emotional effects, however, are highly controlled, not a lot is left to chance, to the user. The architects still wish to dictate life.

224

APRT, Gardenia
Tropical Garden and
Environmental
Information Centre,
2001.

Where the seams and edging in many projects from the 1980s were
diagrammatic and over-simplified, these newer buildings, such as Sanoma
House, Helsinki, by Jan Söderlund and Antti-Matti Siikala (1999) and
the Sibelius Hall in Lahti or the Tropical Garden Centre by APRT Architects
(1997; 2001), attempt to offer more in terms of movement and a complex
assemblage of forms. Large, predominantly cubic forms, these building
innovate in the available glass and steel technology, often reinforcing the
polish and structure in the interiors with careful detailing and the use of

timber. The experience is less linear that it used to be, and when an elegant roughness is opted for, rather than overworked detail, this makes for more interesting and imperfect modernist resolutions. But this is rare.

The manifesto issued in 1980 by the Museum of Finnish Architecture put Finnish architecture into the position of having to continue the conversation. Modernism was Finland's birthright, however ambiguous modern architecture had become internationally. Today there is no agreed finality, nor perhaps need there be. Pluralism lives in much that is contemporary now in Finland, although it is still a pluralism struggled against. Deep within the Finnish culture lies the stranglehold of a strong mainstream. Students in many fields learn the coded mainstream in order to progress; few take any risks. This leaves some mourning the loss of an opposition; the unseen (drawings and projects) in Finnish architecture remains *unseen* (architects such as Pietilä, Launis and others have a significant body of work – pedagogical and professional – explored through drawings, though little attention in such collections has been shown by the Museum of Finnish Architecture as yet). Whether in the new corporate buildings that have filled up Helsinki, such as the Meritorni Tower and the new Nokia Headquarters, both by Pekka Helin (2000–03) in the old wharf area of Ruoholahti, or in some of the new housing developments, movement, ascent, descent, vista and bridges, all sorts of applied tectonic interventions attract the user as if in micro-environments and miniature city quarters. The spirit, though, if compared to any attempt to reflect forest space, is uninviting. Like the latest cell phone and its cartoon-covers, the need to be contemporary and show it has become paramount.

With aesthetic control uppermost, image politics has come full circle from 1900. With Nokia by far the biggest operation within Finland and the biggest influence on both capital and communication patterns, it is now also impossible to ignore the politics of investment within the country. During the 1990s in Finland, the Finnish Central Party was in government. Much of their electorate came from the rural parts of Finland, unlike the Social Democrat Party, which finds its electorate mostly within the cities. To preserve their own power base, it was inevitable that the Central Party would promote the regions, implying also a significant regeneration in creating new labour opportunities within forestry. Timber in all forms benefited. There was thus less incentive to expand the corporate development of the city, the use of steel and glass, until the Social Democrats took over in the mid-1990s.[15]

Along with the huge rise of office buildings and the expansion of Helsinki as an international city, an investment in city values as opposed to more traditional rural values occurred. Cities everywhere in Finland profited by a buoyant economy; a more competitive and efficient building

226

Pekka Helin, Sandels
Senior Citizens'
Housing, Helsinki,
2000.

Kristian Gullichsen
and Timo Vormala,
Biomedicum, Helsinki
University, 2001.

industry had to respond. With Finland sharing the Euro currency, supported by the success of the Nokia empire, Helsinki and its sister cities, Vantaa, Espoo and Kauniainen, started to change drastically in architectural scale. Following on from the debate over Kiasma, much of this development consisted of architecture accommodating grander international style, inviting grander international lives. Encouraged by aggressive tendering practice, a corporate glass and steel architecture supported by various manufacturers began to fill up the prime sites and residual parts of Helsinki. And though we can also observe other types of a more sensitively scaled architecture being built around the country, in relation to the way Finnish architecture is now pictured and the agenda of Modernism, this 'new internationalism' currently remains the rather bewildering architecture through which the shape of Modernism is controlled. Most Finns, rural still, feet-on-the-ground, resist such agenda and orchestrated menus. The architect as lifestyle guru is, up until now, still unacceptable.

The population in the city of Helsinki area has doubled over the last 30 years to its current figure, 559,000. Today the question of administrative reform is topical. Greater Helsinki (including Espoo, Kauniainen and Vantaa) is an area now growing to about one million inhabitants where more than one fifth of the country now lives.[16] This is an administrative region that is likely to expand in the coming years. (In March 2004 a report was published proposing a new urban core – Helsinki, Vantaa, Espoo, Kauniainen – combined with the districts of Kirkkonummi and Sipoo, estimated at 1.3 million about 2020.) City not only became 'country' once more, but the new urbanism began to dominate all political and cultural decisions. This left the core of Helsinki requiring continuous maintenance, change of use and some serious architectural intervention. Espoo, including the expanded and unrecognizable Tapiola Garden City, is spoken of now not only as a bewildering lost forest space, but as a frightening collection of non-centres that make up a city as big as Helsinki. Recent sociological analysis has not been kind to the dreams of the architects. In the 1950s and '60s Sweden was the destination out of Finland when life appeared rough, cold and primitive and an urban civility was desired. Espoo now represents the truth of Finland, a new suburban civility and exile, and, to make matters worse, to many young Finns with their Ikea Modernism and self-assembly lives, it has become Sweden! Only those who know Finland and Sweden well realize what sort of insult this is.[17]

Those unfamiliar with the emerging narrative of a restored modern architecture would see in much of Finland's recent work a 'New Internationalism'. It has been published both at home and abroad often – and sadly consistently – with little serious, constructive and critical feedback. The 'revolutionaries' have established their privilege within an increasingly reactionary profession. Those wishing to see the 'continuum' in Finnish architecture as a modern agenda – an updated history of that modern architecture traced back to the urgent pragmatism and common sense of the 1920s and the *funkis* of the 1930s – read this development as a return to what the Finns have done best, throughout the twentieth century. It is an appropriated, restrained, somewhat strangely sophisticated, high (now synthetic) Functionalism. It is an internationalism that is propelled by received opinion, a reversal of previous sets of values that now promotes spectacle architecture too easily diffused by propaganda and an uncritical media.

This latter-day agenda was helped between 1995 and 2000 by a significant development in the use of steel in architecture, repeating to some extent the *memetic* process recognized in the spread of Miesian architecture in the 1950s and '60s. To go back even further than that, this also repeats the emergence of White Functionalism in the 1930s when a recognizably international style was located within natural settings and landscape. It recalls too the 1940s – the basic module system that could be varied to suit conditions and contour.

To conclude, we might best consider how the partisan manoeuvres towards these revisions within the modern agenda were characterized by the year 1998, the centenary of Alvar Aalto's birth. After years out in the cold, ostracized by an ideologically rationalizing generation influenced post-war by Blomstedt, Ruusuvuori, Mikkola and Pallasmaa, Aalto was eventually rehabilitated, lauded and critically hailed by a whole host of stars. As a representative of the best critical humanism within Finnish architecture, Aalto had found new but old champions. He was reinterpreted by many who once had so much difficulty with his work and persona. He became, to Pallasmaa and thus – *ipso facto* – to many other Finns, the quintessential modernist, the *synthetic functionalist*.

Only not everyone buys this. Perhaps this is as it should be when coats are reversed, agendas re-shift, pick up on previous error, opportunistically redefining their own positions in the present. But as if to remind us to challenge the consensus and nostalgia this implies, at the same time the *New York Times* critic Herbert Muschamp assessed the moment, pointing out that little serious attention had been paid to Aalto's œuvre in relation – synchronically – to more contemporary architecture, and – diachronically – among the wider, collective vision of humanism and organic architecture that emerged in the work and writings of many 'revisionist' architects in the 1950s.[18] Muschamp was right; the discourse had been once again heavily selected and a more interesting enquiry curtailed. Many shared Muschamp's observation and felt that Finnish architecture suddenly changed in the 1990s: it had gone soft; the activists had finally betrayed the very provocations Aalto himself had encouraged in relation to the core Modern Movement. Activism had deflated itself, without moving to newer struggles, newer resistance. This was not tradition, but permanence. Was this another betrayal of an original and 'absolutely' Finnish Modernism?

Is this not the way in which Modernism entered society, the way it progressed and was used to shape the national identity and social development of Finland throughout the twentieth century? In fact, Finnish architects, young and old alike, are behaving in much the same way today towards trends and fashion in architecture as the early pioneers and thinkers did in the first three decades of that century. The type of structures designed and the images produced through the use of steel and glass may appear universal, but they are equally 'national' in their appropriation.

More than 30 years ago, the Finnish architect Matti Suuronen produced the Futuro. From the difficulty of putting a holiday cottage on an awkward site to the architect's experiment with a small semicircular plastic barn emerged the technical and aesthetic idea for Futuro. In 1968 the plastic, 4,000-kilogram, fully furnished pod, button-controlled and with aeroplane steps, potentially dropped down anywhere in the Finnish countryside, virtually had the architect excommunicated. Hard to believe

Matti Suuronen,
Futuro, 1964–8.

when, after all, Archigram in the UK was already producing workable
fantasies that would encourage critics to see architectural use and
utopias in space technology, capsule planning and other such accessories.
But in the context of 1968 Futuro, a divergent aberration, appeared too
dangerous for the Finnish orthodoxy. When the CF00 was carried by heli-
copter across Stockholm, the architect was a sensation. Futuro model
CF10 followed as a form of street kiosk familiar in the Finnish town and
country environments, CF45 became the Venturo apartment house, and
CF100 and CF200 became versions of a petrol station. Over half of the
production of Futuro in 1968 went straight abroad and up to the oil
crisis in 1973 more than 10,000 pods were manufactured in the USA per
year. It is hard to say whether it was the architect or the object that
became too famous. But clearly this assimilation of technology and minimalism, when put against the Constructivist slant favoured in Finland at
the time (Mies crossed with Japanese module planning), was inauthentic.
The serial production made possible by Futuro was in no way professionally respectable or comparable to the serial architectural thinking
propounded and propagated by the younger militants. Suuronen was

Cartoon by Kari
Kuosma, 'The Most
Ultimate Modernist
Façade Innovation
So Far', 1998.

considered a business architect, ignored by
the profession. But in 1998, when Aalto was
celebrated in full unqualified manner in
New York, Suuronen's pod was exhibited at
the Museum of Finnish Architecture.

Futuro is one more story in miniature of
the contradictory trends and promotional
tendencies in Finnish architecture where the
centre is peripheral to another centre. Futuro
indicates the critical difficulty the convergent
culture presents itself when it can so easily
and naively rehabilitate its own shortcom-
ings. As the century closed, a natural resistance to expressive Deconstruction and the
high-tech fascination with steel and glass
could not fail to invite echoes to the industrial aesthetic of the better 'Constructivist'
works from the 1960s and '70s. The taste and
fascination for abstraction mixed with the
allusion to the industrial aesthetic helped to
create a high-tech city image while still offering the public an 'unfriendly' image. Steel to
the public has always been cold, clean and neutral; glass is transparent
fear. They bring no burnish, no blemishes, no history. Usually public dissent is expressed in a more personal way: letters to the editor in *Helsingin
Sanomat* (Finland's biggest daily newspaper, which had itself for many
years narrowed the debate and kept to the consensus-Modernism) or then
in inter-disciplinary seminars like 'Talking about the City', held in Helsinki
in 2000–01 and organized by the Museum of Finnish Architecture.[19]

Steel offers an interesting parallel here to the Futuro story. Although
the use of unprotected steel in supporting structures was generally pre-
vented in Finland by very strict fire safety norms, its use has grown. The
Valio practice attempted to get round such restrictions. In the pioneering cheese factory in Vaarala (1968–72) the supporting steel trusses were
located outside to suspend the roof. Thermal insulation was used as fire
protection between the construction and the inner fire load – arguably
the first use of exterior steel construction in Finland.[20] Visible in international publications resonating with the use of steel, suspended roof
structures and space frames in Europe, such buildings were not readily
'marketed' at the time as part of Finland's image (at the beginning of the
1990s, the market share of steel in office buildings in Finland was about
15 per cent. A decade on that figure is approaching 35 per cent and likely

Valio Practice,
Valio Cheese Factory,
Vaarala, 1968–72.

to rise; in Britain, the same figure approaches 60 per cent). Globalization, an undifferentiated market economy and recent architectural fashion have altered all this.

Besides the pioneering work of the Valio Practice under Matti K. Mäkinen, however, two other buildings bracketed by almost thirty years may help us to understand how this new 'industrial' imaging now frames contemporary Finland's approach to Modernism. A building like Hotel Rosendahl in Tampere by Jaakko Laapotti (1974) was at first considered rather un-Finnish. In relation to the more expressive Modernism and the small-scale modular experiments that had come out of the 1960s, the high-tech was, at the time, considered clumsily 'sterile'. This was not a building published as 'Finnish architecture'. Yet, set this building against one of the iconic buildings of the last few years, the Sanoma House in Helsinki by Jan Söderlund and Antti-Matti Siikala (1999), and we observe similarities. Almost thirty years apart, both buildings appropriated and refined some of the latest technological innovations available abroad. Both are a singular application of a refined tectonics, and both buildings affected the urban context in no small way by breaking convention in their urban siting and setting. The heaviness and robustness of the former building is only emphasized by the double glass façade and the lighter filigree structure of the Sanoma Building. The urbanism represented by both buildings was one redefined by fashion and taste. Both architects believe in the un-talkative, un-analysed product.

The Sanoma Building is designed as a cross-programmed 'mall' to house the nation's largest media operation and newspaper (*Helsingin Sanomat*), a series of shops plus an art gallery and several cafés. It is the ambience, scale and vacancy of the airport brought into the centre of the city. When the Sanoma Building appeared to dwarf in scale the Kiasma Museum, Finland claimed to have an international building. Once more this can be interpreted as a misreading of the theatre of world architec-

Jaakko Laapotti,
Hotel Rosendahl,
Tampere, 1974.

tural images, which are now available to any architectural office anywhere. Although there are many precursors to the double glass façade
(such as Jean Nouvel's Cartier Foundation in Paris), these large steel and
glass buildings have significantly altered the scale and urban image of
Helsinki over the last few years. The differences and nuances between
the works, say, of Pekka Salminen in Helsinki Vantaa Airport (1999) and
Heikkinen's and Komonen's Rovaniemi Airport (1992), would repay
study, as would a serious critique of the way steel is used in a building,
say by Olli-Pekka Jokela in relation to a work by the architects of Ark
House. Suggesting these new institutional and corporate images may fall
short of more exuberant international models does not, however, diminish their invention. In fact, it serves to support the thesis that Finnish
architecture is best when it resists the excess of the original models and
can arrive at a local poetics all its own.

With many more of these *memes* already built nearby and with many
more to come, it is likely that some version of this steel and glass
architecture will play an increased role in the future. More and more

buildings will replicate each other and provide a model for versions in other cities and towns through the effective competition practice still used in Finland.

We have seen how Finnish architecture generally operates, adapting foreign trends and ideas, refining them for their own native idiom. The situation is no different in the new millennium. As Finland progresses it looks as if the Finns may have succeeded and used the modern agenda like no other country. This might be a triumph not easily accepted or quite recognized in the present environment of new urbanism and trans-programmed architectures. But the question remains now as it was in 1904, 1929 or 1956: why and to what extent do these contemporary buildings that are now published represent Finnish Modernism and what relationship do they have with modern architecture? And what can we identify as part of the psychological make-up of Finnish Modernism? Do current buildings bring a fresh intelligence to an architectural style that might be more robust internationally? Or does the new architecture imply an alteration of a known and comfortable order, one that will always have the critical support of the profession and the legacy of past achievement, a version of modern architecture historicized to support a nationalistic urge?

How have architects taken on trend and innovation? It is worth briefly mentioning the work and direction over 30 years of the architects Kaarina Loftsröm, Antti Katajamäki and Matti K. Mäkinen. There is little doubt that, during the 1980s, few had as much power and influence in the building sector as Mäkinen, whose work at the Valio has already been cited. In his capacity as Director of the National Board of Public Building, it is to his credit that many buildings that are now recognized from the 1980s and early '90s were part of a singular and strong-willed desire to steer the national building policy towards high-quality architecture. Loftsröm has been responsible for two of the strongest 'high-tech' image buildings of the 1990s, Innopoli in Espoo (1991) and the Bio Technology Centre in Viikki (1996). The Valio buildings carried out by Mäkinen and Antti Katajamäki in Vaarala (1972) and Jyväskylä (1980) are certainly the solid base from which Katajamäki went on to produce one of his best works, the Oulu Dairy (1983), Futurium Housing (1988) and many more relatively ignored projects.[21] More is likely to come from such divergent talent.

Recognizing that simple honesty is not always as simple as it looks, Mäkinen himself has remained acute to the development in technology and its confusing ambiguities in relation to the modern agenda. Through writing he continually and consistently challenges the architect's profession to understand their own choices, directions and the

Kaarina Loftström,
Innopoli, Espoo, 1991.

fashions involved, even in steel itself. In his favour, like many of the older generation of architects, he believes that changes will produce the right direction.[22]

Like boxers in the ring, these three architects have bobbed, ducked, danced, jabbed, punched and counter-punched. But the sport has remained unchanged; consensus strangely mutes. Established architects have, of course, been able to revise their revolutionary dogma and compete in the corporate boom of the last ten years. Rapidly though, they demonstrated the need to be able to design and build structures to suit a corporate investment culture. Reputed architectural practices headed by two of the signatories to the Finnish Architectural Museum manifesto of 1980, Jan Söderlund (Sarc Achitects) and Pekka Helin (Helin &

Co.), were to become, by the turn of the twenty-first century, two of the largest architectural practices in the late capitalist exercise. Mostly a polished technological rhetoric, a hard transparent aesthetic and applied control of form and finish once more show culture taking control over nature and a conservative logic disguised by international 'memes'. The Nokia Corporation complex, various buildings by Helin and Siitonen, have altered the western approach to Helsinki, while the Media Sanomat Group's Sanoma Building and other buildings by Sarc have helped to restructure prized urban sites into poetic wastelands.

But if all this talk of a revitalized Modernism and a New Internationalism is accurate then we return to the one firm, Heikkinen and Komonen, that has not only been at the cutting edge of this style in Finland, but has expressed a practical and un-theoretic inventiveness to take it further. Beginning in the early 1980s with an appropriated Deconstruction repertoire (punched-out windows, slanted angles, slopes, ramps and shifted axes), their work has refined to include a complexity that is both tectonically inventive and a promise of new programming within architecture. In a range of well-controlled works their minimalism is as refined and mediated as the choice of material and client, but the later work shows spaces relying on more subtlety, more invention. The control of the architect is evident; naivety meets opportunism and clears away sentiment. But sentiment remains, as the lobbying for new work constructs new legends, new validities. As Petra Ceferin concludes her own study of the self-reflexive way in which the Finns have set up expectations of their own architecture, this is the firm that announces on their website: 'We are Finns . . . we just want to make good architecture.'[23]

To bring ourselves up to date, as much as we can remain so, an indication of the range within contemporary Finnish architecture and its contract with Modernism might begin today with the Black House, Villa Sälteskär, in Inkoo (2000) by Minna Lukander and end with the digital creations and fusion of the group Ocean North, the project '60 Minutes' by Casagrande & Rintala for the Venice Architecture Biennale of 2000 and the first-prize project awarded to Jyrki Tasa in March 2004 for a new housing development, Mastokatu, in the Katajanokka district of Helsinki.[24] Everything in between seems to repeat itself; it bobs, ducks, dances, jabs, punches and counter-punches. Although this would and does demonstrate a wide, plural range of work going on, it does actually distort the legacy of Modernism that still takes a hold on the profession.

To make good architecture is not, of course, and has never been, the only action architects take on. A 'legacy' goes backwards as well as forwards. It can also imply a programmatic hold on the present by the past.

Jyrki Tasa, Mastokatu Housing, Katajanokka, Helsinki, competition winning project, 2004.

History is only scantily studied and theory is all but historicized out of any existence, but this does not prevent the influence of strong figures like Ekelund and Bryggman making itself felt through current professors and researchers. Many of the younger architects now acknowledge work from the past century's Modernism in Finland while they seek similar 'timeless' and 'basic' solutions. This agenda echoes the 'eternity of land-scape' and essence-mythology propounded by the rationalists from the 1960s and '70s crossed with the 'natural' sense of the Nordic classicism from the 1920s. The tendency today is to fuse, to synthesize, the softer, humanistic qualities of Aalto with the classical modern spirit of Bryggman, Blomstedt and Revell. Not always regional, not always absolute, but somewhere in between new notions of planning suffer.

A balance, however, to the classical 'modernist' line of some of the larger contemporary civic projects might be achieved by scrutinizing more modest works. Here one senses in much of the unnoticed but highly competently skilled new architecture the subtext within the Ekelund-Blomstedt programme for Finnish architecture. It is a desire for an uninflected, utilitarian architecture that proves as economic and as attractive as some of the larger projects. It is too early to tell, but mention might be made of the 'young' work of architects such as Tuomas Silvennoinen (with his Centre for Orthodoxy and Nature project of 2000), Jenni Reuter (Straw Bale Cabin, in Sattmark, Parainen, West Finland, 1997–9) and Jari Tirkkonen ('Architect's Nest' – an experimental private house project, 2002).

Possibly the Dutch architects over the last decade have been instrumental in exporting their strengths and inviting wider agendas, but in many of the younger architects it is the rational line of Aulis Blomstedt and Aarno Ruusuvuori that has been fused with a softer, even playful materiality and tectonics seen internationally. Whether this suggests new ways of finessing architecture's constant mission, a revitalized but repressed 'nationalism', or is a re-tread of known patterns remains open to debate. Architects are still missionaries, although the task remains domestically scaled and the wider brief for architecture remains closed. In such a tense culture, the award of a competition to an appropriated Gehry assemblage or Libeskind diamond-tilt will momentarily shift the aesthetic paradigm but change little. There is evidence of smaller-scale, sensitive work on sustainability, and the ecological programming in some younger practices proves to lead naturally onto larger civic works, but to go by the Government Architecture Policy Programme, to house and shelter people in a quality environment, inside and out, still remains the mission.

There are faint signs of a counter-Modernism. The young architects educated in the 1990s were the first to have consistently travelled and explored foreign practices. Many have worked with internationally known practices and many have returned and, though struggling with new ideas and the instrumental strategies to get them accepted, things may be about to change. Jyrki Tasa, of all practising Finnish architects, could signal a serious turn in Finnish architecture; the nearest natural talent and natural stubbornness to Pietilä, his plasticity begins to display a control previously seen with the emerging Alvar Aalto. The two houses, Into (1998) and Moby Dick (2003), indicate deft plasticity and lightness crossed with surprising structural invention.

Meanwhile, professional strengths and loyalties continue. Architectural competitions have been important for young architects just as they were throughout the twentieth century. As diversity encourages innovation, as the past is continually negotiated, the lack of universal rules and fundamental truths proves irresistible. Post-humanism, post-ideology, post-theoretical ideas are all being discussed without any

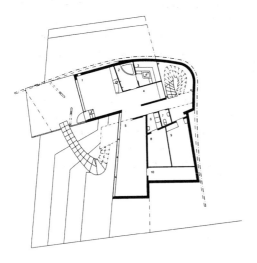

Jyrki Tasa, Moby Dick House, Espoo, 2003, plan.

clear critical direction. Bio-centric approaches combine with cyber-architectural ideas, but invariably the Finnish architect will return to the notion of social progress, shared responsibility, environmental concern and the emerging solidarity with the user and dweller. One young group (HKR) refers to this as post-humanism:

> Ecological thinking is – however – a uniting theme in all our work. Instead of being post-modern, we think of our work as post-humanist. This means that we want to challenge anthropocentric thinking and promote a bio-centric approach instead. We want to emphasize a shared human responsibility over environment and solidarity with nature. Furthermore we think architecture is not simply an activity restricted to the architect. It is as much an activity for those who enter, use and experience the built environment.

There is a stand-off at present, which perhaps echoes the indifference all over the world with the hubris of star architects and their warring ideologies. Coinciding as Finnish architecture now does with a branded, global internationalism, it might also be argued that the huge scale and careful narrow range of international trends have produced a neo-conservative architecture, versions, souvenirs even, of a brave but 'incomplete Modernism'. It is worth recalling Jurgen Habermas's words from his essay 'Modernity: An Incomplete Project':

> Neo-conservatism shifts onto cultural modernism the uncomfortable burdens of a more or less successful capitalist modernization of the economy and society. The neoconservative doctrine blurs the relationship between the welcomed process of societal modernization on the one hand, and the lamented cultural development on the other.[25]

The poet Risto Ahti offers us a vital clue to this incomplete Modernism in Finland in his poem 'Mistakes and Intimidations': 'Just fancy: somehow, through sheer daft youth, someone manages a mistake – and is schooled, intimidated, and shorn of error! But error's what we're looking for – error to shear perfection.' Schooled, intimidated and shorn of error: Synthetic Modernism? Finnish Modernism?

TEKNISKA FÖRENINGENS I FINLAND FÖRHANDLINGAR

ARKITEKTEN

TIDSKRIFT FÖR
ARKITEKTUR OCH
DEKORATIV KONST

ÅRGÅNG XXIII

MAJ
1903

arkkitehti

Julkaisija SUOMEN ARKKITEHTILIITTO (SAFA)

8

SISÄLTÖ:

Tuleva vaihdinvaihto

Kuukausipää
Arkkitehti Väinö Vähäkallio

1936   TOIMITUS: YRJÖ LAINE   TOIMITUSKUNTA: HILDING EKELUND
KAJ YNGLUND · N. E. WICKBERG   CAROLUS LINDBERG · ANTERO PERNAJA

arkkitehti
ark
7·1977
Asuminen
ja
Arava

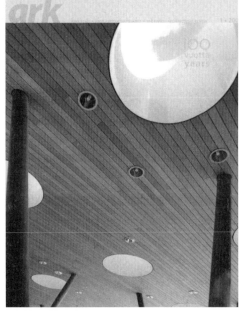

ark

100
vuotta
years

Epilogue

History and the Shape
of Modernism

Some day every pleasure dome turns into
    an underground dungeon, dawn
        casts on the french chalk
the shadow of a grill.
    This time the make-up won't wash off,
and for the last waltz you must always
        bring your own shackles . . . over the congealed
wine-puddles, the broken glass, the torn-up
                visiting cards
    the counts and viscounts you met in the evening
have lost their estates by morning.
Arto Melleri, 'After the Ball'[1]

In 2003 *Arkkitehti*, the Finnish Architectural Review, celebrated 100 years
of existence with a centenary issue. A symbolic starting point was imagined in the profession. Everywhere people were taking stock. Perhaps a
re-evaluation of Finnish architecture was possible. In a closing essay, an
influential figure from the 1980s (as Director of the National Board of
Public Building), Matti K. Mäkinen, scripted the situation as he saw it,
after the ball: 'ageing maestros sell neo-functionalism for housing production and international glass boxes for the business life, while the
younger generation create a more course-grained small-scale architecture.' This is more remarkable in the way that Mäkinen is talking of his
colleagues from the 1960s and '70s. In many ways, he is taking on the
'Finnish atmosphere' – the unspoken closed profession that still dictates
attitudes, positions and history. 'The mantra of our time', he continues,
'is the trinity of economy, growth and competitiveness.' Have we not
met this trinity before – Marx, Modernism and Materialism – a mantra
already identified?

    Ageing maestros and the young; the debate is muted, history distort-
ed. More similar civic courage is necessary to effect serious debate and
change. In another essay from the same issue when surveying the activist
years, Aino Niskanen ended with what we now see as obvious. She noted
how, after the turbulence and rudeness of the 1960s and '70s, a consensus

Arkitekten/Arkkitehti
covers from 1903 to
2003.

took over debate in the Finnish architectural profession. 'When and why', she concluded, 'did we become so polite – or silent?' Again we see how this can distort the history of exchange and ideas and the combat for the agenda within Finnish architecture – the profession is no more polite than it ever was, or silent. Consensus did not emerge after the 1960s and '70s but formed over the course of the twentieth century; it is no privilege of the post-activist years. But consensus always encourages quietism. In political and professional circles it implies the existence of those who speak for others, and results in a loss of civic courage. This is emphasized by the closing words of Mäkinen, who resorts once more to the words of Pallasmaa, uttered some years back: 'In the time of global placelessness and virtual space, Juhani Pallasmaa continues his phenom-enological observations about the thematics of the "home"':

> I might be unjustifiably nostalgic but I'm still of the opinion that architecture can be conciliatory; it can enable a 'homecoming'. Architecture can still create buildings in which we can live with dignity. And we still need buildings which strengthen our view of human reality and the essential hierarchies of life.[2]

Is it really so puzzling why the words of one commentator keep re-appearing as they reinforce the very expectations required from the legend? Has not the profession left itself open to the very control of individual figures? This obeys the logic of self-censorship that sets up 'authority' to act and speak on behalf of others. It operates by loyalty and obedience. It requires a lack of courage. The Museum of Finnish Architecture itself instigated a self-perpetuating promotional process; the current profession echoes the same mechanics. Dignity, strength, human reality, the essential hierarchies, life and the conciliatory gesture: do not Ekelund, Bryggman and Aulis Blomstedt also come readily to mind?

Agendas shift, the shape of modernizing re-forms, and the modern alters its own ideology to survive. The history of Modernism and the Modern Movement in relation to the Finnish architectural profession is also a mapping of the way authority has shifted, programmes altered and architecture gradually developed into a culturally constructed and socially marketable product. Eccentricity is marginalized, wilder pro-grammes are invariably tamed. The normative is suggested, often subtly, and is guided by the power of institution, museum or university. Modern-ism has inspired both critical thrill and considerable ambiguity through-out the world. Its trauma, trace and nostalgia are surely not over yet. Its beginnings are, of course, traceable further back than the inventions and revolutionary moves of the early twentieth century. But ultimately within the words of Pallasmaa lies the strategy of retreat again, echoing a constant recourse to defending the society from the dread or even fear of an invasion. It also retreats from the advances that a changing and challenging brief for contemporary architecture may bring.

Longing for respite from competitive trends does not, however, remove the competition or the trend. The extent to which Finland was seduced by the agenda of Modernism that was embedded in a selected interpretation of the Modern Movement and resisted other excesses has formed the core of this book. For the first 60 years of the twentieth century, a progressive and relatively open modern tune played out in all branches of the culture. In the 1960s 'ecology' became important, along with the first rockets and space-walks on the moon. An awareness of over-population strengthened environmental fears and ecological scenarios. New technology offered others besides architects hope. In the 1970s (possibly dated more accurately to 1967) something international broke the national – the student protest movement. Suddenly, Finland's previous Modernism to some was bogus. The rest is not, as they say, history; it is yet one more narrative.

How far a retooled Modernism remains a suitable vehicle for latent, 'national' identity building remains a question for the profession. The public do not read it so unequivocally. Open and plural the society claims to have become post-1989, but the patterns and aesthetic formalism remain much the same; the paradigm has hardly shifted. Tradition and the modern are now usefully re-scripted and blurred by visiting critics to become the inevitable, fitting agenda for Finland. Meeting the expectations cleverly scripted in advance, this defiantly reinforces the profession's confusion. How long the younger architects will tolerate this conservatism and continuity in myth-making remains also unclear.[3]

This study has also focused on the shadow figures in order to understand how those architects who have not always produced identifiable and conformed œuvres have influenced the shape of Modernism, as much as those whose works have consistently come to the attention of the public both within Finland and beyond. It would be churlish to suggest that the construction of Finnish architecture as legend has only proceeded by marginalizing diverse talents or the shadow-figures we have outlined. Although there is some truth in this, it is never as simple as that. If this study's observations on the unchanging patterns and politics within architecture are anywhere near accurate, things will go on much the same.

Few countries have seen the potential in an architecture set out and defined by the pioneers of the twentieth century and yet been able to co-opt, adapt and refine their own architecture and social objectives to respond to such vision. In this there is no doubting the contribution made by Finnish architecture. Perhaps the luck is coincidence: much of the society had to be developed during the modern century – there really was no choice. Yet the society has made real progress. To those who have lived through the twentieth century, today's Finland in many ways is unrecognizable. In other ways, not a lot has changed. Some cultures succumb to outside pressures, other cultures succumb less; some resist the trends, others reanimate their own lives through these trends.

When asked about Alvar Aalto's immense influence in Finnish architecture, Reima Pietilä used to tell a story about Aalto as a huge tree. The rule of metaphor followed clearly. No one visited that part of the forest. The shadow cast by the huge tree was too dense, the darkness impenetrable. Arrows were fired into the shadow, but the riders, hunters, gatherers and forest-goers never risked proximity. Instead, they baited from afar. On the death of Aalto suddenly the enormous tree was felled. There was a huge clearing. Those who had been comforted in the shadow and silence of the 'master'– those firing arrows into the unknown – suddenly found the sun blazing on their heads. The shadow was gone, the forest open. A silence followed. Initially there was dancing in the architectural offices. Momentarily few grieved, but only momentarily. The gatherers could re-group. History and individuals realigned themselves, opportunities shifted ground; the legend could be reconstructed.

Introducing a more recent critical study of the continuity within Finnish Modernism, Kenneth Frampton identified just that approach: 'the principal heuristic device has been to establish the figure of Alvar Aalto against the general ground of Finnish practice, with the aim of illuminating both figure and ground; first one and then the other, in a kind of alternating critical dialectic.'[4] This coincides with the critical coherence given at the end of the century on Aalto's centenary. The neatness of tying this all up as a 'synthetic Modernism' tends once again to distort the creativity, contradictions and the ambiguities noticed throughout the century. Each committee, institute, jury, governing board and professional colloquy has struggled for its own voice and its own steering mechanisms. The more the twentieth century progressed, the more operative these shadows have become. In music, Sibelius still haunts the culture, though the new generation of composers such as Lindberg and Saariaho have pushed ahead in a remarkable way. In politics, the long reign of careful positioning and mediation practised by President Kekkonen is only now being researched and thus loosening its hold on all relations east of Helsinki and west of Moscow. To say that Finland has always sought the West to escape the density of its eastern neighbour is misleading. Eastern influences have constantly shaped Finland. But in architecture, Alvar Aalto became that shadow that needed stepping on, just as children do in that game where they try to kill each other by catching up with the shadow.

To sketch how Modernism entered the Finnish society, how it was received, restored and then returned, also invites a sketch of the political, social and cultural factors that accommodated this agenda. The political and social history of Modernism remains to be written, but suggestions have been offered; the serious interplay between cultures and ideas, and a history of mentalities that entertain some ideas and not others, remains for the future. But there is little doubting that the larger figure in the twentieth century in Finnish architecture, despite the influence of Mies van der Rohe or Frank Lloyd Wight, has to be Le Corbusier. Up to the late 1950s Le Corbusier's works, books and ideas were constantly monitored, studied and used to shape not only the modern architect's response to modern architecture but the response to society itself. Only in 1956 in Dubrovnik at the CIAM / Team X congress did Le Corbusier begin to hand over control to the next generation. Enter Modernism's other partners, albeit belated in Finland, materialism and Marxism.

Let us remember the Low Temperature Laboratory at Helsinki University is known globally for its work on low temperature physics, while it is the Gulf Stream that keeps the climate milder than one thinks. Nokia today is the world's leading mobile phone supplier, and supplier of mobile and fixed telecom networks. Maintaining a competitive edge has ensured Finns a high-wage, social welfare society, and the country is proud of its ever-increasing gadgetry. Need we distance all this with claims for originality and the critical games and myths that describe things as 'unmistakably Finnish' or 'absolutely original'? Does not our narrative suggest a brighter, more generous understanding of the transfer of ideas; a generosity too that may prove more significant and less divisive in this century than the last?

As in Elias Lönnrot's folk poem from the nineteenth century, the new movement came from elsewhere, 'the dance was not led by me, nor by my partner here: no, the dance was brought from abroad, the caper led from yonder – the White Sea of Archangel, the deep straits of Germany.'[5] The *caper* – what a good term for Modernism and its eternal promises – was brought from even further, from beyond that great Finnish town lost in the Second World War, Viipuri. Beyond even that, beyond possibly Novgorod itself, somewhere far off towards Byzantium. Does this not confirm our initial suggestion at the start of this book that history is a contemporary, unfinished narrative that must engage the very history it looks back on?

This may not proceed quite as imagined. An 'unfinished' Modernism may offer a permanent exercise in nation building and tradition while needing to invent new strategies for borrowed, altered and transformed ideas of architecture. Stability may then depend on the ability to adjust the very stimulus and seduction that comes from external trends and challenges. The corollary, however, must be considered. Without transformation and change, what will become of this 'tradition', this birthright of Modernism? What might happen if external threats are tamed and undermine the cohesion of this national response? Would this imply fake encounters with an outdated modern code? And if Modernism is now considered a tradition, the birthright of the nation, can it still set itself up as a constant attempt to live in a truth and use architecture to go some way towards attaining that truth?

To speak of the modern is both infuriating in its desire to be defined and liberating in a desire to see our own time as consistently and continuously modern. Probably Finland, more than any other nation, due to some instinctive and happy coincidence, still remains modern after all these years. And with the strength of its difference as a small, vibrant culture, with its inner spirit, its *sisu*, with its demand for order, its Hegelianism, with the defiance of a Paavo Ruotsalainen and the sentimentality and effectiveness of the *puukko*-knife, it may still remain open to the necessity of challenging the very repertoire of Modernism and its defiant tradition that it proved so consummate in mastering.

Yet a curious amnesia exists about the 'revolutionary' years in Finnish architecture, just as it does about the notion of a consensus. Certainly to express dissent and want change, to react against the stuffed-shirt mentality, is part of all movements. The young might have been immature in the 1960s, but is the sense of shame something to do with the thinness of ideas, the diagram of an architecture so easily imagined, so lightly held, but so little understood and studied? There is more seriousness in this period that has not been acknowledged or analysed. It was a short period, two or three years, when all careers and lives were put at risk. This is a matter of pride, not shame, and Finnish architectural history would gain immensely if its protagonists could openly explore their positions at this time.[6]

After the ball, after the banquet years, a 'political', 'architectural' correctness put an emphasis on legend, image and identity. There appears to be a prevailing puritan morality within Finnish architecture that, when threatened, often closes up to produce and defend a flawed version of its own history. It looks more likely that if this is indeed a neo-conservatism, it is one that represents a desire to impose strong, stubbornly local conditions of professionalism and pragmatism on trends and fashions that still insist on influencing the way architecture attempts to design and control lives. But architecture is always called to order by a request to move on. In the case of a small, proud, affluent country, communicating with people worldwide, the question is appropriate: is Finnish architecture really still 'modern' after all these years?

References

Introduction: Modern Architecture and the Shape of History

1   Paavo Haavikko, *The Winter Palace* (Talvipalatsi, 1958); trans. by A. Hollo in *Selected Poems* (London, 1974), p. 74.
2   For these and many more such facts, see Max Jakobson et al., *Facts about Finland* (Helsinki, 2000).
3   J. M. Richards, *An Introduction to Modern Architecture* (1940) (London, 1956), p. 9.
4   Two essential volumes that enable the reader to follow the architecture of Finland: *Arvi Ilonen, Helsinki, Espoo, Kauniainen, Vantaa: An Architectural Guide* (Helsinki, 2000), and J. Kaipia and Lauri Putkonen, *A Guide to Finnish Architecture* (Helsinki, 1997).
5   Matti Klinge, *A Brief History of Finland* (Helsinki, 1981), p. 7.
6   'In Switzerland a Swiss asked me all sorts of questions about Finland: Finns – of course – speak Russian; are there artists in Finland? and why on earth do Finns not want to be Russian, since the Poles, after all, have to be Germans? . . . In Florence someone asked me whether there were phonographs in Finland. – That is how it is: no one had heard of it, so it has not contributed anything to the cultivation of the spirit in the wider world.' Joel Lehtonen, cited in M. Niemi, 'In the Public Interest and for Private Gain', in *Matkalla! / En Route!: Finnish Architects' Studies Abroad*, ed. Timo Tuomi, exh. cat. Museum of Finnish Architecture (Helsinki, 1999).
7   For various texts through Aalto's life where he speaks of this, see Goran Schildt's writings, especially *Alvar Aalto in his Own Words* (Helsinki, 1997).
8   Max Jakobson, *Finland: Myth and Reality* (Helsinki, 1987), p. 13.
9   *Sisu* is that extra strength used to explain Finland's unusual achievements, especially for the size of the country. *Sisu* would be useful also as a parallel way to read Marjatta Bell and Marjatta Hietala, *Helsinki, the Innovative City: Historical Perspectives* (Helsinki, 2002), which charts innovation and know-how strategies back to the Finland of the nineteenth century and its unique autonomy under the Russian empire and into the future IT capital, post-Nokia. In all this the creative mythology within *sisu* should not be underestimated.
10 For more detail in relation to political and cultural history, see Klinge, *A Brief History of Finland*. An important historian, he has made accessible to foreigners a rather complex history offering a political and cultural shape.
11 See the work of Minna Canth, Juhani Aho and Teuvo Pakkala.
12 Song-like, sensuous, with its fair share of pathos and didacticism, Leino tried to combine the archaic while reacting rapidly to contemporary social, political and ideological questions.
13 For example, those marketed by the firm Marttiini Ltd, Rovaniemi.
14 Raymond Williams, from *Keywords* (London, 1976), p. 174.
15 'Il apparait aussi humble qu'est modeste la place occupée sur la carte universelle par

le pays qu'il represent. Mais il essaye de donner le mieux possible une idée du carac-
tère distinctif du peuple de Finland'. A. Edelfelt et al., *Le Pavillon finlandais*, exh. cat.,
Paris World Fair 1900 (Helsingfors, 1900), p. 11, trans. from the French by the author.

16 Other important painters from the time were Magnus Enckell, Ellen Thesleff,
Hugo Simberg, Juho Rissanen and Pekka Halonen.

17 See Markku Valkonen, 'Gallen-Kallela', in *Finland: A Cultural Encyclopaedia*, ed.
Olli Alho (Helsinki, 1997), pp. 125–6. For the art of this period in more detail, see
John Boulton Smith, *The Golden Age of Finnish Art* (Helsinki, 1985), and for a
Scandinavian perspective, see The Arts Council of Great Britain, *Dreams of a
Summer Night: Scandinavian Painting at the Turn of the Century*, exh. cat.,
Hayward Gallery (London, 1986).

18 Klinge, *A Brief History of Finland*, p. 91.

19 Louis Sparre (1863–1964) was a Swedish nobleman, close friend of Gallen Kallela
and well-linked to the British Arts and Crafts movement. For a more detailed
account of this collaboration, see J. M. Richards, *800 Years of Finnish Architecture*
(London, 1978).

20 Ibid.

21 The exhibition text just stops short of describing the Pavilion as brilliant imitation:
'mais bien sur, c'était un joli symbole de la lumière' ('but of course, it was a pleasant
symbol of the light'). Taken from my *Sa(l)vaged Modernism* (Helsinki, 2000).

chapter one: Pioneering Finnish Modernism

1 Mrs Tweedie completes her sentence: 'but, – and oh it is a very big BUT indeed,
there exists a Finnish pest'. Mrs Alec Tweedie, *Through Finland in Carts* (1897)
(London, 1913), p. 60.

2 For more on this, see Matti Klinge, *A Brief History of Finland* (Helsinki, 1981),
pp. 75–7.

3 For more, see Olli Alho, ed., *Finland: A Cultural Encyclopaedia* (Helsinki, 1997).

4 The Trade Exhibition of 1889 in Paris, with representatives from Finland. Advertising
Poster, in Max Jakobson et al., *Facts about Finland* (Helsinki, 2000), p. 8.

5 Marjatta Bell and Marjatta Hietala, *Helsinki, the Innovative City: Historical
Perspectives* (Helsinki, 2002), pp. 77–9.

6 I have used Klinge, *A Brief History of Finland*, and Max Jakobson, *Finland: Myth
and Reality* (Helsinki, 1987), and others for this history; the shape of history may
be clear, although the emphasis varies depending on historian, discipline and era.

7 For more important background on this history, see the essays by Jarkko Sinisalo,
'Architects and Building Administration, 1810–65', and Eeva Maija Viijo, 'The
Architectural Profession in Finland in the Latter Half of the 19th Century', in
The Work of Architects, ed. Pekka Korvenmaa (Helsinki, 1992).

8 Bell and Hietala, *Helsinki*, is very useful for its catalogue and deep indexing of
such travels in administration since Finland's engineers, politicians, artists,
experts, teachers and other professional classes all increased their knowledge of
existing ideas and systems abroad.

9 Albert Edelfelt, 'The Decline and Rebirth of Decorative Taste' (1898), in *Vuosikirja
3 / Yearbook 3: Abacus, Museum of Finnish Architecture*, ed. A. Salokorpi (Helsinki,
1993), p. 29.

10 Ibid.

11 Heini Korpelainen, ed., *The Finnish Architectural Policy: The Finnish Government*

(Porvoo, 1999), p. 5.

12 For a more detailed survey of the history of the race, see Peter Hajdu, *Finno-Ugrian Languages and Peoples* (London, 1975).

13 This significantly at a time when Finnish architecture was to move into its more systematic and dogmatic mode, when any form of irrational, sculptural and nature-inspired architecture was blackballed. To continue this pattern and trace Karelia as a liminal zone, see the television documentary films of the architect Georg Grotenfelt, produced from the 1990s.

14 Teppo Korhonen, 'The Architecture of Eastern Karelia in the Eyes of the Finnish Intelligentsia', in *Matkalla! / En Route!: Finnish Architects' Studies Abroad*, exh. cat., Museum of Finnish Architecture (Helsinki, 1999), pp. 92–8.

15 Ibid., p. 92.

16 Commentators such as S. Giedion, J. M. Richards, Kenneth Frampton, Charles Jencks, Malcolm Quantrill, Colin St John Wilson, Scott Poole, Peter Davey and William Curtis would all seek in varying degrees 'something absolutely originally Finnish'.

17 Armas Lindgren remains important, although he has been in the shadow of Eliel Saarinen; Riitta Nikula's excellent exhibition catalogue monograph somewhat redresses the balance: *Armas Lindgren, 1974–1929*, exh. cat., Museum of Finnish Architecture (Helsinki, 1988).

18 One of the strongest and most thorough surveys of this period is Leena Ahtola-Moorhouse, Michael Carapetian and Jonathan Moorhouse, *Helsingin Jugendark-kitehtuuri, 1895–1915 / Helsinki Jugend Architecture, 1895–1915* (Helsinki, 1987).

19 See the entry 'Design' in *Finland: A Cultural Encyclopaedia*, ed. Alho, p. 70.

20 Only in the 1960s when the young militant-rationalists attacked Reima Pietilä (1923–1993) would we hear similar charges, recognize similar tension.

21 The seminal work on Saarinen's Finnish period is Marika Hausen et al., *Eliel Saarinen: Projects, 1896–1923* (Keuruu, 1990).

22 Sigurd Frosterus, 'London Rhapsody' (1903) in *The City as Art*, ed. Liam Kelly (Dublin, 1994); see also Kimmo Sarje, *Sigurd Frosterus* (Helsinki, 2000), an invaluable and long-awaited study on Frosterus's contribution to Finnish society, culture and architecture including his international activities (in Finnish only).

23 For a detailed look at this and how Finland adapted and sought foreign know-how to advance its own development and civic pride, see the interesting discussion, 'The City of Helsinki and the "Urban Question"', in Bell and Hietala, *Helsinki*, pp. 77–100.

24 This is well documented in the various references mentioned here.

25 'He will find a far more reliable point of departure in these engineering products than the Gothic or Renaissance in his endeavours to reflect the spirit of the age – it is there that he will find the seeds, the beginnings, from which his new, dreamt-of style may one day germinate.' Sigurd Frosterus, 'Architecture: A Challenge', and Gustaf Strengell, 'Some Observations on Present Conditions in our Architecture in View of the Railway Station Building Problem' (1904), in *Vuosikirja 3 / Yearbook 3: Abacus*, pp. 48–81.

26 See Marja-Rütta Norri and Wilfred Wang, *20th Century Architecture: Finland* (Helsinki and Frankfurt am Main, 2000), 'Urban Plan for Töölö', p. 150.

27 For more on Jung's revolutionary planning role, see Bell and Hietala, *Helsinki*, pp. 163–4.

28 See the various Helsinki plans and the developments in planning strategies as they reacted to sovereign, plot-defined singular building developments through-

out the century. See also 'Building the Jugendstil Metropolis', in Bell and Hietala, *Helsinki*, pp. 162–71.

29 Asko Salokorpi, *Modern Architecture in Finland* (London, 1970), p. 12. More recently and importantly, Asko Salokorpi, *Selim A. Lindqvist* (Jyväskylä, 2001).

30 In stylistic terms, the question is probably not whether Villa Ensi (1911) may be reminiscent of, or influenced by, Josef Hoffman's work, but whether the unmistakable Constructivist ideal later interpreted from this was that unmistakable!

31 Asko Salokorpi, *Modern Architecture in Finland* (London, 1970).

32 Again consult Ahtola-Moorhouse, Carapetian and Moorhouse, *Helsingin Jugendarkkitehtuuri*.

33 The change in the Helsinki Railway Station in a way directed Saarinen towards urban planning, designing projects for Budapest and Tallinn; in 1912 he received Second Prize for Canberra, which began his international career. The grand Munkkiniemi-Haaga plan (1915) implied a radical growth for Helsinki, which was developed further in 1918 with Bertel Jung in a general plan that developed into the Pro Helsingfors city design.

34 For more on Engel and Schinkel, see *Vuosikirja 3 / Yearbook 3: Abacus*, pp. 14–21.

35 Engel's reference world included Vitruvius and Alberti, just as today's architects often refer back to the 'antique repertoire' of Modernism: Le Corbusier and Mies van der Rohe.

36 Historians such as Ritva Wäre, however, are now revealing a much more studied attempt to follow what was going on at that time, and how influence and assimilation go hand in hand.

37 G. M. Trevelyan, cited in Malcolm Bradbury and James McFarlane, *The Name and Nature of Modernism* (London, 1976), p. 19.

chapter two: Independence: Rehearsals for Modernism

1 Edith Södergran, 'The Land That Is Not', in *Skating on the Sea: Poetry from Finland*, ed. and trans. Keith Bosley (Newcastle upon Tyne, 1997), p. 200.

2 The Social Democratic Party had previously split from the more revolutionary wing that had founded the Finnish Communist Party in 1918; the latter remained illegal until 1944; see Matti Klinge, *A Brief History of Finland* (Helsinki, 1981), pp. 103–6.

3 For more, see Klinge, *A Brief History of Finland*. Also on the legacy of the civil war, see Marjatta Bell and Marjatta Hietala, 'Helsinki Turns Finland into a Modern Society', in their *Helsinki, the Innovative City: Historical Perspectives* (Helsinki, 2002), pp. 173–215.

4 S. Frosterus in Marja-Rütta Norri and Wilfred Wang, *20th Century Architecture: Finland* (Helsinki and Frankfurt am Main, 2000), pp. 121–6.

5 Clearly there are others: Hilding Ekelund, Yrjö Lindegren, Jaakko Laapotti, Toivo Korhonen, Erkki Kairamo and so on to the present.

6 Timo Tuomi, Kristina Paatero and Eija Rauske, eds, *Hilding Ekelund, 1893–1984, Architect*, (Helsinki, 1997), in Finnish, Swedish and English.

7 On a visit to the church of the Eremitani in Padua in 1921, Ekelund wrote: 'Beautiful interior. Kodak in silent activity!' in *Hilding Ekelund, 1893–1984*. An excellent study with new research and critical writing; extract from Pekka Suhonen, 'Helsingin Taidehalli' (Helsinki, 1997), and *Extracts from Travel Diaries*, 27 October 1921 (p. 142).

8 Born in St Petersburg but fled to Finland in 1917, she wrote in German and Swedish, not Finnish.

9   See Pekka Helin's very useful essay 'Liveable Architecture' on Ekelund and housing, in *Hilding Ekelund, 1893–1984*, pp. 194–7.

10 For more detail on this whole issue the reader is referred to Raija-Liisa Heinonen, *Functionalismin Läpimurto Suomessa* [The Breakthrough of Functionalism in Finland] (Helsinki, 1986), an indispensable thesis but only in Finnish.

11 See the various references mentioned in this study for more details on this period, especially the research and texts of Riitta Nikula, Simo Paavilainen and Wilhelm Helander.

12 See Bell and Hietala, *Helsinki, the Innovative City*, for a detailed look at all such fact-finding missions and tours and the relevance of these discoveries to the development of Helsinki as a city, and the subsequent adaptation and dissemination to the whole country.

13 Mika Waltari, *Suuri Illusio* [The Grand Illusion] (Helsinki, 1928).

14 Predictable, probably given the pace of change and the shock with which the agrarian society had to face change, the national works of Sillanpää, Kilpi and Kallas were balanced somewhat by the suspicion and critical irony in the humorous short prose of Pentti Haanpää.

15 See the works of Edith Södergran, Elmer Diktonius and Gunnar Björling.

16 See Riitta Nikula, *Architecture and Landscape: The Building of Finland* (Helsinki, 1993), for an excellent narrative study and for further important details about this period.

17 See the various writings of the two influential figures, Riitta Nikula and Simo Paavilainen.

18 Susanne Salin, 'Nordic Classicism in Hilding Ekelund's Proposed Parliament Building', in *Hilding Ekelund, 1893–1984*, pp. 120–25. See Riitta Nikula's texts listed in the bibliography for a deeper analysis of these differences and her triple division of Nordic classicism.

19 Riitta Nikula: 'thus the leading architects of the capital left their imprint on the remote parts of Finland: the Classicist wooden buildings of the period are beautiful monuments to the ideal of universal education', in Norri and Wang, *20th Century Architecture*.

20 Bell and Hietala, 'Helsinki – a Children's Paradise', in their *Helsinki, the Innovative City*, pp. 175–83.

21 Asko Salokorpi, *Modern Architecture in Finland* (London, 1970), p. 32.

22 There is no doubt that Ekelund's article 'Italia La Bella' in *Arkitekten* (February 1923) was widely influential.

23 I am grateful for the small but timely survey of this and other work; see Timo Keinänen and Kristiina Paatero, eds, *Martti Välikangas, 1893–1973: Arkkitehti* (Helsinki, 1993).

24 For an equivalent journey we might have also considered the work of Väino Vähäkallio as he turned the 1920s into the 1930s with a new approach that trimmed a red-brick classicism into a functionalism to come. However, a welcome study will appear in the near future by Aino Niskanen.

25 Riitta Nikula, 'The Inter-War Period: The Architecture of the Young Republic', in Norri and Wang, *20th Century Architecture*, p. 44, also see Riitta Nikula, *Architecture and Landscape* (Helsinki, 1993), for a detailed and invaluable account of this period's building.

26 For Aalto on the Existenzminimum, see Goran Schildt, *Alvar Aalto in his Own Words* (Helsinki, 1997), pp. 76–8.

27 Salokorpi, *Modern Architecture in Finland*, p. 29.

28 In 1925 there had been the Hangon Keksi Fair, and another advertising fair in 1928, but 1929 appeared to signal the modern, functional change; see Bell and Hietala, 'On the Importance of Exhibitions', in their *Helsinki, the Innovative City*, pp. 211–15.

29 The list of successful competition architects is vast and the current system of open competitions within Finland and the Nordic countries, or Finland and the European Union, still provides a rare gift for each participant. See Pertti Solla, 'Architectural Competitions in Finland', in *The Work of Architects*, ed. Pekka Korvenmaa (Helsinki, 1992), pp. 268–81; see also my *40 Young Architects from Finland* (Helsinki, 2002), pp. 8–11.

chapter three: White Functionalism: The Modern Agenda

1 Arthur Honegger, 'Arvi Kivimaa', in *Skating on the Sea: Poetry from Finland*, ed. and trans. Keith Bosley (Newcastle upon Tyne, 1997), p. 213.

2 Ford Madox Ford, 'Return to Yesterday' (1923), in Malcolm Bradbury and James McFarlane, *The Name and Nature of Modernism* (London, 1976).

3 See Vilhelm Helander and Simo Rista, *Suomalainen Rakennustaide / Modern Architecture in Finland* (Helsinki, 1987), p. 20.

4 Deep structure and surface structure is a critical distinction in Generative Grammar. In the 1950s linguists postulated a theory of a deep, underlying structure for sentences where all factors determining structural interpretation are defined. Subsequently these are converted to surface structures. Transferred to architecture, briefly this implies an underlying structure for the varying surface architectures seen in Modernism. It is particularly useful in the Finnish context for its varying 'styles' within an underlying ideal, a deep structure. See 'Deep Structure' in *The New Fontana Dictionary of Modern Thought*, ed. A. Bullock and S. Trombley (London, 1999), p. 204.

5 Cited in Aski Salokorpi, *Modern Architecture in Finland* (London, 1970), p. 27.

6 See Raija-Liisa Heinonen, *Funktionalismin Läpimurto Suomessa* (Helsinki, 1986).

7 To follow this, see *Alvar Aalto: Between Humanism and Materialism*, exh. cat., Museum of Modern Art (New York, 1998).

8 There are new monographs appearing that begin to confirm just how intricate and at times homogeneous was the development of Modernism in the building of the new republic. For a survey of work by all these architects and the significance to the modern agenda, see Leena Makkonen, *Martta & Ragnar Ypyä* (Helsinki, 1998); T. Jeskanen and P. Leskelä, *Oiva Kallio* (Helsinki, 2000); and R. Nikula, 'The Inter-War Period: The Architecture of the Young Republic', in Marja-Riitta Norri and Wilfred Wang, *20th Century Architecture: Finland* (Helsinki and Frankfurt am Main, 2000).

9 See Göran Schildt, *Alvar Aalto: The Mature Years* (New York, 1991) for events around the 1940s and also for the 'rejection' of Aalto by Finnish architects, especially the agitprop antics of J. Pallasmaa and K. Mikkola in the late 1960s and early '70s. If the USA was suspicious of Finland and struggled to offer post-war support, similar suspicion would be countered against Aalto for his willingness to court the US. The events are confused, awaiting more serious research on Aalto's position and manoeuvrings at this time.

10 See Bruno Zevi, *The Modern Language of Architecture* (Seattle, WA, 1978), p. 198.

11 For a view of this attitude against Aalto, see Aulis Blomstedt's unpublished letter

from the 1940s describing Aalto's 'electric-eel architecture' in my *Grace & Architecture* (Helsinki, 1998).

12 I have discussed this aspect of the 'continuum' in Finnish architecture in my *40 Young Architects from Finland* (Helsinki, 2002).

13 See Vilhelm Helander and Simo Rista, *Suomalainen Rakennustaide / Modern Architecture in Finland* (Helsinki, 1987), p. 21.

14 Märta Blomstedt, Matti Lampen, Olavi Sortta – it is impossible to mention the many Finnish architects involved in this national functionalism. The likes of Aulis Blomstedt, Olli Pöyry, Kaj Englund, Erik Lindroos, Jorma Järvi, Hugo Harmia, Aarne Ervi and Woldemar Baeckman started before the war but carried out most of their works after it. See Kirmo Mikkola, Timo Keinanen and M.-R. Norri, eds, *Funkis: Suomi Nykyaikaa Etsimässä*, exh. cat., Museum of Finnish Architecture (Helsinki, 1981), and an invaluable book, *Arkkitehdiksi sodan varjossa* (Helsinki, 1994).

15 Salokorpi, *Modern Architecture in Finland*, p. 34.

16 According to R. Nikula's account in 'Architecture and Landscape' of Teppo Jokinen, *Erkki Huttunen, 1901–56: Arkkitehti* (Helsinki, 1993), p. 129. For a brief history of the consumer co-operative shops in Finland, see Marjatta Bell and Marjatta Hietala, 'The Co-operative Movement as Civil Resistance', in their *Helsinki, the Innovative City: Historical Perspectives* (Helsinki, 2002), pp. 160–62.

17 Slip-form: a process of sliding, timber shuttering designed to enable concrete to be poured 'continuously' to achieve greater heights and a more economic production.

18 See Jokinen, *Erkki Huttunen*, pp. 111–21.

19 It was renovated by Juhani Pallasmaa in 1995 as was the Glass Palace opposite in 1998, by Lukander and Ilonen; they were both faithful renovations, though somewhat lacking in contemporary interventions and vitality.

20 Bertel Saarnio would later employ and work with the young Juha Leiviskä on Kouvola Town Hall, thereby providing a direct link from the 1960s and '70s to the 1930s. Aulis Blomstedt would identify Leiviskä as an architect 'to watch'.

21 Aino and Alvar Aalto were to travel to the USA for the first time in autumn 1938.

22 I am indebted to the small, timely and delightful monograph by Jokinen, *Erkki Huttunen*, pp. 85–93, although interpretation and emphases are my own.

23 Huttunen is not alone in working this way; other Finnish architects do tend to follow this pattern. Väino Vähäkallio worked for the left-wing co-operative OTK, and after travelling to America discovered ideas that influenced his own factory designs and the 'cubic' countryside OTK shops.

24 However, it is possible that only Alvar Aalto and Matti K. Mäkinen have held such influential positions in the profession after Huttunen; Aalto was for a long time head of the profession and Mäkinen himself was Director of the National Board of Public Building throughout the important civic rebuilding period of the 1980s. During its existence, 1809–1995, the National Board of Public Building (Rakennushallitus) had three of their nineteen directors emerging from the large co-operatives: Vähäkallio from OTK, Huttunen from SOK and Mäkinen from Valio, the dairy co-operative. Not only chief architects, these figures were responsible for all administration, logistics, biddings, contracts, appointments, etc., necessary for national-scale building programmes. In this they resemble the 'supreme builder'; especially essential for the National Board of Public Building and its plan for government and state-subsidized buildings (like the later Heureka Science Centre, 1984, and Kiasma Museum, 1995). See Matti K. Mäkinen's personal and provocative narrative of this history in *Missio* (Helsinki, 2002). Charles

Bassi and C. L. Engel also headed this organization in its Russian empire days. The parallels in terms of power and influence are not as ridiculous as some Finns like to make out.

25 See the volumes *Matkalla! /En Route!: Finnish Architects' Studies Abroad*, exh. cat., Museum of Finnish Architecture (Helsinki 1999), and Norri and Wang, *20th Century Architecture,* for details of study trips, journals and publications.

26 Artek in *Finland: A Cultural Encyclopaedia*, ed. Olli Alho (Helsinki, 1997), p. 29.

27 See Erik Kruskopf, *Suomen taideteollisuus, Suomalaisen muotoilun vaiheita* (Helsinki, 1989), for an important general history of Finnish design (in Finnish and Swedish); also John Boulton Smith, *Modern Finnish Painting and Graphic Art* (London, 1970); Göran Schildt, *Modern Finnish Sculpture* (London, 1970).

28 If so, we might try to uncover those presuppositions in the lives of our ancient or medieval ancestors and perhaps build on this basis a 'history of mentalities' as opposed to the 'history of ideas'; Leszek Kolakowski, *Modernity on Endless Trial* (Chicago, 1997), p. 3.

29 Cited in Vilhelm Helander and Simo Rista, *Suomalainen Rakennustaide / Modern Architecture in Finland* (Helsinki, 1987), p. 21.

30 See P. E. Blomstedt, 'Architectonic Anaemia', in Norri and Wang, *20th Century Architecture*, pp. 128–31.

31 Pauli E. Blomstedt, like those early travelling, predominantly Swedish-speaking, Finnish architects, would remain in 'radical' touch with the changing and challenging international pulse. For more on P. E. Blomstedt, see my *Grace & Architecture* (Helsinki, 1998), and Elina Standertskjöld, *P. E. Blomstedt, 1900–1935: Arkkitehti* (Helsinki, 1996).

chapter four: War: Standardization and Solidarity

1 Bo Carpelan (born 1926), from 'In Dark, in Light Rooms' in *Skating on the Sea: Poetry from Finland*, ed. and trans. Keith Bosley (Newcastle upon Tyne, 1997), p. 223.

2 Henry Bell, *Land of Lakes* (London, 1950), p. 95.

3 See Max Jakobson, *Finland: Myth and Reality* (Helsinki, 1987), and Matti Klinge, *A Brief History of Finland* (Helsinki, 1981), for versions of this period.

4 See Jakobson, *Finland*, pp. 29–36, for an accessible account of both the reality and the myth of these events.

5 For a general view of this period with other figures, see Seppo Zetterberg, 'Finland through the Centuries', in Max Jakobsen et al., *Facts about Finland* (Helsinki, 2000), pp. 45–56.

6 Paul Dukes, 'Foreword', in Bell, *Land of Lakes*, p. 11.

7 See Nils Erik Wickberg, *Ajatuksia Arkkitehtuurista* (Helsinki, 1946), for the main debates during the 1940s including Le Corbusier, Nature-Romance; Aalto-Wright; Japan; Symmetry; Functionalism; Le Corbusier-Palladio; Le Corbusier's letter to students and the important concluding essay, 'Barokki ja Nykyaika' [Baroque and the Contemporary] – Wickberg's analysis of the dynamics of the Baroque would also be important for the emerging debate about Aalto's later 'monumental' works since they would be rejected by the Rationalists.

8 Vilhelm Helander and Simo Rista, *Suomalainen Rakennustaide / Modern Architecture in Finland* (Helsinki, 1987), p. 186.

9 J. M. Richards would sketch out this agenda in his pioneering volume *An Introduction to Modern Architecture* (London, 1956); also see Nils Erik Wickberg,

Ajatuksia Arkkitehtuurista / Thoughts on Architecture (Helsinki, 1946).

10 See Karl-Erik Michelson, 'The Finnish Building Information File', and Erkki Helamaa, 'Building Finland Housing, 1940–80', both in an invaluable collection of essays, *The Work of Architects*, ed. Pekka Korvenmaa (Helsinki, 1992). Also see the important catalogue, Erkki Helamaa, *40-luku korsujen ja jälleenrakentamisen vuosikymmen* [1940s: The Decade of the Dugout and Reconstruction], exh. cat., Museum of Finnish Architecture and The Alvar Aalto Museum (Helsinki, 1983), with an English summary.

11 See Liisa Häyrynen, 'Architects Look Back: The Experienced History of the Architectural Profession', in *The Work of Architects*, pp. 233–53; an unusual research using a historical psychology model (MacKinnon) with more recent theories like the 'intellectual field' from Pierre Bourdieu. 'The 1940s has been experienced variously as sensitivity and honesty, a soft functionalism or a soft romanticism.' Further research indicates that even the term 'romanticism had negative, positive, and neutral meanings'.

12 Viipuri Railway Station (Eliel Saarinen) would be rebuilt after the war in Stalinist classicism. See also the Viipuri Art Museum by Uno Ullberg.

13 Pekka Korvenmaa, 'Destruction, Scarcity and a New Rise', in *Finnish Architecture in the 1940s* (Helsinki and Frankfurt am Main, 2000). I owe my information to this and other texts in English by Korvenmaa, which are invaluable in interpreting this liminal decade and its importance in understanding the shape of Finnish Modernism.

14 Elsi Borg also did the Helsinki garrison buildings in Töölö in a refined, stripped-down Functional style.

15 For more on Elsi Borg, see Maarit Henttonen, *Elsi Borg, 1893–1958: Arkkitehti* (Helsinki, 1995), with an English summary.

16 The soft romanticism of the Children's Castle has become to some a 'terrible romanticism'. See also Häyrynen, 'Architects Look Back', p. 241.

17 Pekka Korvenmaa, 'Destruction, Scarcity and a New Rise', in Marja-Rütta Norri and Wilfred Wang, *20th Century Architecture: Finland* (Helsinki and Frankfurt am Main, 2000), pp. 71–82.

18 See the forthcoming intellectual biography of Aalto, by Eeva-Liisa Pelkonen.

19 For more detail, see Karl-Erik Michelson, 'The Finnish Building Information File', in *The Work of Architects*, pp. 129–37.

20 Known as the (post-war) *Rintamamiestalo* (Front-soldier-house), examples emerged later in districts like Maununneva, Pakila and other (now) older 'semi'-urban areas of Helsinki.

21 Häyrynen, 'Architects Look Back', p. 239.

22 For more on Tapiola and its organization, its housing association, the role of Heikki von Hertzen, etc., see Marjatta Bell and Marjatta Hietala, *Helsinki, the Innovative City: Historical Perspectives* (Helsinki, 2002), and the Tima Tuomi, ed., *Tapiola: Life and Architecture* (Helsinki, 2003), as well as www. weegee/tapiola50 for a new history of the project.

23 See Renja Suominen-Kokkonen, 'Women Architects: Training, Professional Life and Roles', in *The Work of Architects*, pp. 72–89, especially the bibliography. Finnish women were the first European women to be given the vote, in 1906.

24 Wickberg's editorships: 1946–9, 1952–6 and 1958–9.

25 Korvenmaa, 'Destruction', p. 78.

26 The importance of this decade is also confirmed by a most interesting series of interviews from architects and students who were around during the 1940s: Asko

Salokorpi, *Arkkitehdiksi Sodan Varjossa* (Rakennustieto, 1994). Names often left out of Finnish histories but significant later in the profession would be: Elissa Aalto, Ola Hansson, Jonas Cedercreutz, Lars Hedman, Osmo Lappo, Veli Paatela, Erkki Koiso-Kanttila; see Salokorpi for these and others.

27 See Göran Schildt, ed., *Alvar Aalto in his Own Words* (Helsinki, 1997), for a number of such texts around the 1940s and '50s. Also see my *Aaltomania* (Helsinki, 2001) and *Grace & Architecture* (Helsinki, 1998) for more on Aalto's warnings.

28 Korvenmaa, 'War Destroys', in *The Work of Architects*, pp. 114–18.

29 For this 'memetic' process, see Susan Blackmore, *The Meme Machine* (Oxford, 1999), and Nikos A. Salingaros and Terry Mikiten, *Darwinian Processes in Architecture: Datutop 23* (Tampere, 2003).

30 Korvenmaa, 'War Destroys', p. 126.

31 See Erkki Mäkiö, 'Changes in Building Techniques', in *Heroism and the Everyday: Building Finland in the 1950s*, ed. Riitta Nikula, exh. cat., Museum of Finnish Architecture (Helsinki, 1994), pp. 57–64.

chapter five: Expressive Modernism: The Banquet Years

1 Paavo Haavikko, *The Winter Palace* (Talvipalatsi, 1959) from 'The Fourth Poem' in *Contemporary Finnish Poetry*, ed. Herbert Lomas (Newcastle upon Tyne, 1991), p. 124.

2 Matti Klinge, *A Brief History of Finland* (Helsinki, 1981), p. 157.

3 For more in depth on this era, see Sirkkaliisa Jetsonen, 'Humane Rationalism', in Marja-Rütta Norri and Wilfred Wang, *20th Century Architecture: Finland* (Helsinki and Frankfurt am Main, 2000), pp. 83–97.

4 See the survey of the range of public buildings in Sirkka-Liisa Jetsonen, 'Realism or Dreams? Public Building in the 1950s', in *Heroism and the Everyday: Building Finland in the 1950s*, ed. Riitta Nikula, exh. cat., Museum of Finnish Architecture (Helsinki, 1994), pp. 35–56. This is an impressive volume in English and Finnish with an unusual range of essays.

5 Henry Bell, *Land of Lakes* (London, 1950), p. 42.

6 See L. Häyrynen for the 'image' of this era, in 'Architects Look Back: The Experienced History of the Architectural Profession', in *The Work of Architects*, ed. Pekka Korvenmaa (Helsinki, 1992), pp. 239–41.

7 Herbert Lomas, 'Introduction', in *Contemporary Finnish Poetry* (Bloodaxe, 1991), pp. 9–45.

8 Accompanied also by H.-R. Hitchcock and P. Johnson, *The International Style: Architecture since 1922* (New York, 1932).

9 Silvennoinen's Pihlajamäki Housing would also reflect a similar spirit.

10 The nickname was in fact given by Viljo Revell himself to the 'city kortteli' (the mass is akin to Revell's other mega-complex 'city quarter' in Central Vaasa). *Makkaratalo* is now hotly debated. The owner wishes to remove the sausage motif for increased building rights whilst Museovirasto (the Finnish Board of Antiquities) has opted for protecting the building. In reality, Revell took charge of the town planning, Mäkinen the buildings (the suspended construction was influenced by the Marl Town Hall in Germany) and Castren implemented the drafting in Revell's office.

11 See Asko Salokorpi, 'Towards New Achievements', in *The Work of Architects*, pp. 150–67.

12　See also Merja Härö, 'On Systematic Architectural Education in Finland', in ibid., pp. 210–31.

13　There is a detailed and very interesting account of the fluid decisions and controlling statements that make up this appointment in Raija-Liisa Heinonen, *Funktionalismin Läpimurto Suomessa* (Helsinki, 1986), pp. 37–41.

14　See Osmo Lappo, *Johan Sigfrid Sirén: Architect of Form and Responsibility* (Helsinki, 1989); continuity and permanence, two of Sirén's watchwords, are analysed well here.

15　This is corroborated by the writings of Schildt and others, such as Pietilä and Timo Suomalainen. What has often remained unsaid about this is the way that architects were forced to take sides and the way students were not introduced to Aalto's work at all during this time.

16　Marja-Riitta Norri has begun a sensitive enquiry into this in her notes called 'Heroes and Matter' in *Heroism and the Everyday: Building Finland in the 1950s*, ed. Riitta Nikula, exh. cat., museum of Finnish Architecture (Helsinki, 1994) and 'Appreciation', in *Aalvar Aalto*, exh. cat., Museum of Modern Art, New York (1998). The existence of Keijo Petäjä's archive would be also crucial to the understanding of this misunderstanding between the recognized architects from the 1950s and Alvar Aalto. Petäjä was a consummate note-taker, an avid historian and a thorough professional, besides an architect of some distinctive work in the 1950s and '60s.

17　For Wickberg's role in the Museum, in the framed catalogue texts of the exhibitions during the 1950s and early '60s, see Petra Ceferin, *Constructing a Legend* (Helsinki, 2003), pp. 66–8.

18　Harri Kalha: 'The international reception of Finnish applied arts allied them with the national character and natural conditions. In the context of exhibitions, the simplified colour contrasts of Finnish design were explained through the light summers and dark winters; a certain grandeur of expression was explained through the intuitive and emotional quality of Finnish creativity.' 'The Applied Arts: Dreams and Reality', in *Heroism and the Everyday*, pp. 152–62.

19　The various *Finland Builds* catalogues, published by the Museum of Finnish Architecture, are an invaluable resource for researchers wishing to analyse the promotion and image-building of Finnish architecture. See also the recent thesis by Petra Ceferin published as *Constructing a Legend: The International Exhibitions of Finnish Architecture, 1957–1967* (Helsinki, 2003). The writer begins to explore and question the basis of the promoted legend of Finnish architecture and charts the valuable distinctions between those exhibitions meant for home consumptions, such as the *Finland Builds* exhibitions, and those heavily controlled and used to promote Finnish architecture abroad.

20　Cited in S.-L. Jetsonen in *Heroism and the Everyday*, p. 209, from 'Abstract Tendencies in Contemporary Art', *Finnish Art Yearbook, 1956–57* (Helsinki, 1957).

21　Consider Blomstedt and Pietilä; both wrote about and analysed nature and landscape. Both would absorb contemporary theory, philosophy and literature from the 1950s and re-fit them for their own special conditions. Blomstedt read nature as a rational, radical proportional guide; Pietilä attempted a morphological form guide. For more on this, see my *Writing Architecture* (Cambridge, MA, 1989).

22　For much more detailed and a sound analysis about the applied arts and the international imagery, marketing and the new blood of Modernism, see Harri Kalha, 'The Applied Arts: Dreams and Reality', in *Heroism and the Everyday*, pp. 239–43. Refer also to Petra Ceferin, *Constructing a Legend* (Helsinki, 2003), who cites Kalha in her analysis of the construction of the legend of Finnish architecture in the international exhibitions from 1957 to 1967.

23 Film remains somewhat muted with reduced influence in the 1950s. Without any serious state support and with television just creeping in, Laine would follow known genre and produce the classics of Hella Wuolijoki, Väinö Linna and F. Sillanpää for the screen, while 1950s Finnish film has a particular flavour all its own. See Peter von Bagh, in *Heroism and the Everyday*. It would be the 1960s that picked up on the neo-realism of Nyrki Tapiovaara (1911–1940) and his important films of the 1940s, which adapted an impressionistic talent to traditional genres (thriller, epic.)

24 Haavikko has written short stories, novels, stage and radio plays, opera libretti, pamphlets and memoirs, and continues to challenge the Finnish society and language, its versions of history, property, power and propaganda.

25 According to Olli Alho, ed., *Finland: A Cultural Encyclopaedia* (Helsinki, 1997), Stravinsky in the entry on music, neo-classicism, rhythms, colourful instrumentation belongs to the work of E. Rautavaara (*b.* 1928), Uuno Klami (1900–1961) and the modernist Usko Meriläinen (*b.* 1930). The post-war work of Joonas Kokkonen (1921–1996) would be influenced by Shostakovitch and Bartók. Music would go into a twelve-tone period lasting until the 1960s, and the leading figures of a new Modernism would be Erik Bergman (*b.* 1911), whose aleatoric work fascinated many, and Paavo Heinänen (*b.* 1938), who went into a post-serial style after Meriläinen. Important for us here, however, is that in many ways composers and Finnish musicians can be seen to have used their work to challenge their interpretation of Modernism in a much freer way than the architects. But even a diagrammatic mention cannot do justice to the richness that now exists in the culture.

26 See also *Finland: A Cultural Encyclopaedia*, pp. 249–50.

27 Graduated already in 1932, Franck became the designer and later director of Arabia and the Nuutajärvi Glass factory (1951–76). As a teacher at the University of Art and Design (1960–68), Franck's influence, like that of Blomstedt, was crucial and would encourage younger students in design and architecture to take on a more pressing social responsibility. This would emerge soon enough in the 1960s and on into the '70s.

28 See S. Giedion, *Space, Time and Architecture* [1941] (Cambridge, MA, 1949); also see Petra Ceferin, *Constructing a Legend* (Helsinki, 2003), pp. 10–14.

29 Or, as the phrase goes in Finland, 'every Finnish architect carries a little Alvar Aalto in his breast pocket'.

30 For a discussion of this building and its critical response by Frampton, see my *Grace & Architecture* (Helsinki, 1998). In the 1980s Frampton would also begin the critical rehabilitation of Aalto, whose works after the Enso-Gutzeit Building (1962) and Finlandia Hall (1962–6) had been undervalued, considered romantic, sentimental and – strangely – for at least two decades totally un-Finnish!

31 Reyner Banham, 'The One and the Few', *Architectural Review*, 753 (April 1957); also cited in Sirkkaliisa Jetsonen, 'Humane Rationalism, Themes in Finnish Architecture of the 1950s', in *20th Century Architecture: Finland*, ed. M.-R. Norri and W. Wang (Helsinki, 2000).

32 See Ceferin, *Constructing a Legend*. Ceferin's study is invaluable in understanding how controlled the construction of the image of Finnish architecture became. Following this a detailed study of the polemics, politics and agendas of the persons involved would not only give us the link to the next forty years but would explain much of the self-censorship and critical reluctance in the profession over its confused notion of Modernism, absolute versions of it and the everyday agenda.

33 Ibid., p. 148.

34 Almost all surveys of Finnish architecture have these examples, but for more recent ones see Norri and Wang, *20th Century Architecture: Finland* (Helsinki and Frankfurt am Main, 2000), for a balanced view of the other housing developments besides those of the heroes.

35 Consider the works, for example, of Lauri Silvennoinen, Osmo Sipari, Markus Tavio and Heikki Castren.

36 See Sirén's competition sketch for the Otaniemi Chapel and, possibly the most extreme example, Reima Pietilä's winning competition project for Malmi Church (1967); no detail whatsoever is present: all space, all line, all agreed projection.

37 See Norri, *Heroism and the Everyday*, notes on the 1950s for more detail about Imatra and the early years of *Le Carré Bleu*.

38 Including Jan Söderlund, E. Valovirta, Ilmo Valjakka, Simo Jarvinen, Eero Valjakka, Käpy and Simo Paavilainen, Mikko Heikkinen and Markku Komonen.

39 For an interesting discussion, see Ceferin, 'Within Nature's Embrace', in *Constructing a Legend*, pp. 85–94.

40 Forest Space would return as a critical notion in 1997: see the entry on 'Space' and the notion of 'forest space' (written by J. Pallasmaa) in *Finland: A Cultural Encyclopaedia*.

41 See the recent reassessment of the Otaniemi Chapel in Russell Walden, *Finnish Harvest* (Helsinki, 1998); the building is romanticized critically as the essence of the 'forest' psyche. For a forgotten but important book, see Erik Bruun and Sara Popovits, *Sirén, Heikki and Kaija* (Helsinki, 1977), with a foreword by J. Joedicke. Sirén is another Finnish architect of extreme importance but has received relatively little detailed analysis in his own country.

chapter six: Fellow Travelling: Militancy, Mies and Constructivism

1 Pentti Saarikoski, from 'What's Going on Really!' (1965), in Herbert Lomas, *Contemporary Finnish Poetry* (Newcastle upon Tyne, 1991), p. 182.

2 Max Jakobson, *Finland: Myth and Reality* (Helsinki, 1987), p. 13.

3 Wuori was speaking of the time when Stalin expected Soviet forces to be hailed as liberators of the Finnish proletariat, Eero Wuori; Paul Dukes, 'Foreword', in Henry Bell, *Land of Lakes* (London, 1950), p. 13.

4 See Aino Niskanen in *Arkkitehti* (August 1968), p. 82: 'ala rakenna muuta / kuin barricadi'.

5 This useful survey appears in an important review of 100 years of the *Finnish Architectural Review*: Aino Niskanen, 'Utopioista arkeen / From Utopia to Reality, 1967–76', *Arkkitehti* (February 2003), pp. 80–87.

6 Ibid., p. 81.

7 I am indebted to Matti K. Mäkinen for this detail; he recalls being the youngest, accompanied also by Ruusuvuori and Petäjä. Aalto would certainly have not been part of this group.

8 For a full list of the international exhibitions from 1957 to 1967, see Petra Ceferin, *Constructing a Legend* (Helsinki, 2003), Appendix, pp. 197–9. An example of all the classic aesthetically controlled images of Finnish architecture in the 1960s can be seen in the catalogue used in Turin, 10–30 December 1973. Interestingly, again overseen by Ålander and his small group, patronized at ministerial level, there is no index, no details of photography or photographers. Tacit control is the byword – the jury of the exhibition was Adlercreutz, Lappo, Leiviskä, Mikkola, Mosso,

Ollila, J. M. Richards, Riihilä, Vepsäläinen with the shockingly 'unsurprising' position of a woman as secretary, the talented researcher Heinonen. The architect of the show was Paavo Mänttäri.

9 The pig event is legendary but remains indistinct. Sadly, few wish to admit now to this and other events from the time; so ambiguous and obviously painful was this period that as yet no real study or analysis exists. In correspondence with Tapani Launis, who was part of the group that bought the piglet, released it and then sold it back to the farmer the next day, these were heady and accelerating times. So silent and confused has the record become, there is a necessity to revisit this period and listen to those who were actually present, such as Launis, who have not taken the obvious route. Launis is also rare among Finnish architects in that he has continued his engagement in parallel to the profession, teaching at places like the Cooper Union and researching in various parts of Europe. See also Marja Härö, 'Schooling Architects', in *The Work of Architects*, ed. Pekka Korvenmaa (Helsinki, 1992), p. 221.

10 Contacts with Ruusuvuori and Mikkola were important to build careers and positions within the growing hegemony of the Museum of Finnish Architecture and the Professional Association (which also oversaw the *Finnish Architectural Review*). Mikkola directed the young Finnish architects and architectural policies; alcohol, poetry, revolutionary fervour, women and ambition all played their part. When Mikkola died in the 1980s, Pallasmaa not only took over his historian role but began to re-appropriate and re-script his own and Finnish architecture's ideology and history.

11 See J. M. Richards, *A Guide to Finnish Architecture* (London, 1966), p. 85. Also see Ceferin's well-balanced discussion of Richards, Banham and Giedion and their appropriation of Aalto's seduction. Scientific, regional and individual, the Modern Movement had its new trio; Aalto, and the young architect from Turku, Reima Pietilä, would later challenge all three.

12 For more on Suvikumpu Housing, the later addition in the 1980s and other Pietilä work mentioned, see my *Writing Architecture* (Cambridge, MA, 1989)

13 See also my *Writing Architecture*.

14 See Arne Nevanlinna, *Illuusio Arkkitehtuurista* (Helsinki, 1996), pp. 46–7. Also see A. Nevanlinna and A.-K. Nevanlinna, *Fasadin Henki* (Helsinki, 2001), for an important, playful look at the lexicon within the controlled profession of architects at the turn of the millennium.

15 Adlercreutz's wife Gunnel Adlercreutz is also a significant and influential figure and has maintained the profession's contacts with UIA for two decades now. She currently heads the Finnish Building Institute.

16 See Laura Honkasalo, *Sinun Lapsesi eivat ole Sinun* [Your Childhood Was Not your Own] (Jyväskylä, 2003), a novel that charts the 'political' childhood and coded protest of this period.

17 Consider also the Miesian work of Arto Sipinen (Jyvaskyla Library) before his more rhythmic Aalto-esque work (Tapiola Cultural Centre); for this and echoes of Leiviskä's 'verticalism', see my *Sa(l)vaged Modernism* (Helsinki, 2000).

18 See Olavi Laisaari, *Tehokas kaupunki* [The Efficient Town] (Helsinki, 1962); see also Vilhelm Helander and Simo Rista, *Suomalainen Rakennustaide / Modern Architecture in Finland* (Helsinki, 1987).

19 See the memoir by Kalle Holmberg, *Vasen Suora* (Helsinki, 1999). Kristian Gullichsen in a recent note suggests that a fresh confessional tone would explain much about the naivety and passion of this era. See Niskanen, 'Utopioista arkeen

/ From Utopia to Reality', p. 85.

20   Sexism also stylized the rationalism of the time. Ruusuvuori along with Aalto
      represented the deeply chauvinistic side of the architectural profession. Recent
      attempts to raise the game critically and identify Ruusuvuori's thinking distort
      the weight of those years. See Kirsi Leiman, ed., *Concrete Space: Architect Aarno
      Ruusuvuori's Works from the 1960s*, exh. cat., Museum of Finnish Architecture
      (Helsinki, 2000). A selective editing of the aphoristic in Ruusuvuori, this under-
      plays his immense influence and controlled manipulation of the Finnish agenda.
      See also J. Jäppinen and R. Oikarinen, *Gardens of Fiesole: Lifestory of Alvar Aalto.
      Vol. 1: 1898–1927* (Jyväskylä, 1998), in comic-book form.

21   In Ruusuvuori's words: 'Architecture underwent a decisive revolution during the
      1920s and 1930s. The masquerade was over. The organic connection of form with
      action as well as respect for the inherent beauty of structures were the factors
      which turned architectural design into a process evolving from inside out. Thus
      the outer form became the organically growing manifestation of the inner spatial
      arrangements and structures. Its function was to directly reflect these internal
      incidents.' (From Aarno Ruusuvuori, *Structure is the Key to Beauty*, catalogue as
      part of the *Five Masters of the North*, Museum of Finnish Architecture [Helsinki,
      1992], ed. Norri and Kärkkäinen, with Peter Celsing, Sverre Fehn, Knud Holscher
      and Hogna Sigurdardottir-Aspach.) The other important publication on
      Ruusuvuori to appear in the 1990s was Kirsi Leiman, ed., *Concrete Space: Architect
      Aarno Ruusuvuori's Works from the 1960s*, exh. cat., Museum of Finnish
      Architecture (Helsinki, 2000).

22   'A kind of craze was born, that only Miesian buildings were suitable for social
      uses. People began to say there was no point in competing anymore, since the
      competitions were not producing alternative architectural models.' Ruusuvuori,
      Structure, p. 50.

23   These buildings are also historically significant for the way that architects have
      either continued or altered their own architectural rhetoric and tectonic control
      over the last 40 years. For more on this, see my essay *Critical Steel, Steel Images*
      (Helsinki, 2002).

24   It would be worth looking at the urban development and its legacy, Lars Hedman,
      'Architects as Urban Planners in the 1950s and 1960s', and also Jere Maula, 'Architects
      and Urban Developments in the 1960s and 1970s', in *The Work of Architects*.

25   Although at this time one might have anticipated more buildings with steel
      cladding, the holiday cottage on the Turku archipelago, Maja Pöllö (1971, Esa
      Piironen), remains a rare example of the use of corrugated steel for cladding,
      possibly a distant trace of later work by Glenn Murcutt in Australia. Even the
      architects designing with Constructivist echo at that time would have probably
      stopped short of using such material in the natural context. Instead, most were
      adapting and innovating Miesian aesthetics for their own wooden constructive
      'Japanese' dreams.

26   A similar simplicity and clarity was created by the same architect, Ola Laiho,
      in the Lutheran Church built in Vuosaari in 1969. External panelling, floor and
      ceiling used plywood boarding. Simple steel detailing for the cross and altar
      made this church perhaps the best example of resonance and invention within
      the Miesian idiom.

27   For an earlier, lengthier version exploring some of these ideas, see my *Sa(l)vaged
      Modernism*.

28   Göran Schildt, *Alvar Aalto in his Own Words* (Helsinki, 1998).

29　See my *Grace & Architecture* (Helsinki, 1998) for Timo and Tuomo Suomalainen, and *Timo Penttilä*, exh. cat., Royal Institute of British Architects (London, 1980), with an introduction by Vittorio Magnago Lampugnani.

30　Kalervo Siikala would identify this in the late 1970s: 'Finland's world renown as an architectural pioneer is based on a few magnificent exceptions to its general rule of standardised, tasteless and unimaginative buildings, all of them a great injustice to their natural surroundings.' See also the latest work to try and express the mechanics of these myths and planning strategies: Kaj Nyman, *Sinisilmäisyyden aika* ['Blue-Eye Years': Planning Myths, 1950–2000], (Helsinki, 2003).

31　Although 'Structuralism' on hindsight should be kept to the direction of philosophy, from Saussure to Lévi-Strauss, there is a historical use of the -ism term in Finland as the literal application of material constructions. This usually mistakes the literal identification of steel construction, which is uncomfortably linked to 'structure' and the 'structuralist' thinking itself.

chapter seven: Deconstruction and Reconstruction

1　Pentti Saaritsa, 'Hommage au Travail des Chiens', from Herbert Lomas, *Contemporary Finnish Poetry* (Newcastle upon Tyne, 1991), p. 214.

2　For a clear view of this exchange, see J. Pallasmaa, 'Vastapoli', and the response 'Vastavuuspeli' by R. Pietila in *Arkkitehti* (June 1966).

3　The Japanese magazine *A+U* (Tokyo) became very important as a vehicle of the new throughout the late 1970s and '80s. Most offices subscribed to the journal and new American works were lavishly photographed and displayed. The architects' interviews became required reading. For a view of these changes in Finland during the 1980s, see the design magazine *Muoto*, published by Ornamo, the Finnish Association of Designers. Under the editorship of Heikki Hyytiäinen and printed by Valtion Painatuskeskus there was much new experimental work in design, architecture, advertising and fashion as *Muoto* became a meeting point for young new designers and design writers.

4　Statement by the Finnish participants in the Europe–America Architecture Seminar on the Future of the Modern Movement, 19 September 1980. For more on this, see my *Sa(l)vaged Modernism* (Helsinki, 1999). The Second Alvar Aalto Symposium in Jyväskylä 1982 continued this dialogue under the heading 'Classical Tradition and the Modern Movement'. Matti K. Mäkinen was chairman and opened the symposium, while Juhani Pallasmaa delivered the closing words. The symposium also coincided and was shaped somewhat by the publication in 1980 of *Farväl till Funktionalismen* [Farewell to Functionalism'] by Gunnar Asplund's son Hans.

5　Bertel Jung, 'Functionalism', *Arkkitehti* (1930), p. 59 (in Finnish).

6　For a sensitive English-language overview of the decades 1970–90, see Marja-Riitta Norri, 'Interpretations of Contemporary Reality: Sketching a Portrait of Recent Finnish Architecture', in Marja-Riitta Norri and Wilfred Wang, *20th Century Architecture: Finland* (Helsinki and Frankfurt am Main, 2000), pp. 107–17.

7　This is not well documented as yet but the events surrounding the Nokia Headquarters competition(s) in the early 1980s and the rivalry between Penttilä and others, such as Pallasmaa, Helin and Söderlund, would also indicate how the agenda for Finnish Modernism was shifted from the more solid pragmatic realism advocated by Penttilä to the leaning towards poetic structure and tectonic symbolism that emerged from these architects. Penttilä would take up a profes-sorship in Vienna, occupy Otto Wagner's room in the Academy and have very little to do with Finnish architecture henceforth. For more hints on this, see my *Sa(l)vaged Modernism*.

8 See my *K / K: A Couple of Finns and Some Donald Ducks* (Helsinki, 1991).

9 For a general survey up to this moment, see Markku Valkonen, *Finnish Art over the Centuries* (Keuruu, 1992), in Finnish, German, French and English.

10 For more on these buildings and Pietilä's re-emergence, see my *Writing Architecture* (Cambridge, MA, 1989). Frampton identifies what many other Finnish architects have not been able to put into words but have similarly felt: 'with the exception of his New Delhi Embassy and the Finnish President's Residence he [Pietilä] fell into one digression after another'. Frampton, Foreword to M. Quantrill, *Finnish Architecture and the Modernist Tradition* (London, 1995).

11 Signs of this can be seen in Finland: *Nature, Design, Architecture*, exh. cat., Museum of Finnish Architecture (Helsinki, 1981).

12 Kenneth Frampton, 'Towards a Critical Regionalism: Six Points for an Architecture of Resistance', in *The Anti-Aesthetic: Essays on Postmodern Culture*, ed. H. Foster (Washington, DC, 1983), pp. 16–30. Relate this to *Alvar Aalto: Between Humanism and Materialism*, exh. cat., Museum of Modern Art (New York, 1998), and the various essays by Frampton, Reid, Treib and Pallasmaa as they continue to read the authentic modern in Aalto, picking up from Frampton's original 'critical regionalist' thesis.

13 For more details of this and an analysis of Frampton's critical writing on Aalto's Säynätsalo Civic Centre, see my *Grace & Architecture* (Helsinki, 1998).

14 Since the 1980s Pallasmaa has literally guided the phenomenological debate with-in Finnish architecture. He became the main figure in resisting the contemporary and realigning Finnish architecture theoretically. For this shift to 'interpretive' mode, see *The Two Languages of Architecture* Abacus 2, MFA yearbook, Museum of Finnish Architecture (Helsinki, 1981). For more on Pallasmaa's role in Finnish architecture, see my *The End of Finnish Architecture* (Helsinki, 1994), *Sa(l)vaged Modernism*, and *Aaltomania* (Helsinki, 2001).

15 For more figures, see Max Jakobson et al., *Facts about Finland* (Helsinki, 2000).

16 Works from Helin and Siitonen, Käpy and Simo Paavilainen, the Valio Office (Mäkinen, Löfström, Katajamäki), Nurmela, Raimoranta & Tasa, Kairamo, Gullichsen & Vuomela, 8-Studio (including Kaira, Mahlamäki, Lahdelma) Kareoja & Jokela, Wartiainen Architects, Söderlund & Co., Penttilä and Saari, Piironen, Airas & Järvinen, Ilonen, Erholz and many others range from an assimilated postmodern repertoire to a refined, restrained late Modernism and on to what some see as a neo-Constructivism.

17 Dominique Beaux attempted to chart the 'other' marginalized direction in his *Les Chemins de L'Après Aalto, pour une architecture humaine*, exh. cat., L'Institut Finlandais (Paris, 1993) – the works of Pietilä were put alongside Adlercreutz, Mikola-Saurama-Tervaoja, Monark, NVO, Serola-Autio, Studio 8, Valovirta, Leiviskä, Grotenfelt, Louekari, Littow, Järvinen and Airas.

18 For further details on these two important buildings, see my *Writing Architecture* and *Sa(l)vaged Modernism*.

19 See Anna-Maija Ylimaula, ed., *The Oulu School of Architecture* (Helsinki, 1993), in English and Finnish. Architects who have contributed to this significant move-ment include: Reijo Niskasaari, Keijo Niskasaari, Lasse Vahtera, Jorma Öhman, Pekka Littow, Ilpo Väisänen, Kaarlo Viljanen, Anna and Lauri Louekari, Heikki

Aitoaho, Päivi Jääskeläinen, Seppo Huttu-Hiltunen, Heikki Taskinen, Juha Pasanen, Jouni Koiso-Kanttila, Marja and Pekka Laatio, Kyösti Meinilä and Aulikki Herneoja. See also Lauri Louekari, ed., *Pohjoinen Arkkitehtuuri 1* (Oulu, 1994), for new works from the north and new architects out of Oulu and Vaasa. The recent editor of the *Finnish Architectural Review*, Harri Hautajärvi, himself an Oulu graduate, has begun to redress this balance in recent issues, publishing projects from all over the country. These architects have also been responsible for a serious documentation of the local crafts of building and materials.

20 It is important to remember that one of the architects on the jury of the Seville Pavilion was Kristian Gullichsen, a 'manifesto' member. Gullichsen was a highly respected professional figure who would, throughout the 1990s, play a significant role in reshaping Finnish Modernism, not only through his own buildings and office, but through his various roles in the society and as juror on many competitions in the decade. His statements about the Kiasma Museum and his briefing for the Canberra Finnish Embassy competition are crucial for anyone wanting to trace this development. His office remains committed to a revised Constructivist architecture of high quality, along with colleagues such as Timo Vormala (and the late Erkki Kairamo).

21 See also the official publication for a sample of the 'national-image' politics that accompanied the Finnish Pavilion at Seville Expo 1992, *Contrasts and Connections*, ed. Heikki Kunnas and Juhani Pallasmaa Asiakirja (Helsinki, 1992).

22 *Datutop* has an impressive collection of issues and is indebted to the work of Jorma Mänty, Kari Jormakka and others.

chapter eight: Late Modernism, Critical Humanism

1 Risto Ahti, 'Mistakes and Intimidations', in Herbert Lomas, *Contemporary Finnish Poetry* (Newcastle upon Tyne, 1991), p. 239.

2 A note in the us *Metro* free magazine, 8 October 2003: 'Finland least corrupt . . . according to an anti-corruption group which released a survey yesterday . . . Finland was the world's cleanest nation and Bangladesh the most corrupt.'

3 For more such figures, see Max Jakobsen et al., *Facts about Finland* (Helsinki, 2000).

4 Matti K. Mäkinen acted as vice-chairman of the jury and thus led most of the meetings, and the future Director of the Museum, Tuula Arkio, also had a strong role in the process. Along with Wartiainen and Tasa, it is likely that there was not a strong fascination towards a fading 'modernist' iconography. The results of the Kiasma competition produced a backlash from the architectural museum headed by M.-R. Norri. Wartiainen responded as it was played out in the *Architectural Review* (London). Perhaps to allay these differences and cool tempers, Pallasmaa was appointed the 'associate' architect to Steven Holl. A history of this period and actual events is yet to be revealed, so closely do Finns seem to need their professional secrecy. Hopefully this will change. For more on this debate, see my *Sa(l)vaged Modernism* (Helsinki, 2000).

5 For more on Leiviskä, see my *Sa(l)vaged Modernism*. Also see *Juha Leiviskä*, ed. M.-R. Norri, exh. cat., Museum of Finnish Architecture (Helsinki, 2001); Malcolm Quantrill, *Juha Leiviskä and the Continuity of Finnish Modern Architecture* (London, 2001). For the 'expressive' context, see Philip Arcidi, 'Latter-Day Expressionists', *Progressive Architecture* (September 1992); connections made

between Reima Pietilä, Gunnar Birkerts and Juha Leiviskä.

6   For musicality and the continuity of 'Modernism' narrative, see Quantrill, *Juha Leiviskä*.

7   From J. Pallasmaa, 'Space', in *Finland: A Cultural Encyclopaedia*, ed. Olli Alho (Helsinki, 1997), p. 296.

8   Pierre Bourdieu, *Neo-Liberalism, Utopia of Unlimited Exploitation, Acts of Resistance* (New York, 1998).

9   See Marja-Riita Norri in the *Architectural Review* (1995, collected issues) with a response by Kaj Wartiainen; see also *my Sa(l)vaged Modernism* for more on this exchange.

10   For a reaction to the confused planning process behind this building, see J. Jauhiainen and V. Niemenmaa, 'Yhden muuton genealogia: Tieteen tilan teknologioiden suunnittelu ja hallinta', *Alue ja Ympäristö* (31 January 2002), pp. 38–53, and, by the same authors, 'Läpinäkyvää suunnittelua? Esimerkkinä Helsinking Yliopiston Physicumin suunnittelu ja rakentaminen', *Yhteiskuntasuunnittelu*, xxxix/4 (2001), pp. 7–22.

11   For a useful survey of work throughout the 1990s, see the books of architectural photography by Jussi Tiainen: *New Finnish Architecture* (Helsinki, 1996), *Finnish Architecture, 1994–1999* (Helsinki, 1999), *Helsinki: Contemporary Urban Architecture* (Helsinki, 2001) and *Helsinki* (Helsinki, 2004). Also see Tiainen's photographs in *Kiasma* (Helsinki, 1998).

12   Including the architects Louekari, Littow, Viljanen, Aitoaho. Also see L. Louekari, ed., *Pohjoinen Arkkitehtuuri 1 / Architecture of the North 1* (Oulu, 1994), with English summaries.

13   For this see the immense range of buildings produced by Mahlamäki and Lahdelma as part of the 8+Studio architects from Tampere (which also included P. Kareoja and O.-P. Jokela) in the 1980s and then as a duo in the 1990s.

14   See my *40 Young Architects from Finland* (Helsinki, 2002). For ARRAK, see my contribution to *10x10* (London, 2000); also for connections to this group, see Riitta Kuusikko, *Andreas Alariesto, 1900–89* (Oulu, 1994).

15   Later, with the introduction of the Green Party to the government, investment and interest shifted to protect the forest and develop city culture; the result was less risk, more compromise. In the year 2001 the 'Greens' threatened a delay, to some a timely revision, of the corporate images that looked likely to fill remaining prime sites in Helsinki.

16   For a welcome look at the growth of the capital in the nineteenth and twentieth centuries, see Marjatta Bell and Marjatta Hietala, *Helsinki, the Innovative City: Historical Perspectives* (Helsinki, 2002).

17   For this 'Swedish' insult and other aspects of Ikea Modernism, see T. Nevanlinna and J. Relander, *Espoo: Totuus Suomesta* (Tammi, 2000). This is, of course, the unofficial view. Tapiola recently celebrated its 50th anniversary with some fanfare. For this and all things contemporary connected with Tapiola, see http://www.weegee.espoo.fi/tapiola, where history, plans, multi-media presentations all put a rather strange, uncritical and non-contextual gloss on this forest drama.

18   For Muschamp's comments in the *New York Times* and more detail, see my *Aaltomania* (Helsinki, 2001).

19   'Talking about the City', *Helsinki Forum* (1 November 2000–25 February 2001), Museum of Modern Architecture, Helsinki, in English and Finnish: an excellent publication outlining the current inter-disciplinary debate and promising more

openness and more challenge.

20 For more on Mäkinen, Valio and the branding of steel in Finnish architecture, see my *Critical Steel, Steel Images* (Helsinki, 2002).

21 See Eeva-Liisa Nikula and Jukka Laukkanen, *An Architect of the Times: Antti Katajamäki* (Oulu, 1998).

22 More recently, *Arkkitehtiuutiset* (September 2003) Mäkinen has challenged the architects to take more contemporary responsibility and suggests a restructuring of the whole association, so outdated and irrelevant it appears it has become.

23 Petra Ceferin, *Constructing a Legend* (Helsinki, 2003), p. 150.

24 I began to suggest this range in my *40 Young Architects from Finland*.

25 Jurgen Habermas, 'Modernity: An Incomplete Project', in *The Anti-Aesthetic: Essays on Postmodern Culture*, ed. Hal Foster (Washington, DC, 1983), p. 7.

Epilogue: History and the Shape of Modernism

1 Arto Melleri, 'After the Ball', in Herbert Lomas, *Contemporary Finnish Poetry* (Newcastle upon Tyne, 1991), p. 287.

2 Matti K. Mäkinen in 'Signs of the Times', *Arkkitehti* (February 2003), p. 95, citing Pallasmaa from *Arkkitehti* (January 1994).

3 See the recent publication, which goes some way to confirming these patterns: Sirkka-Liisa Jetsonen, *Sacral Space: Modern Finnish Churches* (Helsinki, 2003), photographs by Jari Jetsonen and essay 'The Beauty of Hidden Order' by Fred Thompson, who worked in Ruusuvuori's office in the 1960s.

4 Kenneth Frampton, 'Foreword', in M. Quantrill, *Finnish Architecture and the Modernist Tradition* (London, 1995).

5 Elias Lönnrot, 'The Dance', in *Skating on the Sea: Poetry from Finland*, ed. and trans. Keith Bosley (Newcastle upon Tyne, 1997), p. 96.

6 The names of the protagonists from this period are obvious and have been mentioned in this text. They are also mentioned in my book *Sa(l)vaged Modernism* (Helsinki, 2000) and to some extent in *Aaltomania* (Helsinki, 2001). I would urge others from that time to come forward as interest grows to try and understand what this 'Finnish atmosphere' is: its power, creative influence and repressive tendencies.

Select Bibliography

Ahtola-Moorhouse, Leena, Michael Carapetian and Jonathan Moorhouse, *Helsingin Jugendarkkitehtuuri, 1895–1915 / Helsinki Jugend Architecture, 1895–1915* (Helsinki, 1987)

Alho, Olli, ed., *Finland: A Cultural Encyclopaedia* (Helsinki, 1997)

Amberg, Anna-Liisa, et al., *Eliel Saarinen: Projects, 1896–1923* (Keuruu, 1990)

Beaux, Dominique, *Les Chemins de L'Après Aalto, pour une architecture humaine*, exh. cat., The Finnish Institute Gallery, Paris (1993)

Bell, Henry, *Land of Lakes* (London, 1950)

Bell, Marjatta, and Marjatta Hietela, *Helsinki, the Innovative City: Historical Perspectives* (Helsinki, 2002)

Blackmore, Susan, *The Meme Machine* (Oxford, 1999)

Bosley, Keith, ed. and trans., *Skating on the Sea: Poetry from Finland* (Newcastle upon Tyne, 1997)

Boulton Smith, John, *Modern Finnish Painting and Graphic Art* (London, 1970)

—, *The Golden Age of Finnish Art* (Helsinki, 1985)

Bourdieu, Pierre, *Neo-Liberalism, Utopia of Unlimited Exploitation, Acts of Resistance* (New York, 1998)

Bradbury, Malcolm, and James McFarlane, *The Name and Nature of Modernism* (London, 1976)

Bullock, A., and S. Trombley, eds, *The New Fontana Dictionary of Modern Thought* (London, 1999)

Carpelan, B., et al., eds, *Hufvudstaden* (Helsinki, 1974) [in Swedish]

Ceferin, Petra, *Constructing a Legend* (Helsinki, 2003)

Connah, Roger, *Aaltomania* (Helsinki, 2001)

—, *Critical Steel, Steel Images* (Helsinki, 2002)

—, *Grace & Architecture* (Helsinki, 1998)

—, *K / K: A Couple of Finns and Some Donald Ducks* (Helsinki, 1991)

—, *Sa(l)vaged Modernism* (Helsinki, 2000)

—, ed., *Tango Mantyniemi* (Helsinki 1994)

—, *The End of Finnish Architecture* (Helsinki, 1994)

—, *40 Young Architects from Finland* (Helsinki, 2002)

—, *Writing Architecture* (Cambridge, MA, 1989)

—, 'That Sweet Blind Point: Towards an Uninflected Architecture', *10x10* (London, 2000)

Dreams of a Summer Night: Scandinavian Painting at the Turn of the Century, exh. cat., Hayward Gallery (London, 1986)

Foster, Hal, ed., *The Anti-Aesthetic: Essays on Postmodern Culture* (Washington, DC, 1983)

Giedion, S., *Space, Time and Architecture* [1941], (Cambridge, MA, 1949)

Haavikko, Paavo, *The Winter Palace: Selected Poems* (1958), trans. A. Hollo (London, 1974)

Hajdu, Peter, *Finno-Ugrian Languages and Peoples* (London, 1975)

Heinonen, Raija-Liisa, *Functionalismin Läpimurto Suomessa* (Helsinki, 1986)

Helamaa, Erkki, *40-luku korsujen ja jälleenrakentamisen vuosikymmen*, exh. cat.,
     Museum of Finnish Architecture and The Alvar Aalto Museum (Helsinki, 1983)
Helander, Vilhelm, and Simo Rista, *Suomalainen Rakennustaide / Modern
     Architecture in Finland* (Helsinki, 1987)
Henttonen, Maarit, *Elsi Borg, 1893–1958: Arkkitehti* (Helsinki, 1995) [with an
     English summary]
Hitchcock, H.-R., and P. Johnson, *The International Style: Architecture since 1922*
     (New York, 1932)
Holmberg, Kalle, *Vasen Suora* (Helsinki, 1999)
Honkasalo, Laura, *Sinun Lapsesi eivat ole Sinun* (Jyväskylä, 2003)
Jakobson, Max, *Finland: Myth and Reality* (Helsinki, 1987)
—, et al., *Facts about Finland* (Helsinki, 2000)
Jansson, Tove, *Comet in Moominland* (London, 1951)
Jäppinen, J., and R. Oikarinen, *Gardens of Fiesole: Lifestory of Alvar Aalto. Vol. 1:
     1898–1927* (Jyväskylä, 1998)
Jencks, Charles, *Modern Movements in Architecture* (London, 1971)
Jeskanen, T., and P. Leskelä, *Oiva Kallio* (Helsinki, 2000)
Jokinen, T., *Erkki Huttunen, 1901–56: Arkkitehti* (Helsinki, 1993) [with an English summary]
J. S. Sirén: Arkkitehti / Architect, 1889–1961, exh. cat., Museum of Finnish Architecture
     (Helsinki, 1989)
Kaipia, J., and L. Pitkonen, *Guide to Finnish Architecture* (Helsinki, 1997)
Keinanen, Timo, and Kristiina Paatero, *Martti Välikangas, 1893–1973: Aritehti*
     (Helsinki, 1993) [with an English summary]
Kelly, Liam, ed., *The City as Art* (Dublin, 1994)
Klinge, Matti, *A Brief History of Finland* (Helsinki, 1981)
Kolakowski, Leszek, *Modernity on Endless Trial* (Chicago, 1997)
Korpelainen, Heini, ed., *The Finnish Architectural Policy* (Porvoo, 1999) [English edition]
Korvenmaa, Pekka, ed., *The Work of Architects* (Helsinki, 1992)
Kruskopf, Erik, *Suomen Taideteollisuus: Suomalaisen Muotoilun Vaiheita* [Finnish
     Industrial Art: The Events of Finnish Design] (Helsinki, 1989) [in Finnish
     and Swedish]
Kuusikko, Riitta, *Andreas Alariesto, 1900–89* (Oulu, 1994)
Laisaari, Olari, *Tehokas Kaupunki* [The Efficient Town] (Helsinki, 1962)
Leiman, Kirsi, ed., *Concrete Space: Architect Aarno Ruusuvuori's works from the 1960s*,
     exh. cat., Museum of Finnish Architecture (Helsinki, 2000)
Lomas, Herbert, *Contemporary Finnish Poetry* (Newcastle upon Tyne, 1991)
Louekari, L., ed., *Pohjoinen Arkkitehtuuri 1 Architecture of the North 1* (Oulu, 1994)
     [with English summaries]
Magnago Lampugnani, Vittorio, ed., *Timo Penttilä*, exh. cat. [RIBA] (London, 1980)
Mäkinen, Matti K., *Missio* (Helsinki, 2002)
Makkonen, Leena, *Martta & Ragnar Ypyä* (Helsinki, 1998) [with English summary]
Mikkola, Kirmo, Timo Keinanen and M.-R. Norri, eds, *Funkis: Suomi Nykyaikaa
     Etsimässä* exh. cat., Museum of Finnish Architecture (Helsinki, 1981)
Nevanlinna, Arne, *Illuusio Arkkitehtuurista* (Helsinki, 1996)
—, and A.-K. Nevanlinna, *Fasadin Henki* (Helsinki, 2001)
Nevanlinna, T., and J. Relander, *Espoo: Totuus Suomesta* (Tammi, 2000)
Nikula, Eva-Liisa, and Jukka Laukkanen, *An Architect of the Times: Antti Katajamäki*
     (Oulu, 1998)
Nikula, Riitta, *Armas Lindgren, 1874–1929: Arkkitehti / Architect*, exh. cat., Museum of
     Finnish Architecture (Helsinki, 1988)

—, *Architecture and Landscape: The Building of Finland* (Helsinki, 1993)

—, ed., *Heroism and the Everyday: Building Finland in the 1950s*, exh. cat., Museum
of Finnish Architecture (Helsinki, 1994)

Norri, Marja-Riitta, ed., *Juha Leiviskä*, exh. cat., Museum of Finnish Architecture
(Helsinki, 2001) [in Finnish and English]

—, and Wang, Wilfred, *20th Century Architecture: Finland* (Helsinki and Frankfurt
am Main, 2000)

—, et al., eds, *Talking about the City* (Helsinki, 2001)

Nyman, Kaj, *Sinisilmäisyyden Aika: Blue-eyed Time* (Helsinki, 2003) [in Finnish]

Outhier, Reginald, *1736–1737: Matka Pojan Perille / Journal d'un Voyage au Nord*
(Helsinki, 1976) [Finnish edition of French original]

Pallasmaa, J., *History of the Museum of Finnish Architecture*, exh. cat. (Helsinki, 1980)

—, and H. Kunnas, eds, *Contrasts and Connections*, exh. cat., Seville (Helsinki, 1992)

Quantrill, M., *Finnish Architecture and the Modernist Tradition* (London, 1995)

—, *Juha Leiviskä and the Continuity of Finnish Modern Architecture* (London, 2001)

—, *Pietilä: Context and Modernism* (Helsinki, 1984)

Richards, J. M., *A Guide to Finnish Architecture* (London, 1966)

—, *An Introduction to Modern Architecture* (London, 1956)

—, *800 Years of Finnish Architecture* (London, 1978)

Salokorpi, Aski, *Arkkitehdiksi Sodan Varjossa* (Helsinki, 1994)

—, *Modern Architecture in Finland* (London, 1970)

—, *Selim A. Lindqvist* (Jyväskylä, 2001)

—, ed., *Vuosikirja 3 / Yearbook 3: Abacus, Museum of Finnish Architecture*
(Helsinki, 1993)

Sarje, Kimmo, *Sigurd Frosterus* (Helsinki, 2000)

Schildt, Goran, *Alvar Aalto in his Own Words* (Helsinki, 1997)

—, *Alvar Aalto: A Life's Work* (Helsinki, 1994)

—, *Alvar Aalto: The Mature Years* (New York, 1991)

—, *Modern Finnish Sculpture* (London, 1970)

Standertskjöld, Elina, *P. E. Blomstedt, 1900–1935: Arkkitehti* (Helsinki, 1996)
[with English summary]

Tiainen, Jussi, *Finnish Architecture, 1994–1999* (Helsinki, 1999)

—, *Helsinki* (Helsinki, 2004)

—, *Helsinki: Contemporary Urban Architecture* (Helsinki, 2001)

—, *Kiasma* (Helsinki, 1998)

—, *New Finnish Architecture* (Helsinki, 1996)

Tuomi, Timo, ed., *Hilding Ekelund, 1893–1984: Architect*, exh. cat., Museum of
Finnish Architecture (Helsinki, 1997) [in Finnish, Swedish and English]

—, ed., *Matkalla! / En Route!: Finnish Architects' Studies Abroad*, exh. cat., Museum
of Finnish Architecture (Helsinki, 1999)

Tweedie, Mrs Alec, *Through Finland in Carts* (London, 1897)

Valkonen, Markku, *Finnish Art over the Centuries* (Keuruu, 1992) [in Finnish,
German, French and English]

Walden, Russell, *Finnish Harvest* (Helsinki, 1998)

Waltari, Mika, *Suuri Illusio* [The Grand Illusion] (Helsinki, 1928)

Wickberg, Nils Erik, *Ajatuksia Arkkitehtuurista / Thoughts on Architecture* (Helsinki,
1946) [in Finnish]

Ylimaula, Anna-Maija, ed., *The Oulu School of Architecture* (Helsinki, 1993)

Zevi, Bruno, *The Modern Language of Architecture* (Seattle, WA, 1978)

Acknowledgements

In the course of writing this book I have benefited from a number of excellent new studies by Finnish and international scholars. I have also benefited from older studies and the privilege of re-reading. There is now on Finnish architecture a developing and significant critical archive. Many have helped me in this, offering advice, contacts and suggestions. Where help has come in the form of books, references or insights, these occur in the notes. I have however chosen to write between the lines of such existing studies for two reasons. Firstly, it is important to re-assess accepted critical opinions in relation to the contemporary moment, and secondly, artistic influence has often been denied as part of a serious critical study. Over the many years I lived in Finland and since, I have had the pleasure of sharing my ideas with many people. It would be impossible to mention them all, but all know the conversations we have had, the help they have given. I thank each and all here, and know they will forego the convention of identifying them individually.

It remains to make the obvious but important point: the book is my own, thus the errors too. Thank you all.

Photo Acknowledgements

The author and publishers wish to express their thanks to the below sources of illustrative material and/or permission to reproduce it.

Photos courtesy of the Alvar Aalto Museum: 69, 143 (right – photo: Martti Kapanen); ARK magazine: 240; ARRAK/Matti Karjanoja: 193; photos courtesy of the author: 18, 26, 35, 36, 38, 39 (above and below), 61 (right), 65 (right), 131 (above and below), 144, 161 (above), 166, 174 (above), 183 (below), 194 (left and right), 199, 201 (above and below), 202 (above and below), 205 (left), 207, 212, 215, 219, 220 (below), 235; Finnish Defence Forces Education Development Centre: 101 (photo T. Nousiainen); Heikkinen & Komonen: 184; Helsinki City Archives: 64 (right); 65 (left); 103; HKK: 186; Kalevi Keski-Korhonen: 160; Lahdelma & Mahlamäki: 224; Lehtikuva Oy: 12; Juha Leiviskä: 217; Monark: 205 (right); Matti Niemi: 214; Raili & Reima Pietilä: 180; Museum of Finnish Architecture (Suomen Rakennustaiteen Museo): 10, 11, 13 (left and right), 14, 21, 22, 23, 29 (photo Nils Wasatjerna), 32 (photo Kari Hakli), 33 (photo I. K. Inha), 37 (photo Studio Granath), 41, 42 (above and below), 43, 49, 51, 52, 54, 59 (right – photo A. Salokorpi), 60, 61 (left – photo Foto Roos), 64 (left), 68, 71, 72, 75 (photo Gustaf Welin), 76 (photo A. Pietinen Oy), 78 (right – photo H. Iffland), 80, 81, 84 (photo Eino Mäkinen), 87, 88, 90 (photo Kari Hakli), 91 (below – photo Foto Roos/ SRM), 92 (above – photo Foto Roos, below – photo Kolmio), 96 (photo H. Iffland), 97, 98 (photo H. Iffland), 99, 105, 106 (above – photo Fred Runeberg, below – photo A. Vahlström), 110 (above – photo G. Vaskainen), 112, 113 (below – photo Olli Lehtovuori), 121 (photo H. Havas), 123 (photo A. Matilainen), 124, 128 (photo Aerofoto), 130 (above – photo H. Havas), 132 (below left – photo Foto Roos, below right – photo H. Havas), 135, 136, 140 (photo Arne Ervi), 141 (photo A. Pietinen), 146 (photo Heikki Kaitera), 147, 148, 149, 150 (below – photo P. Ingervo), 151, 152 (above – photo P. Ingervo, below – photo H. Havas), 153, 156 (photo Simo Rista), 162 (photo Simo Rista), 165 (photo Juhani Pallasmaa), 171 (photo Risto Kamunen), 172 (above – photo Bengt Anderson, below – photo Heikki Kaitera), 174 (below – photo H. T. Lehmusto), 175 (above – photo A. Pietinen), 177, 178 (photo Hede Foto), 182 (right), 188, 217 (below), 233 (photo Simo Rista); Timo & Tuomo Suomalainen/Fethulla: 191; Matti Suuronen: 230; Jyrki Tasa: 200, 210, 237; Jussi Tiainen: 8, 46, 66, 67, 83 (above and below), 142, 143 (left), 213 (left and right), 216, 220 (above), 225, 227 (left and right); Valio/Matti K. Mäkinen: 232; and Kaj Wartiainen: 198.

Index